16/-

c/-

MADELEINE'S JOURNAL

Books by Mrs. Robert Henrey

THE LITTLE MADELEINE (*her girlhood*)

AN EXILE IN SOHO (*her adolescence*)

MADELEINE GROWN UP (*her love story and marriage*)

A FARM IN NORMANDY *and* THE RETURN (*the birth of her child*)

MATILDA AND THE CHICKENS (*a winter on her farm*)

A JOURNEY TO VIENNA (*the making of a film*)

PALOMA (*her story of a friend*)

LONDON (*with water-colours by Phyllis Ginger*)

MADELEINE'S JOURNAL (*her contemporary diary*)

MADELEINE'S JOURNAL

by

MRS ROBERT HENREY

LONDON: J. M. DENT & SONS LTD

For

ETHEL LINDER REINER

CHAPTER I

THERE IS not much news this week: nylons are in the shops for the first time, though it is thirteen years since they were introduced to the world, and the price of knitting wool has come down, but the wool stays in the shops and the nylons also, I fancy. Those of us who could afford to, bought our nylons in the black market, or stocked up in Paris or Amsterdam, or had them sent over by gentlemen friends from America. Sugar and butter are rationed, but in a little while we shall buy both as easily as in Paris or New York. Meanwhile the Germans are kind: being wealthy, they send us their surplus delicacies. In London the insufferable queue lingers on, whether for the half-empty bus or for the egg which once a week the grocer's assistant hands us with a snarl. Is it relatively fresh, foreign, or 'sealed'? We are not supposed to ask. But to-morrow, hurrah! Even by the time you read these words, eggs will be plentiful. Rationing will have come to an end. How amazing! These absurdities out of *Alice in Wonderland* will merely leave behind them two lines in this journal. What a picturesque, nonsensical era! Happily our 'to-days' are outmoded faster than the season's Paris hat which I am not allowed to buy for want of currency, for the Government having taken half our earnings prevents us from spending the remainder as we please. But to-morrow these things also will be different. Income tax will have come down and we shall be allowed to travel where and how we wish—even to Canada, lovely member of our Commonwealth family, and to the United States where they also speak our own tongue. Our intelligence may thus at long last be counted more vital than our 'exports,' cliché-ridden word of no meaning to the feminine mind.

To-day the editor of Burke's *Landed Gentry* announces that more than half the 5,000 landed gentry mentioned in his book no longer have any land. This strikes me as curious and sad, but we are at the beginning of a new reign and some of London's noblest buildings have been very cleverly cleaned on the outside and look nice in the sunshine.

Mrs. Terry, whose husband a former titled family's manservant is in charge of the maids in my block of flats, comes to give me a hand once a week. She arrives pushing her carpet-sweeper rather as if she were going to mow a lawn, and is always in an excellent temper. One of the daily maids has just had a baby. We have all been waiting for this news since she was obliged to stop working because she was so big that she could not see her toes. The symptoms, I am assured, were not quite the same as for all the other millions of women who have babies. I eagerly acquiesce. Symptoms never are the same, at least in our imagination. That is why the subject is more than usually inexhaustible. We needed to know what the mother, the mother-in-law, the grand-mothers, and the district nurse had to say about it. What poetry, what wealth of detail, emerge from these discussions! What delightful points of comparison! What a desire for individuality!

'Well, it's a boy!' declared Mrs. Terry, and at this she seemed greatly relieved, for the woman in question lived in what we so horribly call a 'pre-fabricated' house, and already she had two little boys. Would not a girl have been nice for a change? No, that was not the point.

If the baby had been a girl, Mrs. Terry explained, it would have complicated life in this uncommodious home. The baby girl would have needed a room of her own!

So baby girls could no longer be mixed with baby boys! What progress we had made since my girlhood when the new-born was put on a pillow on the parents' bed! Mrs. Terry, between a pull and a push of her droning machine, shouted:

'You ought to see the cot! My! It's wonderful: tiny coloured sheets and the sweetest eiderdown; just like a doll's bed, madam!'

There was a pause and then:

'Oh, but——' and here Mrs. Terry stopped the machine, which was much too noisy for a sustained conversation: 'Oh, but it was really the baby's father who was the star of the performance. He went to the hospital and waited timidly in the corridor like they do on the films, feeling a bit of a brute. You know what they are! Then one of the nurses came to fetch him and pushed him into the room, and another put the baby, all wrapped up, in his arms. It appears he was ever so embarrassed with all those women. He said: "Why, ladies, this is my first baby!" "And what about the others waiting for you at home?" they asked. "Yes, of course," he answered, "but the two others were born when I was serving overseas, and I never saw them till they could walk." Well, madam, it does bring the war back to one, doesn't it? Still, we are ever so happy that everything turned out so well, and one of the aunts bought a brand-new perambulator and wheeled it herself, still tied up in brown paper, through the streets.'

Mrs. Terry switched on the machine again and changed to more general topics.

Some people claim that London has become a very dull city to live in. A young queen will renew its

*

brilliance, say others, but the aristocracy that should logically flourish under a monarchy has gone to rear pigs in the country. Their ancestral homes are sold up, and even the Duke of Wellington, though keeping a tiny corner for himself, has handed back No. 1 London to the nation that gave this Piccadilly mansion to his illustrious forbear. London is presumably too expensive for aristocrats. Mayfair where you once found them has become offices—and so the Queen reigns but her nobles, poor dears, are plundered of their castles and chased out of town. They do not enjoy the same respect as the throne and are fair game for all of us. And yet who can tell that they will not produce a share of the adventure-loving youth of the new Elizabethan age?

Are we still adventurous or have we lost the fun of it? A young woman writes in a serious London newspaper that, amongst the under twenty-fives, to confess to any desire for fame and fortune is regarded as naïve and immature, if not positively anti-social. Is it also wrong to be young and feel one's blood tingling? Could falling in love be equally anti-social? That might turn London into a very dull city, but I do not believe that London is dull. Even in its moments of crisis it is the most truly magnificent city I know, but its people react differently to social changes from those in other countries. It rather enjoys bouts of restrictive Puritanism, and even its women, who are more feminist than feminine, are apt to suffer queues and food shortages too gladly because it makes them feel good to have done their duty. A judge of appeal who jumped on a bus between official stops was told by the conductor: 'Hi! You can't do that! You're trying to dodge the queue,' and he jumped off obediently though there was plenty of room inside.

A very delightful friend with whom I sometimes lunch at the Ritz was telling me that she had attended a church service at which the 78-year-old Earl of Athlone and

Princess Alice were present. As soon as the service was over a number of dignitaries hurried out to see the distinguished couple into their car, but they could not find them and there was no royal car. My energetic friend took a No. 9 bus, and there suddenly in the crowded interior she saw the earl and the princess with a companion who, on peering into her purse, found that she had no money to pay for these illustrious persons. My friend offered the fare; then decided she ought to make some sort of curtsy to the Earl of Athlone who, seeing her, tried to respond in the confined space at his disposal. He tried to put up his arm but it was difficult, 'and,' she added, 'he was of an age and rank accustomed to large and roomy cars.' They were going back quite simply to Kensington Palace. One might think it strange that Queen Mary's brother could not have borrowed a car from his sister at Marlborough House, but on reflection, these are the very people who are most insistent on not giving trouble.

Though Mrs. Terry only stays an hour, I find it impossible to concentrate during the rest of the morning. We have talked about too many things. The alternative to work is a walk along Piccadilly.

Piccadilly is easier to walk along than Bond Street where, if they were intelligent, they would prevent all traffic as in the main shopping street of Amsterdam. Then Londoners, and people who come to London both for business and amusement, could saunter from end to end not merely on the pavements but in the centre of the road, talking, thinking, and unhurriedly looking into the shop windows. The answer would probably be that to ban traffic would be undemocratic, but it is in the most democratic countries that the central shopping streets are most luxurious, and it is in the interest of the many that foreigners should be lured to London.

I was therefore walking along Piccadilly, the only equivalent to the Roman market-place in this gigantic city which is London, when on the pavement at the base of a shop window, was one of those open trap-doors through which goods are taken down to the cellar. Two gentlemen wearing dark overcoats and Homburg hats, walking very quickly just ahead of me, were eagerly discussing business, when one of them removing a lighted cigarette from between his lips threw it aside with a deliberation that showed how suddenly the nicest things can cease to please. What contempt there was for the unfortunate cigarette in the arrogant flick of his wrist! What a lightning gesture! Would he, I wondered, as suddenly cast off his wife if he had half a chance!

The stub remained quivering on the edge of the gaping cellar, sending up into the cold spring air a gentle wisp of blue smoke. If a sudden gust of wind had come billowing up the street, it would have needed only a few moments for the abandoned cigarette to take its revenge like a spurned woman—not with an attack of nerves, or with threats or tears, but by lighting a fine fire in Piccadilly.

The south side of the street, about three hundred yards of it, is the place to see our elegant women. Women whose husbands run limousines at the expense of the firm have mink coats; others, like myself, are in tailor-mades. Mink is the outward sign of success in New York and London; in Paris the elegant woman displays the town's ever-changing fashions but a fur coat hides everything. As I am a Londoner, at least by adoption, mink remained an unsatisfied ambition till I walked one day into Fortnum & Mason's and spent half the royalties of my latest book on a platinum mink tie to wear with my tailor-mades.

Gwen, my Canadian friend who lives in Arlington House, meeting me at the corner of Bury Street, asks if I have noticed how difficult it is to do anybody a kindness. Gwen is not afraid to show that she is kind-hearted.

'In Toronto,' she says, 'we are very anxious to be of use to one another. It comes to us when we are children because of the snow and ice in the streets. Somebody slips; we run forward to see if we can be of any help. It's natural, is it not? But here in London, the person willing to accept help is far more difficult to come by. Practically I am reduced to guiding people with white sticks across the road. They are the only ones who do not refuse the proffered arm. The others, especially the elderly ladies, appear to take it as an insult. It's rather sad because when I am old myself, if I still live in London, nobody will ever offer to help me across Piccadilly. When the traffic lights change suddenly I feel panicky even now.'

My mother-in-law who lived in the country came up to town to consult her oculist. Terrified by the traffic in Wigmore Street, which she imagined to be growing more perilous every time she came to town, she remained on the edge of the pavement in silent prayer. Suddenly a man took her arm. He was a flower-seller who had left his stall to take her across the road. My mother-in-law told me this story sitting by her fire in her comfortable house where nothing ever came to disturb her but the wind in the trees and the cries of the birds. She called this adventure her 'little miracle.'

'So you see,' I said to Gwen, 'London is a strange place. Sometimes it doesn't happen, and then suddenly it does.'

IF REALLY there are modern equivalents to the great Elizabethan seafarers, these intrepid adventurers are never quite, in the new Elizabethan age, where one expects to meet them. Yet judge, I pray you, if they still exist.

Here was another Monday and I was ironing a blouse while Mrs. Terry dusted the room. She began by telling me that she was one of six girls and there was mum who was seventy.

'As we, the girls, are all over forty,' she declared, 'it's nice still to be able to say: "We're off to visit mum!" or "Mum came along yesterday." Then again we plan a long time ahead what to give her for Christmas and for her birthday.'

Mrs. Terry swept non-existent dust off several bottles of perfume. I watched her anxiously from behind the flex of the electric iron, that flex which is always getting in the way of the most delicate pleats.

'Because of the old age pension,' she said, 'mum has means of her own. She never needs ask us for anything. She can spend her money in an hour, a day, or a week—or she can put it aside. She has everything to make her happy—but no, sitting in her comfortable house she gets bored.

'And it all came about because of our youngest sister, the one we call baby, who some years ago accompanied a lady to America as her personal maid. Once a year

the lady would come back to England for a holiday,
and she brought her maid; then suddenly the lady came
home for good. We all thought that baby would
settle down comfortably near mum, but she had grown
to love New York and soon she was back there, not
only in a good job, but married.

'She loves her husband and is very happy, but as a
matter of fact all mum's daughters are happily married.
It seems that our marriages merely increased the size of
mum's family. When America came into the war our
baby sister quite lost her head at the thought that her
husband might be sent to the Pacific or even to Africa,
and as just then there was an appeal for women volun-
teers, she signed up, and there they both were sitting at
home expecting to be sent off in the same direction.
Simple folks think in simple ways, and they were simple
people in love.

'Her husband was rejected at his medical but our young
sister passed A1 and was drafted to a training camp in
Louisiana. She spent the next two years trying to get
home to her husband.

'The trouble was that all this time mum was without
news. The war ended. They had changed their address.
We asked the British Embassy to trace them. They were
back together, still perfectly happy, but had just been
too lazy to write.

'Last Christmas, Will, my American brother-in-law,
decided to give mum a lovely present. He wrote to say
that if she and all of us would get together on a certain
day and at a certain hour, he and his wife would telephone
to mum.

'What a to-do! What joy! Mum and her five
daughters, and all their children and the husbands waiting
by the corner near the fire for the telephone to ring.
Fancy us, madam, like film-stars talking over the telephone to New York! When at last it rang, and the

operator said to mum: "I have a call for you from New York," we all started to shake a bit, and then we heard an American accent at the other end, but it was Will (whom none of us had ever heard talk), and we all tried to grab the receiver from mum, but none of us could say anything because we each had a lump in our throats. We cried too. Mum cried. But it was lovely, and when it was all over we each remembered what we had wanted to say.

'About a week after Christmas, mum broke the news that she was going out to work. She was to help with the washing-up every night in a club, and with this money added to what she would save from her pension she intended to take the clipper to New York. She wanted to see her daughter and get to know her son-in-law, and nothing would stop her.

'She had worked it all out. It will take her until September to save the money, and then off she flies—with the diplomats and the film-stars.

'So mum works till ten every night. The manager of the club, when he discovered she was seventy, offered to send her home every night in a car, but mum said: "And whatever do you suppose my daughters would say if they saw me driving home with a man!"'

I have a friend called Sonia with whom I relax on the telephone after a hard morning's work. We generally talk for an hour, which is annoying for those who want to ring us up, but Sonia and I have known each other since as girls we rode on the roundabouts on the fair ground on which the Dominion cinema now stands in Tottenham Court Road. We were both so gay and exuberant that the roundabout man, noticing that our laughter was good for business, gave us one free ride in two. The undecided lookers-on, especially if they were young men, rode after us on the wooden animals and then offered us huge boxes of chocolates tied up with vivid ribbon. We were certain of having a wonderful time for a shilling, and invariably when Sonia and I telephone to each other I begin by saying: 'Do you remember how we used to slide down from the tower on the magic carpet, and how high the tower seemed to us?' and Sonia answers: 'Do you remember when we won two powder-boxes but the powder was so white that when we dabbed it on our faces we looked like clowns?' And as we talk of those days they seem as fresh as the first armfuls of lilac in May.

From this we pass on to more serious subjects: which are the best nylons, for instance, and what we intend to do this spring about hats.

'Hats are too expensive in London,' says Sonia, who is very pretty. 'To feel happy about one's hats one should have scores of them as we used to have before the war. Each time one felt a bit depressed one bought a new one. The spleen is a heady thing. Depressions are fostered in the brain. Quick! Buy a new hat! The mere sight of one's head looking different is enough to make one happy again.'

She broke off to speak to somebody. Questions and answers reached me in a distorted, unintelligible way, and it was some time before she returned to the telephone and said:

'It was the coal-man. How one has to pander to him! My coal fire is my great joy. Electric fires and gas fires are not the real thing. They heat one in sections, but a coal fire never has the same appearance five minutes on end. The flames shoot up and quarrel. Then they go down and sulk. It's all so delightfully alive and there's something of England in the days of her splendour. One sees old prints, doesn't one? Big rooms and coal fires and . . .

'But what a business getting coal! I need two sacks

a week, but last week none came so I went to complain to my coal dealer. Guess, my dear, what the woman had the effrontery to say. She said: "I understand you haven't been kind to the delivery man." "How could I be?" I answered. "I was not at home when he came. He left the coal with the housekeeper." "That's just it," she said. "The delivery man was not pleased to find you out."'

'Well!' I laughed. 'You certainly have a way with men.'

'Don't be silly!' exclaimed Sonia. 'It's for the two half-crowns he expects me to give him. So the woman at the shop said: "You understand, madam, all those streets round Grosvenor Square are very awkward for our delivery men. The embassy staffs will leave their cars parked on both sides, so the poor man has to leave his horse and cart miles away. It worries him, you see. Then he has to carry the sacks one at a time across his back, and then there are the stairs to climb. You see, madam, we can't oblige him to call on you. He likes to go to some of our customers and nothing will make him go to others, but of course, if I were to tell him that next time you will promise to be at home, I might persuade him to call.'

'So you were keeping your promise,' I said.

'Did you hear him?' she asked. 'He was blaming the diplomats, saying that they were the only ones to have any money, and what did I think of the blooming cars they brought from America, and what business had they to prevent George and him from drawing up to the kerb. George is his horse. He said he would have bashed their faces in, but where were they? Not one had the courage to remain with his motor-car. The motor-cars were all empty and it was like trying to pick a quarrel with a row of coffins. The housekeeper and I were shaking all over, not knowing whether we were to blame the coal-man,

George, or the diplomats. And it cost me ten shillings—
five shillings for last week and five for this. How are
things with you?'

'I've been saving money,' I answered. 'I saw an
advertisement in *The Times* for some *crêpe de Chine* at
3s. 10d. a yard. I dressed immediately, hurried to Oxford
Street, and by teatime I had made myself a magnificent
blouse for 5s. 9d. Yes, my dear, for exactly 5s. 9d.'

Sonia gave a little gasp of jealousy.

'But of course you haven't washed it yet?'

'It was the first thing I did, to try a small piece to see
how it washed. Magnificent! And one can iron it
like real silk.'

'It will split.'

'What does that matter?' I asked. 'I shall be tired
of it by then. Could you buy a blouse for 5s. 9d.?'

'It's only ninepence more than I give the man for
bringing up my coal,' reflected Sonia, 'and the coal
goes up in smoke! I'm not lucky just now, and what
makes it worse is that I have a little coterie of friends
who are all in the money.'

'Tell me!' I coaxed, settling down comfortably in
bed.

'A few days before Christmas I decided to pay a visit
to the Italian grocer's in Soho. The newspapers had
been talking about the financial situation, and appeared
to think that foreign produce might be affected. So, as
you can imagine, I immediately wanted to stock up with
olive oil and that delicious Roman-made spaghetti that
owes its goodness to the waters of the Tiber. My
friend Constance and I went off together, but Constance
is wealthy and I began to suspect that my excellent idea
of buying provisions in Soho might be more profitable
to her than to me, for whereas she can order things by
the dozen, I must be content with one at a time. Then
again, because she orders so much, the grocers deliver

the goods, while I who buy so little am obliged to carry everything.

'We spent a good hour going from shop to shop; still friends, smiling at each other, though half my face was far from amiable as, very apologetically, she bought up all the spaghetti, declaring she knew I would not mind. Well, my little Sonia, thought I, next time you would be wiser to keep your ideas to yourself. It was nearly one when we had finished, but Constance said: "It's much too late to go home. Let us go to a restaurant, and you shall be my guest."

'My dear, I forgave her everything. We went to a place where they serve steak, neither horse nor reindeer, but English or Scotch beef bought on the "black" and while it was cooking we went to the bar. In due course they came to tell us it was ready. Constance, by some awkward movement in getting up, overturned a heavy metal stool which fell against my leg. I nearly fainted with pain—the metal was so cold and hard, but I quickly recovered and thought no more about it.

'The next morning my leg was worse, but as there was not even a bruise I tried to tell myself that it was merely stiff. All the same I was miserable thinking of the Christmas shopping.

'I telephoned Constance. Her maid said she had gone to Paris. You, of course, were in Normandy milking cows or writing a book. By Christmas Day I was howling with pain, and in the afternoon the doctor came. There was a hidden abscess. A surgeon had to cut it open and give me penicillin; that is how I spent Christmas Day.

'By the time I was well again both you and Constance were back in town, and to add to the irony there never was a shortage of spaghetti or olive oil, so I had merely wasted my money.'

'You spoke of a coterie of wealthy friends,' I interposed. 'Tell me about the others.'

'Not now,' said Sonia. 'Try to come round to-morrow afternoon. There will be a palmist from the west country. I pay her fare but she's amazing.'

I was intrigued by Sonia's palmist. I am tempted to believe in fortune-tellers, but I fear they can only give me bad news. In my girlhood they prophesied good things; my black bread was to be turned to white. Since then I have known the joys of motherhood and as much white bread as I could eat. I would not like to take the risk of being told that my bread must become black again.

As the weather was fine I crossed Park Lane for a stroll in Hyde Park. An almost regal nurse had peeled an orange and was pushing it, slice by slice, into the mouth of a child wrapped up to his neck in a large pram. The little boy's hands were under the dark blue coverlet and he looked like one of those farm animals that one fattens with food from a spoon. He opened his mouth, closed it; reopened it, reclosed it. He was taking his daily vitamins, a good, obedient child, enjoying his first lesson in discipline. I expect he is tucked up early each evening for the sake of his nerves. At six he will go to a preparatory school, at thirteen to a public school, and at nineteen he will be ready for the army and an enemy bullet. How glad I am to have been born a girl!

There were no more rabbits in the Dell and very few riders in the Row. I crossed Knightsbridge to look into the windows of the stores. There was much yellow to evoke the coming primroses, and there were dresses made of tulle to make any young girl dream. There was also a wedding dress decorated with orange-blossom on a headless mannequin: let us hope that this decapitated bride will at least manage to keep her heart!

The noise of traffic is like the growl of thunder, but a thunder poisonous with fumes. The double-decked red omnibuses shake even the great store windows, and almost every bus is empty. Yet there are moments when one pays no attention to noise or smell. At one store the luxurious stocking department is quite deserted; the girls stand with folded arms behind smart counters. Only a few weeks ago I was laughed at when I asked for nylons, but as I had a charge account I was sent an occasional pair in the colour and thickness that the firm chose to allot me, but which unfortunately proved too short, too long, too thin, too thick, too light, or too dark—and I spent infinitely more money than some of my friends, who paid three pounds a pair in the black market for exactly what they needed. It is absurd to be honest when the law is in itself a crime, but governments invariably impose their vexations on women. Now that nylons are back nobody seems to want them; in six months' time there will be a new shortage and we shall waste precious hours searching for them.

On Sonia's birthday I telephoned to wish her many happy returns; I had not gone to consult the palmist but I was anxious to hear what had happened.

'My bad luck continues,' said Sonia, 'but for the others it was an avalanche of joy.'

She laughed, happy to give me a long telephonic account of the proceedings.

'I served the coffee and handed the cakes round,' she began, 'but of course I heard every word. It was not dishonest of me to listen. We don't set out to be secretive; in fact there is an advantage in being over-heard, for if one is quite alone with the palmist one forgets a great deal of what she says, whereas if several friends are together one can compare later on.

'Edith is the palmist. She claims that our lives are

reflected in the palms of our hands. She bends over one and sees things.

'Constance was the first to consult her. You know, my dear, Constance is really old enough to be our mother, and yet when you hear her talk you would think she was on the right side of thirty. That just proves that success can even keep the years back. She has money in the bank; not thousands and thousands but enough to be very comfortable. She has an excellent modern flat and a maid.

'Edith peered into her hand and said:

'"Lady, you are not young, and yet before spring turns into summer you are going to marry a man much younger than yourself. Heavens, lady! How he loves you! How he loves you! How he loves you!"

'My dear, she said it three times just as I have said it to you. We were terribly impressed. Just think of it, at her age.

'Constance sipped some strong coffee to help give the impression that she was quite calm: you know what it is when one suddenly wins a lot of money at Deauville. One wants to pretend that one is not shaken. She put down her cup and said: "Go on, please, Mrs. Edith!" '"I cannot go on," said Edith. '"I merely see your wedding and a journey."

'"Of course, Mrs. Edith! You mean the honeymoon?"

'"No," answered Edith, "there is no honeymoon. There are journeys. I see a ship arriving in hot countries. Oh, you have no idea, ladies, how pretty her future has become! Ah, here comes something else. I see money . . . and lots more love . . . and then more money. Heavens! How the man loves you!!"

'"Well," said Constance, taking a pound note out of her bag to pay the clairvoyant, "why should I not admit everything? True enough, I am going to marry a man I have known for some time. In fact, I tried to put him off. I have no particular advantage in being Mrs. X more than Mrs. Z. I have no relations to worry about and then, as you know, there is a little money in the bank.

'"But this man is so desperately in love with me that he wants to show me to his friends and to his partners in business; and, after all, if that is what he wants, why should I refuse him such a tiny pleasure? I said yes—I would marry him. It does not make me love him any more or less, but it appears that it will add to his happiness to give me his name."

'She is still charming,' admitted Sonia, 'and after [all why should not this man be in love with her? She has rather nice dimples, white teeth, beautiful hair, and is as gay as a really happy woman, a woman who does not bother too much about her age and does not try to hide it. I like that in a friend. A woman who tries to hide her age is a difficult woman to get on with. If she hides that she will hide other things, and then one loses in her company all the fun of intimate confidences.'

'What did Edith tell the others?' I asked.

'There is Flora. She also is rich . . . rich. . . . Money cascades over her like the bubbling waters of the Niagara. I will tell you about her, but first let me tell you what the palmist said to me:

'As usual, she said, I was running, running after money. Indeed, she is right. That is what I spend my life doing. "Oh!" she exclaimed, peering into my hands. "Look at this! You are going to have an accident."

'"That," I said, "must refer to the one I had before Christmas, the abscess on my leg."

'"No, it is not that one," said Edith. "It is another. I think it would be wise for you not to do any spring-cleaning this year—and beware of steps. I can see you tumbling downstairs. . . .   Oh! and here is your arm in a sling."

"'My goodness!" I exclaimed.   "First I am laid up with a bad leg, and now you foretell me a broken arm! I have half a mind not to pay you, Mrs. Edith!"'

'You understand now,' I said, 'why I was so unwilling to consult your clairvoyant, but before you ring off teach me the best way to use up the giblets of a fowl.'

Sonia is a wonderful cook.   Flattered by my question, she asked:

'Do you know how to make a risotto?'

'I know how to make a stew of onions, rice, and butter,' I answered guardedly.

'Possibly. Anybody can do that, but do you cook the rice in water?' she queried.

'Yes,' I agreed.   'That is how I generally cook it.'

'You are wrong,' she said.   'Your rice should cook in butter.   Put two ounces of butter in a saucepan with a finely cut onion, and turn slowly with a wooden spoon so that your onion becomes brown and not black.   Add to this a full cup of rice which has been washed three times in boiling water to remove every particle of dirt and glue.   Stir your rice with the butter and onion slowly over a very low flame until the rice swells, and then add some of the *bouillon* from the adjacent saucepan in which your giblets and chicken legs have been boiling. In about forty minutes your risotto should be ready. Remove the giblets and chicken legs from the adjoining saucepan and put them on the risotto.   A turn of the wrist to the pepper mill, and there is a dish fit for a queen!'

'Well, so long,' I exclaimed, 'and thanks for the recipe.'

CHAPTER III

RAIN HAS been falling all night and yet spring is in the air. The flower-seller and his wife who have their pitch against the low wall of a bomb site in Curzon Street have spread tulips in tins all along the pavement. Berkeley Square is rainswept; Bond Street is slowly changing from the low red-bricked thoroughfare of nineteenth-century fashion to something much more modern. Its old character is more difficult to find; its new one is not yet apparent, though the magnificent Time-Life building, evocation of Fifth Avenue, suggests that the narrow street of Nelson's time is gradually becoming an American colony. There are fewer coats of arms above the little shops. I used to buy my gloves from a court glover, long things for evening wear that buttoned up the arm. Branches of multiple shops are creeping in, and we see the same dresses offered to us everywhere. French jewellers, however, bring us luxury, luxury that is not afraid to make itself visible, diamond brooches worth £20,000 and which, I am not ashamed to say, I think devastatingly beautiful. The picture galleries complain that old masters are not so easy to come by. They are being siphoned into the museums. There I go to see them, but a little sadly. Desultory crowds file past them as in Moscow. Pictures painted for real people that once graced lived-in houses are now safe but cold, like tombstones in a cemetery. They have reached the highest honours and like human princes must suffer boredom.

Here is Oxford Street.

The purpose of my expedition was to buy knitting wool. I sew my own lingerie, make my own dresses, and knit my own woollies. Wool, silks, and materials are therefore my passion. The girl behind the counter, though young and pretty, had an untamed cockney accent, the sort the B.B.C. loves to put over the air in its music-hall and plays. The continental stage has its lovers and mistresses; New York has its gangsters; London has the character with the cockney accent. Having chosen the colour of my wool, I took a skein of it to my pretty assistant who asked me sweetly, because I was nearer the pigeon-hole than she was, to go and collect the amount I required. I then bought another piece of silk to make a blouse.

'Will it wash?'

'Perfectly, madam.'

This was a good thing, for on my way home the rain fell in torrents and the material was soaked through the paper bag.

The afternoon post had brought me a letter from my son, and the house carpenter was waiting to put up a curtain-rod in the kitchen.

While the carpenter was at work I read my son's letter. Eighteen months at a preparatory school in Kent had undoubtedly influenced the workings of his mind. Women from all time, and in almost all countries, are not considered competent to discuss the education of a boy. Certainly there came a moment in my life when I was suddenly aware of the ocean that separated my entirely feminine mind from that of my schoolboy child.

On Sunday he drove up to London with the son of the ambassador of Pakistan to lunch at the embassy.

This social call appears to have been a great success. There was the fast American car, the ambassadress wore a sari, and there was curry for lunch. He telephoned during the afternoon, but as a grown man would telephone rapidly from some business appointment without giving details. His letter now glows with wonderment as if he had made a journey to the East. There was also a Persian school friend who brought back from Teheran 10 lb. of caviare, 'which luckily,' says my son, 'the English boys do not like so we ate it all between us.'

I asked the carpenter if he would accept a cup of tea, and added:

'I'm ashamed to trouble you for such a little job. When I was a young married woman all the window-frames were made of wood. It was nothing to put up a curtain-rod. I used to do it myself. One hammered a nail into the woodwork and then, if one wanted to change anything, one just pulled the nail out. Now it's all steel.'

'Yes,' laughed the carpenter. 'Wooden window-frames are becoming rare, like a great many other things. The result is that when people want a carpenter they have a job to find one. Skilled carpenters are the exception. The raising of the school age is partly to blame, because young men in long trousers are too proud to serve as apprentices.'

He sat down with his back to the refrigerator and continued:

'When I was a little boy the winters up north were hard and it was our job to sweep the snow away before starting work in the morning. And you'll laugh, madam, but the nails were so cold that they used to freeze our fingers, and we cried! Those were the hard days—the good days. We learned our craft, and I might tell you, madam, that there was nothing in wood from the roof of a house to the mast of a schooner that I did not learn how to make.'

Still young-looking but almost bald, he sat on the edge of the chair holding his cup of tea over his white apron, legs apart, head bent down. He sipped his tea very slowly, continually bringing out some unexpected phrase:

'When my wife and I go on holiday we visit the houses the various councils put up. I suppose it seems funny to you, but we get a lot of fun in seeing the little differences from one house to the other, and then we take a look at the old cottages with the lovely beams and oak floor-boards and carved stair-rails.

'There are still men of my age who know how to work. A foreman can tell by just standing in a corner and keeping his eyes open, which are the men who know and which do not. The company that owns this building still has a block of flats made entirely of wood. I was sent to mend something there the other day, and the foreman, after watching me a few moments, said: "There's a job in the City I bet you'd like?"

'"What sort of a job?" I asked.

'"Making pews for an old Wren church that was 'blitzed.' A real, lovely job," he said, "and mark you, they are making them just as good as in the old days. But they'd better hurry up and rebuild their old churches or all the good craftsmen will be dead!"'

He sipped his tea again. Then stirred it. I watched him fascinated, I who drink off a cup of tea in half a minute, anxious about a night-dress half ironed or milk on the fire. But my carpenter stirred slowly—slowly. He continued:

'Unfortunately the big companies employing carpenters of their own no longer have any discernment. They argue that a good carpenter and a bad carpenter add up to two carpenters, and each gets the same wage packet. The good carpenter will often finish off the

work of the bad carpenter. This happens to me every
day. But whereas in the old days I would have scolded
the bad carpenter and told him where he had gone
wrong so that next time he would have done it right,
now I just do his work without saying anything, for if
I scolded him I would be labelled a bad comrade!'

As soon as he had gone I took my baby Singer out of
the box and put it on a table by the window. I was
full of joy at the thought that I might have enough
material not only to make my curtain but also to cover
a lampshade. How I love my baby Singer. What a
splendid thing is progress! Alas for the sailing ships
and the City pews, an electric sewing-machine is the
thing for me! I love to make my lingerie by hand,
experimenting with all the different stitches, sewing with
fairy needles, but for dresses and curtains and lamp-
shades, hail to progress and an electric machine!

The carpenter came back the next morning with the
rod cut to the right size, and I was unable to resist the
pleasure of running up the curtains immediately to see
if he liked them.

He said they were very pretty, and he even gave me a
new idea for the hem which I had not finished. I thus had
the satisfaction of discovering that one does not always
humiliate a man, even an Englishman, when one talks to
him about such feminine accomplishments as sewing.

Now I must get Sonia to talk to me about her friends.
This is the subject that fascinates me.

'How is Constance?' I asked.

'Oh, my dear!' cried Sonia, 'I must tell you the most
shattering thing! For some weeks after our séance with
the palmist I kept on ringing her up in the hope of
seeing her again. She pretended to have a cold.

'"I am not fit to go out," she said, "and I am going through all those provisions we bought in Soho before Christmas."

'Well, as you know, I keep away from my friends when they have a cold. It is not because I am hard-hearted, but I always catch everything.

'Suddenly the other day she rang up to ask if she could come to have tea.

'She arrived wearing dark spectacles and a light scarf over her hair. She sat down in my best arm-chair and said:

'"Well, there it is. We are to be married at the end of April."

'Constance removed her spectacles, and I gave a cry of surprise. My little Madeleine, it was amazing. I do not know how to tell you. The story about her cold was an invention. She had been to the most famous plastic surgeon in London and he had lifted her face. If I had not seen her sitting in front of me in my best arm-chair, I would not have believed it possible. I have never seen anything like it in my life. She is incredible, Madeleine. She has grown younger in an exquisite way; I mean that she has grown younger and yet retains the soft qualities of experience and age. Her features are not those of a silly young woman. That would have been ridiculous on a body which after all is not that of a girl. Her face is the sweet face of a woman of forty.

'"You see, Sonia," she said to me, "on thinking it over I did not want my future husband to regret having married me. He might so easily have done so at the end of a year. As you know, it was not I who insisted on the marriage, but as he wanted it I felt I must do the honest thing and try to give him something worth having. This famous surgeon is a man of extraordinary comprehension. He inspected me very closely, and then we both sat down in his consulting-room and talked things over. We discussed what was possible and what was not possible. I never expected that a man could do so much for a woman. Only, my little Sonia, for ten whole days and nights after the operation I cried my soul out. If only you had seen the cuts and stitches and bruises. You understand? I had lost faith. I did not believe the wounds would heal. I had fallen into the hands of a charlatan, I thought, and I shall be permanently disfigured. I cried and cried. There are doctors and surgeons, I argued, who play on the credulity of stupid, vain women. They ask huge fees and—is there anything more ridiculous in the eyes of a man than a woman who wants to regain some part of her youth? You fool! You poor fool! And then, to whom could I turn for sympathy? It was no good going back to the surgeon. He would merely put me off with a tale, or his secretary would tell me he was booked up for days or weeks ahead. If I had told you, Sonia, you would have laughed at me. So I stayed in my flat with my invented cold until suddenly, towards the beginning of this week, the marks began to disappear: I could see an improvement almost every hour. There now remains only the tiniest scar above my left eye. That is the reason for my dark spectacles. Tell me truthfully, my little Sonia, do I look younger?"

'That is what she said to me, and I exclaimed:

'"Oh, yes indeed you look beautiful!"

'"My little Sonia," she said archly, "I did so want to keep my dimples. To begin with they give me a gay and happy expression, and then . . . I suppose they are a memory of my girlhood. The surgeon said: 'But of course, dear lady, we shall leave your dimples; or if you prefer it, we could make you new ones for the same fee!'"'

CHAPTER IV

HERE COMES Mrs. Terry again, pushing her sweeper with one hand and holding a freshly ironed night-dress in tissue-paper in the palm of her other hand. She delivers my night-dress and asks happily:

'And how are you, madam?'

During the war Mrs. Terry and her husband had one of the loveliest flats in the building, a penthouse flat on the sixth floor which was too near the searchlight-swept, silver-balloon-dotted sky to be popular with those who feared the nocturnal air-raids.

Peace brought the Terrys down to the basement. Their apartment is just as comfortable, no less modern, but they look up at the road through an area. Mr. Terry has his office next to his flat, and it is from his office that he sends forth maids to various apartments up and down the busy building. I am a spoilt woman. Mrs. Terry looks after me personally.

Occasionally I pay them a visit towards teatime. Their kitchen is the sweetest place, smelling of newly baked cakes. While the cakes are cooling on the white cloth, Mrs. Terry irons or mends. Her husband's delight is to do the manly jobs about the flat, to arrange things for her, mend the radio or change the water in the aquarium.

And as they are childless, there is Fluffy.

The previous summer, the Begum Aga Khan and I, having gone off for no reason at all to the Cat Show, she fell in love with and bought a Blue Persian kitten to accompany her on her travels.   Out of jealousy, some weeks later, I bought one also, not at the Cat Show but from a young woman exhibitor who lived a long way up the Edgware Road.

I brought the kitten back in a basket to my flat, and each morning while I was writing, she purred softly, but the time came when I was obliged to go over to my farm in Normandy, and if she came with me she would not be able to come back.   So I asked Mrs. Terry to look after her.

I understand now why cat-breeders hate to sell their pedigree kittens to women like the Begum and me who are always travelling.   They say that we are not dependable, that however much we may fall in love with a kitten, one day we shall take an aeroplane or an ocean liner and abandon it.   In the case of the Begum, because of her exalted position, there had been a positive reluctance on the part of the owner to sell her the kitten. Fortunately Simba, as the Begum's kitten became known, grew up the happiest of cats.

By the time I was back in London, Fluffy had made her home with the Terrys, and it was touching to see Mrs. Terry trying to discover what I was going to do. 'I suppose you will be wanting her back, madam? Mr. Terry and I will be broken-hearted.   He has taken to her so, madam.   And so have I.   It is as if we had a child.'

What could I do but abandon Fluffy to her new home? And then the Terrys have a caravan where they go every week-end, and Mr. Terry takes his daughter-cat in a magnificent, specially designed basket, and on their return I hear all about it.   The caravan, with other caravans, is in the middle of a big field.   On Sunday mornings the men go to the local inn while the women discuss their children and their washing-machines.   Mrs.

Terry has a young niece who is to attend a school for domestic arts. When Sally is eighteen she will know all about running a house, and she will then be qualified to fill a post worth eight pounds a week.

Mrs. Terry is very impressed by her niece's promising career. Already she is very brilliant at school. It is one of the wonders of modern times that girls are proving themselves cleverer than boys. Her mother, says Mrs. Terry, serves her as if she were a princess with breakfast in bed on Saturdays, and on Sundays while Sally does her homework father helps mother with the washing-up.

Mr. Terry is not in favour of this excessive feminine education, but Mrs. Terry, remembering her own beginnings, is impressed by the money that Sally will earn at eighteen, and she says that amongst the people she knows, the women are much more education-minded than the men.

Sonia asks me on the telephone how I would translate the colour magenta into French.

'But you silly, it's the same thing.'

She appeared surprised.

'What would be another word for it—mauve, violet, cyclamen?'

'No, purple would be nearer. It suggests a maiden aunt or a Victorian grandmother. I think a not very pretty ambassador's wife might appear at a court function in it. Why do you want to know?'

'I met a man at my little club in Soho last night who is in the export trade. He wants to compile some catalogue, but he can wait. Would you like to hear about Flora?'

'Why, yes. I am longing to hear about her.'

'You remember that I told you that she was very rich? Some time ago her husband bought a beautiful new house in Ireland. Now would it not be wonderful to have a husband like that—a husband who suddenly bought you a house and opened the sluices of the nearest bank so that you could furnish it just as you pleased?'

She laughed and went on:

'Some women really are lucky. This one, for instance, was not born here. She arrived from the Far East when she was a girl of fifteen, just early enough for her voice not to be hardened into the groove of her own language. She learned to speak English without any accent at all, but her mind remained practical. The amount of arithmetic she has taught me is amazing. One has quite a wrong impression of arithmetic at school: we dream all day while the mistress works out profit and loss on the blackboard; if five eggs cost eightpence, how much will ten cost? It is a logical sequence to the alphabet and King Alfred burning the cakes. In real life, arithmetic does not seem to matter much. One earns a five-pound note, and when it is spent, that is an end to it. I have never kept an account-book or tried to remember at the end of the day how much I have spent. When there is money I spend it, when there is none, I put off buying what I need: a loaf of bread, a lipstick, or a new hat. There was nothing like this about her. She had been poor as a girl. She intended to make a fine marriage.

'"Every sort of husband," she says, "can be found in the heart of London. There are poor men, of course, but there are also millionaires; the millionaire needs to go out just as much as the poor man." Believe me, she knows what she is talking about. She may have come here from a long way off, but she has studied this lovely city of London and knows the wonders that abound here.

'Yet this is what makes me so angry: why did I never see all these things? What was the matter with me? It must be a question of luck. Some of us merely meet the milkman, the crossing-sweeper, or the policeman; others run straight up against the bored millionaire who is suddenly intrigued by the shape of our nose or the turn of our lips. But Flora——'

'What does Flora say?'

'Flora has an answer to everything. She says: "Of course! Of course! You are jealous; you merely think: 'The woman is lucky!' Well, yes, in a way I am lucky. What have I that you have not? Nothing, my dear, but the will to succeed. One rainy night on my way to the cinema I met a man who needed cheering up. I charmed him because I was something he had not guessed existed; he whose business deals in millions suddenly switched his interest to me."'

'So that comes of walking out in the rain!' I said.

'He married her,' said Sonia, 'and gave her the wonderful house in Ireland. Imagine buying everything new! Do you appreciate the rebirth of one's mind, the pure joy of no longer seeing muslin curtains seeped in London fog, of going to the stores and ordering everything, everything new? After that Flora telephoned every day from Ireland: the house was magnificent, the carpets were laid, the curtains hung, the linen put away, but soon Flora had nothing to do and she was bored. She used to say: "Life has taught me everything except to do nothing." She bought a few shares on the stock exchange and, naturally, made money. Then one day some stock she had bought went down a few points. I have never heard a woman in such a panic. "But what does it matter?" I asked her: "it makes no difference at all to your fortune. You are just as rich as ever." "It is not that," she answered. "What worries me is that this might prove the beginning of the end. If success has a beginning, the same must apply to poverty."'

Sonia laughed:

'Are we ever satisfied?'

CHAPTER V

I WAS TO have my portrait painted for the summer exhibition at Burlington House. I fought against the idea at the time. I even had an attack of nerves in Curzon Street and cried, which is not the way a modern woman should behave, but as Flora would have said, almost anything can happen in the heart of London.

I had no direct excuse for being so difficult, but there hovered at the back of my head a rather poignant conversation with a French playwright for whom, before the recent war, I had a great affection.

Francis de Croisset was the author of a hundred charming plays which seemed, as indeed they were, made specially for the Paris boulevards. They were subtle, not harsh, full of clever effects, and, of course, interpreted by those wonderful French actors of the day. De Croisset had come to believe in his characters: bold some of them were, delicious lovers were others. His own exclamations were always gay and unexpected. Of a woman he had always loved but who had refused to have anything to do with him, he said quizzically: 'She is no longer young, but each time I meet her something goes bang in my heart; women who have withstood a man's advances have a charm all their own.

'When I was young,' he went on, 'to conquer a lovely or witty woman seemed the most worthwhile thing in the world. I would have done anything. Yet when I was little, I do not recall having any special ambitions, but later they came surging up. Social success I have had (it was necessary then): President Wilson was my guest after the First World War; fame I have, and that particular delight of seeing an audience laughing at one's play when unseen one is at the back of a box.'

'Do you realize,' I exclaimed, 'that for the first time you are talking to me about yourself! I should like best to hear about those fabulous real people of the Boulevard St. Germain you married into, those witty descendants of the Marquis de Sade; and then about your fellow writers, France, Proust, and Marcel Prévost. It is wonderful to create characters, but will you not also write your autobiography?'

He looked at me obliquely and answered:

'Young woman, when a man writes his autobiography or sits for his portrait, it is time for him to die.'

He added:

'Do I appear to you so old, so written out?'

He was sensitive about his age and I had vexed him terribly. The joy went out of our evening. He was a successful writer, an affectionate and true friend, but a snob, not out of snobbishness but out of necessity. We are too hard to-day on the snobs of yesterday. They were the curators of a witty, polite, and gracious way of living that it is fashionable, for the moment, to criticize. But de Croisset had not found it easy as a young man to be accepted by the literary *salons* of Paris in the nineties, and he might not have liked to let us into the secrets. He died a year later. His plays are out-dated but his memoirs would have been passionately interesting.

I was foolish to allow this incident to come between me and the painting of my portrait. De Croisset was talking about men, not women. Women, from girl-hood, are always writing their memoirs and having their portraits painted. So I capitulated and took the train for Salisbury.

Wilfrid de Glehn, R.A., was the artist. His portraits of women were a feature of the summer show. The moderns thought him uninspired because he made a true likeness, painting after the fashion of Sargent. I believe his work has not yet been fully appreciated. His colours are sombre and classical, and long experience with nudes, for which as a young painter he was famous, gave him respect for the female form.

I had made it a condition that I should be painted in a coat and skirt with a hat. At this, of course, he fulminated, for artists are always afraid that in a few years our hats will seem ridiculous. They are wrong: even a nude is dated by the way a woman does her hair, whether it is short or long. There is nothing wrong in a portrait being dated. Indeed it adds to its value. A writer or a painter is more likely to live if he reflects the fashions of his time. Toulouse-Lautrec and Steinlein, by immortalizing the women of Montmartre and the Moulin Rouge, have immortalized themselves, whereas G. F. Watts and Burne-Jones spurned the feminine fashions of Victorian London and are less sought after to-day.

The truth is that most men consider that there is something flippant in a woman's hat. Their manliness seems to make it necessary for them to laugh at what for us is so important. A hat portrays an age. It is as if Gainsborough had mocked the women of his generation. What inspires a hat? Mme Agnès, a great modiste, once said to me: 'It is in the air. It is in the street. I pick it up unconsciously.'

To all but a few men, however, women's hats are ridiculous, and yet it is most often by a hat that we first attract them. At all events de Glehn capitulated.

We had arranged to meet at the station barrier. What did each of us expect the other to look like? I saw an elderly man with a young, rose-tinted skin and very blue eyes. He wore plus-fours; a white dog was at his feet. He held out his hand, quite sure that it was I, and after exchanging the usual greetings we went to his car.

Sitting in front with him, the dog on the seat behind, I began to feel intimidated.

'I am nervous,' I confessed, 'and I know that you are going to find me terribly ignorant about painting. I have the irregular sort of face that I believe only Renoir could have painted. You don't mind my mentioning Renoir? It is merely to make an excuse for my face.'

'No,' he answered, laughing. 'We may even get on very well together, for we have disclosed a mutual admiration. I shall bear the great Renoir in mind. Yes, perhaps you would have been his type. You were born in Montmartre, I believe?'

He looked at me sideways.

'Ah!' he exclaimed, seeing the hat-box on my knees. 'Inside there, I presume, is the famous hat. I must tell you seriously: I am far more afraid of the hat than I am of your face. Oh, the maddening complications of a woman's hat! I do hope you will not decide to change the ribbons, or the flowers, or the feathers, or whatever it may be, between every sitting? That would make my life singularly difficult. But,' he added, warming up, 'why, in the name of heaven, be painted in a hat! Is not a woman's hair both her modesty and her pride?'

I took no notice of this outburst, and catching sight of the glories of Salisbury cathedral fastened my eyes upon them.

'Oh, how magnificent!'

'Yes, yes!' he cried approvingly. 'Magnificent, in-deed! You may well say so! I am indeed relieved that you are an appreciative woman. In a few moments we shall see the spire to better effect, and every time I see it I thank God that it was not caught by a stray bomb.'

* B

The country was beautiful. I loved specially the long, low walls built of black and white stone and covered with thatch. Fine estates had tall trees. A signpost read: To Stonehenge. This must be Thomas Hardy's country, I thought.

De Glehn, perhaps because of what I had said about Renoir, now continued the conversation in French which he spoke without any accent, explaining that he had spent a good deal of his childhood at Le Havre before studying art in Paris.

'Le Havre had a considerable English colony,' he said. 'We had our clergy, our lawyers, and a consul. The shipping lines had English agents; the warehouses English managers, and though the colony kept to itself the children mixed with French children, growing up bilingual.'

These memories pleased him. He wanted to tell me about his boyhood, and went on:

'My mother was a fine painter. She and other painters used to wander along the coast with their canvases and colours. On one occasion she came back to tea with a picture she had just painted at Ste Adresse, but the canvas was very strange, roughly torn at the edges and of unusually fine texture.

'"What is this canvas?" we asked.

'"The canvas?" she echoed, embarrassed. "Well, I had the colours, the brushes, and the easel, but nothing on which to paint"—she paused—"there was nobody about so I removed my cambric drawers and painted on them."

'"Oh!" we exclaimed in delight.

'"Please!" she urged. "Why waste time talking about my drawers? It is the picture that matters."'

The artist and his wife made me very comfortable in their beautiful house. The studio was a converted barn

half-way down the drive; the back of the house over-
looked a croquet lawn and distant fields. The house
itself was old-fashioned and utterly delightful, the sort
of house one imagines people enjoying in a more
leisurely age. De Glehn had bought it during the war,
his house in Cheyne Walk having been destroyed in an
air-raid.

Mrs. de Glehn, an American, is herself a fine artist.
Their pictures filled the rooms, but there were many
others by Sargent, with whom they had been on intimate
terms. Husband and wife were excellent musicians and
both admired the stories of Henry James. They had
used all their talents to decorate this new home. I have
a recollection of large low rooms with whitewashed
walls quite covered with paintings in light frames. The
bricks of the fire-place were painted white and there was
an edging of Burne-Jones blue which de Glehn had put
on himself, using up an old tube discovered in his studio.
No interior decorator would have dared this stroke which
the painter did out of devilry, but these personal touches
were everywhere. A garden table had been very effect-
ively painted by him in emerald green.

Mrs. de Glehn I thought lovely, her features so finely
cut that there was the clarity, the smoothness of porcelain about them. Her eyes were very dark and she
looked at one ardently from under the prettiest white
hair. She could very well have come out of the pages
of Henry James, for though born in America she had
travelled widely as a young woman in Italy, in Spain,
and in England. Her drawings were truly beautiful,
and her husband had a great regard for her opinion on
his painting: he invited her criticism, then violently
defended himself, rebelling at every phrase, seeking to
prove her wrong, shouting, sulking, arguing, breaking
out from behind barricades, skirmishing, plunging, and
retreating. He never admitted she was right—he was

too much the master of the house—but soon his wife's criticism would take effect and he would quietly slink off and alter his picture.

His studio surprised me. I had expected an enormous room drowned in sunlight, and instead it was in the even light of the north. One lost nothing of blue sky and sunshine, but they reached one filtered and softened. The walls were covered with pictures, and indeed there were so many that one ceased to see them. He painted me by the door to which steps led up. There was always a good fire and his dog slept in a corner, its nose between its paws. After long periods of immobility I used to envy the dog, which could change its position if it wanted to. Sometimes it would leave its corner and go to the door, whereupon its master, putting his brush on his palette or in his mouth, would open it for his favourite and then return to work. A few minutes later there would be a scratching at the door; then the master would again put his brush in his mouth or on his palette, and let the dog in. I chiefly longed to stretch my neck, but I was afraid to change my pose. Nevertheless I learnt to speak without moving my eyes or my head or my hands, and this, for a woman as excitable as I, was no small feat.

I would not have believed that so old a man could be so young. He used to dance in front of the canvas. He would come, he would go, his arm would stretch out, and then one heard the grating of the brush. The colours that he ground and mixed added their oily smell to the fumes of the fire; and interminably, seated on my chair, I would look obliquely (to give a good stance to the back and narrow my waist) at the blue sky beyond the window.

Mrs. de Glehn used to come and fetch us at one. She would talk about the flower-beds and the state of the front lawn, but the moment always came when her eyes would turn to the canvas, and that is what the painter, respectful, tender but ready to revolt, was waiting for.

I would choose this moment to step down from the dais and, without looking at the portrait, I would call the dog and run down the steps into the open air. I was hungry and the garden smelt delicious. I would then go up to my room and take off my hat with the curious feeling of having returned from a social call or from church.

At lunch the master looked a little sulky. His wife remained the admirable, the charming hostess. There were two men guests, expert fishermen, whom I only saw at meals. Conversation, I am glad to say, veered from painting to fishing. Then, after lunch, as in an Edwardian house party, we played croquet till de Glehn would exclaim:

'Now, Mrs. Henrey, we must go back to work.'

I went upstairs to put on my impeccable sapphire blue tailor-made, and my adorable hat of matching felt with its sweeping curve of pheasant feathers, one dyed brilliant red, seemingly growing out of the body of a tiny bird with soft down and bright eyes. The tiny, exotic bird looked incredibly real and yet it was but a fairylike assemblage, feathers and down, against the rim of the felt by the cunning fingers of the great Madame Agnès.

'Truly this hat,' thought I, 'has a right to immortality.'

It had been my first Paris hat after the liberation. Paris had suffered cruelly whatever people may say, but Paris had wisely kept its dressmakers and modistes, its precious stones, its feathers, its flowers, and ethereal veils. My Paris hat made my breasts swell with love and pride. I felt at the sight of it an indescribably sweet fervour, as I once felt about Napoleon's famous hat when I saw it behind the glass case at the Invalides.

The studio door was open and the master was standing

in front of his easel. I half expected him to say to me, as Louis XIV said to Madame de Maintenon:

'Madame, you almost kept me waiting!'

Yes, indeed. I had dreamed a little about my hat. My thoughts were in the rue St. Honoré. I climbed on to the dais, and my neck arched itself into the right position. Already my body seemed accustomed to its twisted immobility. De Glehn painted silently for a few moments, and then said:

'I am pleased. My wife likes the portrait. That is vital. Any picture she does not like is a complete failure as far as I am concerned. Few people realize what we go through—the failures, the disappointments. You tell me you like Renoir, that you adore Rembrandt. Of course, and why should you not? The museums of London, Paris, Amsterdam, and Madrid have the cream of what the great masters painted, but have you ever wondered how many canvases they spoilt? Sargent, whom I venerate, had moments of utter depression. We suffer abominably.'

'Why do you suppose you are the only ones?' I asked. 'What about the musicians, the dressmakers, the writers? And do not I too have my moments of despair. Whatever one writes has been better written before.'

There was a wide swish of the brush against the canvas.

'There!' he exclaimed, delighted. 'That was the start of your jacket. Sapphire blue is a lovely colour, dark but luminous as night.'

He stepped back, and I noticed that he was shod in good, stout, walking shoes. Cycling or golfing plus-fours showed his legs to advantage. Here he was, practising the ballet steps again; if painting really makes a man suffer it also keeps him fit.

'Oh,' he agreed, laughing, 'I don't suppose we suffer so much as I pretend. No, on the whole we have a

wonderful life. Sargent and I used to arrive in quite
new countries and paint the most enchanting pictures,
but the country we liked best was Spain. The women
were exquisite to paint. They had character and beauty
combined. I think that in those days the Spaniards
were the least ambitious people in the world. Perhaps
they were happy to be rid of their once great empire,
for if you no longer have an empire, who can come and
take it away from you?'

'You can fight amongst yourselves,' I said, thinking
of the civil war. But the master was remembering the
women whom Sargent and he had painted.

'The Spanish and the Italian women are naturally
beautiful,' he said. 'English women have perfectly pro-
portioned bodies: my best nudes were done from English
girls. American women have lovely hands—these are
the women I prefer, for, as you are aware, I married one.
American women——' He paused.

'But I am afraid that it was in France that we saw the
least beautiful women. For instance, on one occasion
we made a journey into the Auvergne——'

'Oh, come!' said I, vexed, having taken this last part
as an insult to myself. 'What do painters know about
beautiful women? Their tastes are not the tastes of
other men; see, for instance, in a modern picture gallery
what uncouth, ungraceful women most of them seem to
paint!'

'We may not look for the same qualities,' he said.

'Then how, as an artist, do you judge a woman?'

'Oh, personally,' he said, laughing, 'I automatically
see her in the nude. I judge her breasts, her hips, her
legs. Don't blush! I am aware that a man has to be very
careful when he discusses art. Women are so sensitive.
They think that they alone should measure out to perfection. And you do not need to tell me that you also
are not envious of every other woman you meet? French

women are never satisfied. Men are much luckier. We can get on with our work without worrying about our legs or our waists.'

'It is true,' I admitted, 'that I spend a good deal of time being jealous of other women. I scrutinize each one, and if she has lovelier hair or bigger eyes, my day is spoilt. I would eagerly steal these good points from her. But as for men being luckier, I'm glad you think so. I have no desire at all to be a man, and will remain with my feminine reactions and rather mean jealousies. On the other hand, when the painter looks around for a model does he really need to consider her hips? Our hips can easily be made small or large according to the dress we wear. If women in Paris are rather elegant (in spite of your unhappy journey with Sargent into Auvergne) perhaps the secret is that the Frenchwoman, her hairdresser, her dressmaker, her modiste, her jeweller, and everybody else who looks after her are great artists. So why do painters so often believe that art excludes elegance?'

'Toulouse-Lautrec——' he began.

'All the impressionists of his school,' I put in, 'painted little women with cute hats and amusing faces. The bar of the Moulin Rouge, for instance. . . .'

A car had drawn up on the gravel of the drive. We heard the scrunching of the tyres on the gravel, and Mrs. de Glehn came up. She said it was teatime, and that her husband had no business to keep me sitting so long. 'The poor woman will be quite dead!' she exclaimed. 'I thought we might take tea to our two fishermen who have certainly no intention of coming back. Mrs. Henrey would have an opportunity to see the surrounding country.'

The country was indeed delightful. One heard the pitiful cries of sheep being shorn, cries of fear against the drone of a machine. 'I hope we have no cruel winds,' said de Glehn, thinking of the lambs. We left the car in a lane, and in single file, like Red Indians, walking on tiptoe we crossed a stretch of meadow to the water where Dr. Bourne, the great heart specialist, without uttering a word waved affectionately. His hat was pulled down over his forehead, and beside him were several spectacles, even a pair of pince-nez, to magnify the flies or other objects that he was fixing to the end of his lines. He looked very serious in spite of being so far away from his hospital.

We laid a sheet on the grass to sit on, and his wife Margherita (she was from New Orleans) came to talk. She was without make-up and very dark, and her beautiful dark eyes were soft and inquiring. She was a very learned woman, and, knowing this, one would not have begun by discussing dresses, or shoes, or lipsticks, but one soon discovered that no subject got on her nerves. She showed a delightful interest in every topic, and then again she was immensely tender. There was none of that slight superiority that as a sex we are apt to acquire when we get a name for being clever.

De Glehn said to me:

'She is what I consider a beautiful woman. Her eyes are the mirror of her soul.'

He had known her for some time, he said, not so many years. No, it was not really a question of time, but he knew her well. It was *une affaire de cœur*, he said. Truly an affair of the heart!

I looked at him uncomprehendingly.

A niece of Mrs. de Glehn had been threatened with rheumatic heart disease, and Geoffrey (this was Dr. Bourne) had been wonderful. He saved her, and from then on the two families were close friends. 'I told you,' he said, smiling, 'that it was an affair of the heart.'

The doctor came along in a furious temper. While

we had been talking in whispers, a woman and her children had noisily crossed the bridge over the river. She had ruined his entire day! Certainly, if it had not been for the woman and her silly children, he would have caught an enormous fish. He had a secret conviction that the fish was likely to rise.

'Come and have your tea,' said his wife.

The doctor was quickly calmed, but now that we all had the right to talk, it was he who remained rather silent. He was not a man to accept failure.

It was delightful by the river, but a cool wind brought us back to reality. We must not catch cold; the tea-things were put away and we rolled up the sheet. The two cars were in the lane, and as I had come here with the de Glehns, it was decided that I should go back with the Bournes. The doctor was now very gay and drove slowly to enjoy the scenery, but after a while we came upon the painter changing a tyre. 'Shall I help you?' asked the doctor. 'No! No!' exclaimed de Glehn. 'It's already finished!' He was putting back his tools, youthful and quick at seventy-seven, while half a dozen young boys from the village were watching him with their hands in their pockets. We had pulled up in spite of his assurance that he needed no help, and now Dr. Bourne was with him and the painter was explaining how it had happened. 'I had stopped,' he said. 'There was a curious noise under the car'—and suddenly he had crawled under the body, so that all one saw of him were his stockinged legs and stout walking shoes emerging from underneath.

'He's amazing,' said Margherita, and she made a sign to her husband to come back. She thought the painter might become annoyed if we insisted on wanting to help. It's so good to be able to look after oneself. So Dr. Bourne came back into the car and Mrs. de Glehn waved us farewell, with a smile to Margherita, which between women meant: 'Yes, leave my husband alone. I know how to look after him.'

We drove for a few moments, not very fast. 'If Wilfrid is ready,' said the doctor, 'he will soon pass us. If we don't see him we'll make some innocent excuse and go back.'

We had not long to wait. He passed us gaily, driving very fast! There was an air of triumph in his passing.

It was still light while we had dinner, so that as soon as it was over Dr. Bourne exclaimed: 'I am going back to the river!' We all felt that he was determined to succeed. A moment later his car sped over the gravel of the drive. We went into the drawing-room where de Glehn played a sonata on the piano, and at nine o'clock we put on the radio to listen to the booming of Big Ben. Dampness lay over the grass in the garden and big birds flew low. The painter went back to the piano. He played superlatively well. We were three women listening to the master strike the keys in the grand manner, and I think we all admired him. There was a flower design on the chintz curtains, and there was a sofa with a great many bright, cool-looking cushions. I thought again about Henry James; it was the scene in this drawing-room that evoked him—the painter of seventy-seven playing a sonata on the piano and the three women listening to him, a woman artist, a woman learned in the scientific way, and a woman writer. Henry James would have gathered us all up into a short story. We the women would have been spurned in love and then, in turn, we would have spurned. Or perhaps it would have been a ghostly story with an eerie ending. I looked out through the window, half expecting to see an apparition. Night was falling quickly. There were no more birds and I could no longer distinguish the lawn. How would Henry James have finished the story? Where would we all be in just a few years' time? My eyes now roved round the room; the pictures were in light frames. There was a magnificent portrait of Mrs. de Glehn as a very young woman with dark hair. The expression on the face had not changed. The music came to an end and we the women went up to bed.

I had not been in bed very long when I heard a soft voice on the stairs calling out: 'Jane! Jane!' I slipped a pink dressing-gown over my night-dress and peeped out into the landing. Dr. Bourne was there holding a very large plate on which leaves had been strewn, and on these was a superb trout.

'Oh!' I cried, 'what a beauty!'

But the beauty of the fish was as nothing compared to the joy on the face of the fisherman, and when Mrs. de Glehn arrived to contemplate the prize, the doctor said modestly:

'I knew I would have luck to-day. Good night.'

CHAPTER VI

BREAKFAST is at nine. Margherita and her husband came down one after the other to the round table where Mrs. de Glehn and I are already seated. Then it is the turn of the master, who strides in with his dog at his heels. He bids us good morning rather absently and lifts the bundle of letters from the side of his plate. He is very much the head of the house and we feel that his letters must be very important. Men's letters always look more important than those we receive. They demand gravity.

He fingers them, turns them round, and opens one or two. At times he looks anxious; at others he will give a little exclamation of relief and mutter:

'Ah! That one is only a bill.'

Obviously bills have no terror for him. He seems to have banished fear now and hands the whole sheaf of opened papers to his wife who is busy pouring out the tea. Margherita is very calm. She has no letters to read and shows no interest in the newspaper, but the sight of us all at breakfast in this big light room with the sun streaming in from the garden, this evocation of Henry Jamesian prosperity, the whiteness of the linen cloth, the beautiful china and silver—all this together seems to please her. She looks round at us: her husband, the heart specialist, behind his newspaper, the painter and his dog, his artist wife, and then, turning her lovely dark eyes on me, she smiles.

47

Her husband either has his head behind the newspaper or bends down to drink his tea, but there he is, back behind his paper.   I watch him for a moment, amused. Margherita catches my eye again, and her look is full of a serene gaiety.   Suddenly her husband explodes.   Margherita, without changing her expression, waits.   'We have this every morning at breakfast,' the soft, dark, intelligent eyes seem to say.   'We're going to have some fun.'

Her husband's outburst is a scathing commentary on the day's news.   There is something eighteenth century about his vituperation.   Heavens!   I would never have imagined that this great specialist could prove so inflammable.   I love him for it.   I have always admired violent men.   I think it was because my father was so. A man who works himself up into a great rage gives a picture of welcome virility in a world in which our men are often too reasonable.   Strong feelings are seldom displeasing to women.

Now that the doctor has spilled his venom, he looks happy again and his eyes meet those of his wife who declares that, of course, she agrees with every word. She is proud of him.   He has said it all so well, but a woman knows that nothing will ever change.   We are too wise to waste our energy on politics.

'I think,' says Margherita, 'that I shall put on some warm clothes to-day.   There still seems to be a cold wind.'

The master lays his napkin on the table and goes out with his dog, and suddenly I feel a stranger in a strange house.   It is curious how this feeling can suddenly come over one, even in a friendly house.   I miss my household duties and those three hours that at home I assign myself each day to write.

Margherita was right.   The sun was out but the wind

was cold. I walked round the garden and, returning by the back of the house, discovered the cook in her kitchen. She was a middle-aged London woman who had never left her native city till the de Glehns were bombed out from Cheyne Walk. She invited me in, proud to show me her Aga cooker and her lovely airy kitchen whose walls were all hung with pictures by the master. She loved them, she said, and in winter they made splashes of colour.

The kitchen was warm and I was suddenly cheered by the womanly activity of its pots and pans. This, no doubt, was what I had missed. I stayed some moments talking, and as I left came upon de Glehn, his dog at his heels, returning to the house by the back way.

'We'll start work in five minutes,' he said. 'I have just lit the fire.'

I walked slowly to the barn, and having climbed up to the studio began to examine the portrait. This was the first time I had given it any serious attention. There were no hands yet, merely trails of flesh-coloured vapour emerging like comets from sapphire blue sleeves. The door opened, and suddenly the master was beside me.

'Well?' he asked, with the forced joviality that a man employs when he talks to a little girl. 'How do we find it?'

'Oh!' I exclaimed, 'I adore my hat. It's as if I owned both the original and a copy. Madame Agnès would have been delighted.'

'Yes,' he admitted as I took my seat on the dais. 'There is no question about it: the hat is graceful, but who was this woman, who was this Madame Agnès?'

'A woman of amazing beauty,' I said, 'or at least that is how I like to remember her.'

He looked up, intrigued. He was doing my hands, and they were the most difficult.

'Did she lose her beauty?' he asked.

'Yes,' I answered. 'She became—well, one could hardly bear to look at her. She became almost a monster.'

'For heaven's sake,' he said, 'tell me the story.'

'I first saw her one Saturday morning in her *salon* in the rue St. Honoré. I had started from London in the *Golden Arrow* the day before. Those week-ends were lovely things. Nobody had yet made a religion of austerity, and this fashionable train, with its arm-chairs and exquisite food, brought together, like a club, men of position and charm and women with beautiful coats, pretty hats, and crocodile handbags. It was like a travelling Ritz. One met men who were not with their wives, and wives who obviously had left their husbands at home.'

'Oh yes,' cried the painter, 'I also remember those days. The aeroplane was not the fashionable route. There was the quick, delightful sea crossing and the French restaurant car with roast chicken and peas, and by seven o'clock one could be having an apéritif in the Champs-Élysées.'

'On Friday nights,' I went on, 'I liked to go to the latest play in one of those tiny, stuffy theatres where the audience and the actors seemed to be all huddled together, and during the interval one might come across Lord Castlerosse whose conversation had the wit of a play by Oscar Wilde. His diary in a Sunday paper, with vivid portraits of millionaires, artists, princes, and the great operators of Wall Street, will one day rank with the memoirs of Lord Hervey or the best of Thackeray. He was a great writer who took to the pen by accident, and in fifty years' time somebody will rediscover him and make his work immortal. He was picturesque and vigorous like the doctor at breakfast this morning. That is where one realizes that a woman can never write as powerfully as a man. It is vexing to be girt about with limitations. There was a description one Sunday of the

Aga Khan that made me determined one day to approach that powerful and amazing prince.'

'You will be making me wish I was a writer instead of a painter,' said de Glehn.

'Have no regrets. We don't choose,' I laughed. 'Personally I should have liked to be Melba.'

'Why Melba?' he asked.

'To see results,' I said. 'If not Melba, an actress or a dancer. I should like to cash in quickly on the effort.'

'Go on with your story,' he said.

'I kept the Saturday free for shopping, and always my first desire was to buy a hat. I cannot recall exactly how I was first introduced to her. I merely remember the impact she made on me. She already had a great name, but I suspect that there was no particular moment when she discovered her skill as an artist. Almost before she walked she must have played with pieces of ribbon and tulle. Her eyes were of such a personal blue that there is no word adequate to describe them. Perhaps one could say that they were the blue of periwinkles except that these modest flowers change their intensity with the brightness or cloudiness of the day. Her blue was of the very softest. One seemed to find it even in the rays that emanated from her. Felt and straw were so perfectly dyed to her order that one might have supposed they had been plunged into the depths of her eyes. One spoke of Agnès blue as one talked of Nattier blue. She had what the French call *une tête à chapeau*. This, of course, is perfectly distinct from beauty. It merely means that the woman in question is pretty in whatever hat she wears, even if it is shaped like a flower-pot. Other women have not the soft contours necessary. Hats diminish their beauty instead of enhancing it.

'She worked in a fever of seasons and showings. Great dresses are occasionally born in a man's brain, but in Paris the best-loved hats, the prettiest, are always invented by women. Only a woman can put together these ethereal nothings and place them gently and understandingly on our heads so that we exclaim at their loveliness. I never knew her jealous of another woman's looks, but then she probably considered that she was more than partly responsible. She made them beautiful: even an ugly woman, if she has the right sort of head, can look lovely in a hat. Mme Agnès dispensed beauty as a gardener scatters drops of iridescent water from his watering-can on his thirsty flowers. On leaving her one felt new, transformed, enchanted, and brave; there is nothing more important for a woman than to feel sure of herself.

'Mme Agnès and I became close friends, and when on one occasion she came to London to show some hats, we went everywhere together. She had brought a different evening dress for each night of her visit, and they were all the masterpieces of such brilliant women as Mme Vionnet and Mme Jeanne Lanvin. She had complete faith in the taste of women. She believed with all her deep understanding of Paris that women are supreme in helping women to conquer men—that to reach Adam we must pass through the hands of Eve. It was, I think, the fact that she and I were both so ultra-feminine that we understood each other so completely.

'I remember her best one evening at supper. She was talking of love, and her pretty, clever hands seemed to be writhing. Her arms were still plump and young, though her breasts, in the superb *décolletée* of her dress, had the fullness of maturity, ripe desirable fruit. Her skin was the colour of rose petals and this was independent of make-up, for one seemed to see the warm, eager blood flowing in the veins. As she spoke to me privately, softly, on this eternal adorable question, I had the impression of hearing her heart beat. Her thick, vigorous hair was done into a myriad little curls and dyed the very colour of her blue eyes. This bold coiffure, the tenderness and excitement in her gaze, the veins obedient to some memory or thought passionately colouring the white skin, the quick lowering of her long lashes, the splendour of her dress—all this had a full, intense sensuousness that made the most delightful and disturbing picture in the world.

'I next saw her in August. I had gone to Le Touquet for the week-end. When in other parts of the country orchards and fields were scorched and yellow, Le Touquet with its pine forest and carefully watered flowers, its splendid hotels and elegant casino, was very pleasant. The people one met all, for the moment, had money. They had come from Brussels, Paris, and London and were careful about their appearance. The age of the slovenly traveller was not yet upon us.

'I walked out of the Hermitage wearing for the first time Mme Lanvin's perfume—Mon Péché. I love a new perfume. I become so accustomed to my own favourites that I end by no longer being aware of them. The people with whom I had lunched were intrigued by the electrically propelled scooters then the rage, that one drove silently through the shopping streets or down to the beach. We hired several and cruised lazily round in the sunshine.

'I had gone back to the hotel and was leaning over my bedroom balcony gazing into the wide avenue, when suddenly from the direction of the sea came an American roadster travelling at high speed. What a noise it made! A dark man wearing a sleeveless pullover was driving, and next to him, like a ship's figurehead, bending forward into the wind, her curly blue hair shimmering in the strong light, sat my lovely Mme Agnès, beautiful, radiant, contentedly feminine.

'Where were they going? I am not sure, but a few

weeks later Mme Agnès was thrown burning out of this car on to the side of the road, while the driver was found dead beside her.

'Is there anything more cruel for a woman than to lose her beauty? Months later Mme Agnès, still covered in bandages, left hospital. Her blue eyes alone had not suffered. All Paris had sent her flowers, spring flowers, for winter had come and gone, and spring was with us again. The great modiste had inspired herself with these bouquets for her spring collection. Every hat she made had flowers, the tenderest flowers; each model was a cry of hope, but when at last her bandages were taken off, and she saw that it was no good hoping any longer, that the scars would not disappear and that she had become dreadful to look at, all the joy went out of her heart.

'We were separated during the war. I saw her just after the liberation. She had changed yet again. Her scars were deeper. Sometimes she came up behind one to adjust a hat on one's head, but as soon as she caught sight of her face in the great mirror, she would turn away and call one of her girls.

'Yet she was still interested in fashion, but whereas before her disfigurement each model was first tried on her own lovely head, she now stepped into the role of a spectator. Half her face was cunningly hidden by wide-brimmed hats of straw or felt. One caught oneself momentarily admiring them; then seeing the ravaged face, one turned away in pity and horror.

'Paris was still full of soldiers. The war was scarcely finished but in Mme Agnès's *salon* there were already feathers, ribbons, and flowers. I tried on several hats, but this was the one that I lost my heart to. The moment it rested on my head I seemed to rediscover all the song and colour of Paris. My breasts swelled with gratitude, and Mme Agnès, seeing me so happy, insisted

on making me a present of the hat.   It was her last gift.
She died soon afterwards, but this blue felt, this bird
with its vivid wings, evokes for me all her genius.'

The portrait, as I have said elsewhere, now hangs in my
flat in Shepherd Market with the beautiful G. F. Watts of
Lady Lindsay of Balcaress which I removed from the
Tate Gallery.   The artist warned me that I should pass
through periods of liking and disliking it.   I am not sure
that the hat is not what I like best, which shows how right
I was to insist on wearing it.   The artist steadfastly
refused to reproduce the true colours of my make-up.
My lipstick and nail varnish are so different from reality
that I am in revolt every time I look at the picture.   That
part of a woman which decides how she shall paint her
face or her hands is an important key to her character.
I am continually being tempted to take the canvas out of
the frame and make up my face.   I would like also to add
my pearls, and put more life into my eyes.   In truth, I see
a continual conflict between the dauber which every
woman is on her imperfect person, and the artist who
tries to convey his impression of her on canvas.

CHAPTER VII

ABANK WHICH is not my own has sent me the prettiest brochure telling me why a woman should have her own banking account. My feminity has clearly been taken into considera- tion by the directors when drafting their clever invitation, for on the cover two pink roses are photo- graphed beside a leather-covered cheque-book just the right size to slip comfortably into my handbag.

I am, on the whole, rather flattered by this attention. It is as if a stranger had suddenly noticed that my dress was becoming or had turned round in the street to take a second look at me. One is always pleased to be courted. A silent homage makes a difference to one's entire day.

The booklet assures me that my account will not be subject to my husband's scrutiny, and this is encouraging, for until a relatively short time ago women writers in France could be forced to abandon their royalties to their husbands. Governments alone now reserve the right to look into our accounts and take what they think fit.

My mink tie is the only tangible benefit of my royalties. By far the largest part of one's net income goes in un- exciting ways, and I well understand that most women are content to let the men do the worrying. Only one thing would give me any pleasure, and that is to spend £100 frivolously during a single afternoon. It might, as Arnold Bennett once suggested, stimulate my creative ideas. But no, not if it was my own money. A woman hates to squander what she has earned. At the end of my spending bout I might be exhilarated for a moment, but I would soon be miserable.

And so I vacillate between alluring skeins of knitting-wool and lengths of *crêpe de Chine* and end, reasonable woman that I am, by spending nothing at all. All the same I am thankful to be a woman if only for the joy of stroking lovely, shimmering materials in the big stores. Surely no man can obtain such acute satisfaction by having a drink at his club or buying a new pipe?

My own bank is in the Strand and I shall not change. Messrs. Coutts rears its important façade between tiny old-fashioned shops. In one of these, for instance, are trays filled with brown bulbs which, if one had the earth to put them in, would break out into superb gladioli; then there is the passport photographer who within two hours gives you three portraits for ten shillings, and a silversmith who besides his silver sells—but to whom?—murderous double-barrelled guns.

The doorkeeper bids me good morning and asks if I am keeping well. We discuss the weather and I inquire how he has spent the week-end. Was he in his garden?

'No, madam,' he answers. 'As a matter of fact I did my washing and my ironing. Yes, madam, I had to come to it after the death of my dear wife. She used to do everything herself, and so after she had gone I had not the heart to send my washing to the laundry. I tried to remember, madam, how she did it. All my married life I had seen her on washing days bending over the soapy water but I never really looked carefully. I had taken it for granted that she would always be there. And it looked so simple. Occasionally on my return from the bank she would say: "I have done all the washing to-day!" and I would see it hanging up on the line, or perhaps already ironed and placed on the kitchen table. Everything looks easy, madam, till one tries to do it. So I bought powdered soaps in cartons and read the instructions on the back. The secret is to take your time. For instance, you must not put the linen dirty into boiling water for fear of boiling the dirt in . . . but here I am teaching you, madam! I expect you are not above doing a bit of washing yourself? At any rate,' he continued, 'I carry on with my dear wife's occupations and in doing so I think about her. There is also the mending and the cooking, but the mending is nothing for an old soldier.'

He whispered as if this was too important to bandy about:

'We were married for forty years. That's a big slice of happiness, isn't it?'

'Oh!' I cried. 'If God were only to give me as long!'

There was the prettiest fire in the hall and a wicker-hooded chair from which he had risen at my coming. How curious that in this temple of money the janitor should go home to do his own washing, to cook his lonely meal in a house without echoes!

Every morning in a corner of the big room the directors hold what I think is a meeting. I see them seated at a round table looking solemn, even the young ones. What do they discuss? These are things that a woman will eternally have to guess at. Conversely I doubt if any banker, in spite of two pink roses or three crowns, would be even vaguely aware of the financial ability of such women as Henriette.

Annik, who used to dress our hair, showing me a photograph of her, brought her to my mind. Though such incidents take place in the heart of London, their cosmopolitanism gives them a strange, unreal tang. They often merely provide a little feminine gossip.

Henriette was twenty when she first came to London, and she both lodged and plied her trade in one of the quieter streets behind Hanover Square. Of her girlhood I know nothing, or at least all I know is that poverty and beauty had grown up together so that at twenty her beauty was ready to wipe out her poverty.

A girl begins in Henriette's profession as another might start in music or dancing. She needs patience and fortitude; the rest is a matter of natural ability. Every profession calls for certain qualities or defects. Some professions are greatly admired: this one is considered very reprehensible outside its own environment, but just as great dancers and great actresses are often predestined, those who succeed in this profession have quickly shown signs that they are specially equipped for it.

Thus it is a question of aptitude and desire; seldom one of constraint.

Henriette was hard working and lazy. She was too lazy to get up early every morning and work in a shop, but she had the perseverance to go out into the street in all weathers, either walking very fast along the same pavement, or remaining motionless on the doorstep that led to her apartment.

She was known to other women as being the most beautiful and the most successful of her vintage, just as in quite another world—in society—some débutante will steal all the thunder, not only of the season she is presented at court, but of several subsequent seasons. One could make a list of these society girls quite well, just as others could name instantly those who like Henriette were outstanding.

Henriette, therefore, made her living out of the thing we call love. She dispensed it but she had never been touched by its magic. She was like a beautiful violin from which nobody had as yet drawn sweet and passionate

c

notes. She used to listen to the interminable stories that we all like to tell about this burning subject, but she used to say that as far as she was concerned she could do perfectly well without it.

She had, of course, her manager, whom she would have been glad to love if love had been at her command. She liked him very much, but with her head rather than with her senses. She gave him everything she earned, which is the inescapable, primordial law, but as it was understood that they would eventually live together and own an hotel on the Riviera, and that every year for this purpose they put more money aside, her contractual obligations never seemed heavy.

She had three weeks' holiday in the summer like a typist, and her dresses were very modest but her fur coat was of mink, worth several thousand pounds, for it was not only useful in her profession but was a big lump of capital pleasantly put aside. She had other investments of a similar nature, for they realized that when they bought their hotel in the south of France they would become like other people and have income tax to pay.

Henriette, who was only twenty-one when I first knew her, loved to talk about her future, this intriguing metamorphosis which she hoped would happen when she was about thirty. Her hotel was going to face the sea, and she would have a nice apartment with built-in cupboards, and in winter her mink coat would lift up her social status when she called on the notables and their wives.

Her dreams, those of any young woman, were less ambitious than mine at her age, for I then expected life to provide me not only with a little mink but with far more complicated things, things that now that I am obtaining them, bring me as much torture as satisfaction; but Henriette was simple.

She was also sufficiently reasonable not to worry when her friends told her they had seen Henri, her manager, with another girl. Henri and Henriette, they had the same name and their thoughts were identical—only sensually Henri was much more in love, and finding so little response in Henriette he used to say: 'I expect you work too hard. It will be different when we retire.'

Then Henriette would laugh, and her immense black eyes that so often looked hot with promise would become cold and sarcastic and her lips would curl over perfect white teeth, as she exclaimed:

'Believe what you will. It's all the same to me. Perhaps I wasn't made for that sort of thing!'

Henri at this would become furious, and after failing bitterly in certain exploits in the course of which he tried to demonstrate real inventive genius, he felt like a wild animal beaten by something weak and unresponsive. Then he would bite her and slap her, but she, turning her implacable eyes on him, would answer:

'What a brute you are, my poor Henri. You know it's not my fault.'

He would go back to Paris and Henriette would tell her friends how violent he had been. Some would say: 'There must be something unusual about you two!' Wiser ones: 'You're lucky!' and yet others: 'No, no, you're not lucky. No woman can live without that.'

Superbly indifferent to what any of us said, she played cards with her maid, reminding me of an actress waiting in the wings for her call. Her maid might easily have been her mother, her aunt, or her grandmother—any of those female relations who sometimes accompany young actresses to their dressing-rooms. She never took long to forget Henri's anger, for she did not love anybody or anything deeply enough to worry. She was not a bundle of sensitivity as I was. Her mother in France

merely reminded her of poverty, though I doubt if her
girlhood was exactly miserable in every sense, for she
was already so pretty as a schoolgirl that her mistresses,
she said, petted and spoiled her, and never blamed her
for not knowing her lessons. She rejoiced in thinking
of the girls from school who by now were probably
workmen's wives or serving in shops while she had her
mink coat and bright prospects for the future.

She loved hats and putting little bundles of notes
aside for Henri to collect on his next visit. Though
prettier than all the other women she was not greedy
with her customers, and if it had not been for Henri she
might have got into trouble with those who accused her
of bringing prices down, but she answered haughtily:

'If you're not satisfied, why don't you work a little
harder?'

When, on the first day of that historic September, the
'phoney' war started, Henriette remained in London.
Business was a little uncertain: there were vexations like
the 'black-out' to contend with, but gradually things
became better. Heavens! There were enough men
about—men of all sorts, men in uniform, and so many
civilian husbands who had sent their wives to the country
and who were slowly forgetting them. Henri was called
up in France. There were no leaves for him. Then
the war started properly, and Paris collapsed. Most of
Henriette's colleagues, frightened of what would happen,
took the last boat back to France; and after that England
was cut off from the Continent.

Henriette thought she loved Henri better at a distance.
Their temporary separation would ultimately make no
difference to their having an hotel on the Riviera. Thus
she worked for him loyally, scrupulously, and soon she
was making so much money that she divided it up into
bundles and put it into different safe deposits. Safe
deposits, she argued, were like money in a stocking

under the mattress, but protected by steel doors. She
bought a large diamond and this she wore, enjoying the
cold blue-white beauty of the faultless stone, cold like
herself. Its value was greater than many bars of gold,
and she had the Frenchwoman's ingrained appreciation
of precious stones.

Thus she was free now, tied only to Henri by financial
integrity. Of the very few other women of her race
left in London, not one thought like she. They were
miserable thinking of their men, fearing that they might
be deported or shot, or even fall in love with other
women, but for Henriette these problems did not exist.
Her path was clear.

Her black hair was now so long that it reached her
magnificent shoulders. She reminded me of poems and
pictures of Salome, but a Salome with neither jealousy
nor hate nor love. Yes, I used to think, Henriette is
enjoying her freedom!

Her manner of life had been changed by the air-raids.
Nocturnal life, as it used to be, had become diurnal.
Instead of going out into the streets when darkness fell,
she began to show herself as the smart restaurants
emptied after lunch. She worked tirelessly till the sirens
went. Then all the ladies met in a sumptuous shelter
under a large building in Regent Street. Each brought
with her a small wicker basket packed earlier in the day
by her maid and containing a bottle of wine and a cold
chicken. For the first time for many years they went
to bed at a reasonable hour and slept calmly the whole
night through. They must have struck other people as
looking rather unusual, for though they had no make-up
and wore slacks, they never removed their magnificent
mink coats, too valuable to be left even for a moment
out of sight. Some without make-up looked like other
women, but Henriette with her long dark hair looked
astounding. I never knew a woman to worry so little.

'And why should I?' she asked. 'I sleep with my coat
and my diamond, and my money is in vaults about town.
There is nothing but my lingerie and a few dresses at
the flat.'

Their maids were here also, those Belgian or French
maids, aggressive, thick-spoken but faithful, who followed their mistresses respectfully between the flat and
the shelter with the mattress tied up in a bundle. Oh,
strange London scenes that we have so quickly forgotten! The maid carrying the mistress's bed, walking
a few paces behind her. Tell me if there is not something of ancient Rome in this? Who would have thought
that such simple out-of-door scenes would be enacted
under our modern civilization? 'Take up my bed,
Louise, and let us be going home, for the first finger
of rosy dawn points above Conduit Street and the all-
clear siren has just sounded.'

'Are they not polite and gentle?' you would hear
people say as they went off. Others would pity them,
calling to mind some amazing invention of the male
novelist who is certain he knows all about them and
knows nothing at all. At the corner of Regent Street
twin policewomen in tin hats and serge skirts would
smile good morning.

As the night raids became less violent, these restful
evenings in the Regent Street basement ceased to charm.
Sleep would not come. Each knew that she was wasting
her time. Henriette slipped out on the excuse of
examining the night and found it clear, and the guns
distant. Then she and her colleagues, one by one,
returned to their flats to exchange their slacks for a dress
or, as the weather became warmer, a blouse and a tailor-
made. The streets round Hanover Square became again
the theatre of their nocturnal activities.

The raids were not quite finished, but Henriette had
no fear. She was young, wealthy, and beautiful. Are

these not the three gifts that every one of us would ask of our fairy godmother—youth, riches, beauty?

Her maid Clara did not share her mistress's tranquillity. On the contrary her mind was full of lamentable tales, for every Saturday night, according to custom, she went back to her own quarters in Camden Town where she heard the latest gossip.

'You should spend the week-end here,' Henriette would say. 'It would keep your mind off the war.'

Henriette's birthday was in July. Clara gave her a dozen red roses and jugged her a hare in wine: they would eat it together before Clara went back to Camden Town, for it was Saturday. Henriette opened a bottle of champagne—these small celebrations between mistress and maid do not lack verve, for the maids have stories about their youth, or about other maids who recount the secrets of their mistresses. Henriette, too, was nicer than usual. It appeared that her family was still alive and for the first time she talked about them. Then she said: 'I usually take my holidays in July. It's a pity I can't go to France.'

They played cards, and then Henriette said to Clara:

'I shall only go down into the street once, so as soon as you have done the washing-up you can go back to Camden Town.'

'Thank you, madame,' answered Clara.

Henriette, in her dressing-gown, went into the bedroom where she did her hair and painted her face. Saturday night was unpleasant. The streets invariably looked as if Sunday had already begun, and what with July being so dusty and the nights taking so long to fall, she was unsettled. She put on a white blouse and the skirt of her black tailor-made, and chose a small straw hat from amongst those she had bought in Paris before the war. 'I'll only go down once,' she repeated, as if to fortify her resolve. 'Only once.' And she looked at herself in the mirror, arranging her hat, softening her hair.

'Where's my key, Clara?'

And quickly she ran down the wooden stairs on her high heels.

Now she was in the street, taut, ready for what might happen. In her hand she grasped a long electric torch from which she had removed the magnifying lens. Thus the edge remained naked and sharp, sharp enough if the torch were properly handled to make a weapon almost as deadly as the knife of the apache who put his girls to work at Clichy or St. Denis, teaching them their business. In London a torch was an innocent-looking thing and did in fact, in addition to being a weapon, have its more normal use of shedding a ray of light on any strange impediment that might make her stumble on pavements known so well. It was she who had found the secret, the usefulness of the naked torch, but all her compatriots had quickly followed.

To work off the warmth engendered by the champagne she walked quickly as far as the steps of St. George's, Hanover Square; in peace time smart weddings took place here, débutantes were married to Guards' officers; at night one met one's friends there and talked a moment by the great stone dogs outside the front entrance. Henriette found a colleague who had just arrived from Conduit Street where she lodged. 'It's my birthday,' said Henriette, and she told her that Clara had made jugged hare. Henriette looked as pretty as any débutante who had ever walked down the steps all in white with a veil and orange blossom, and she was only twenty-two. 'But my shoes pinch,' she said.

'And so do mine,' said her companion. 'And high heels are giving me varicose veins.'

'What I'm thinking of,' said Henriette, 'is a cool beer on the terrace of a Paris café and then I could slip my shoes off under the chair. I keep on thinking of Henri this evening.'

'I shall go round by Bond Street,' said her companion. 'This place is like a graveyard.'

And she hurried off.

But against the high-pitched hammer blows of the woman's heels as she hurried away there came another sound, slower, more rhythmical, the sound of a man's footsteps, walking easily from the direction of Regent Street. The man stopped in front of a motor-car dealer's and lit a cigarette. He was a foreigner, some officer in one of the continental armies. She had been forewarned that such was the case by a slight metallic sound in his slow, mannish step. Foreign officers wore much heavier shoes than English officers. Now that his cigarette was alight he went on but stopped again in front of a famous hairdresser, where the plate glass having been smashed there was a tiny window like a guillotine in the centre of the boards. The officer was having an evening stroll. She went up to him and said:

'Allo, chéri!'

'Hallo,' he said, 'I hadn't noticed you. Where do you come from?'

'From the other side,' answered Henriette with a backward movement of her head which might refer to her flat or to her native city on the other side of the Channel.

'From France or from Belgium?' asked the man.

'From France,' said Henriette.

'Oh,' said the man, 'I'm from Belgium.'

He looked down at her, and she asked:

'Viens-tu?'

He merely slipped his arm in hers and accompanied her. She put on her torch and shone it against the sides of the houses, and as she put her key into the front door of the house where she lodged, she was suddenly afraid

* c

that he might go off and leave her there. But the man had nothing else to do. He was far from his own home and was merely engaged in killing time until he in turn might be killed.

Clara was still there. She had finished the washing-up and had slipped into Henriette's bedroom to put away her mistress's dressing-gown and her slippers which she had left lying about. When the man said good evening to her she suddenly caught in his 'Bon soir' the accent of her native province and she exclaimed:

'You are from Brussels?'

'Yes,' he answered.

Then Clara burst into tears, thinking of her country, her city, her streets, and her loved ones.

Henriette said softly:

'You can go now, Clara. I shan't go out again to-night.'

And then, turning to the officer, she added:

'Give her the half-crown you would normally give her when you leave.'

'No!' exclaimed Clara, vexed. 'I won't take his half-crown. Good night, madame.'

'Oh, and before you go, Clara. Is there anything left to drink? I'm thirsty.'

They went into the kitchen but there was only half a bottle of beer. Henriette poured herself out a glass of cold water from the tap, but the man was delighted with the beer. He had put his cap and stick on the table. There was still a pleasant smell of jugged hare about the house. He felt suddenly at ease.

Clara now got her things together, ready to go. She looked like a pack donkey. She was small and carried a great multitude of cloth bags in each hand so that one had the feeling that she was off on a long, long journey, perhaps right across Europe and North Africa to the Belgian Congo. She was in a state of continual alarm, especially about air-raids, so that at the beginning of each week she brought her treasures from Camden Town to Hanover Square, and on Saturday night took them all back to Camden Town, adding to them any food or wine that her wealthy young mistress might have given her in the course of the week.

Henriette listened to the banging of the front door, and then led the man into the bedroom. . . .

Strangely enough after it had happened she did not bother to dress again but remained on the bed, contented and supple.

The man was still stunned by her beauty. He suddenly asked her how old she was, and then added:

'There's no point in even asking you. You're a mere girl.'

She flared up.

'I'm twenty-two this very night,' she said, 'and by "girl," do you mean I haven't any experience? If you hadn't shaved from the first day I started this business, you'd be walking on your beard!'

'You young hyena!' he said, laughing, and sprang off the bed.

'Where are you going?' she asked. 'I thought you were not in a hurry?'

'I'm not in a hurry particularly,' he answered quietly, 'but I live in Kensington and if I miss the last bus I shall have to walk.'

'Stay till morning,' she said. 'I shall only be twenty-two once.'

She got up and went out into the landing to bolt the front door. Then she inspected the black-out curtains. The police were fussy: she used to have to go down three flights of stairs to answer the imperious ring and it always ended by having to offer the policeman a whisky. She looked round the kitchen to see if everything was

in order and then came back into the bedroom. The
man was on the bed—asleep.

She glanced at him in a satisfied, proprietary way, and
picking up his trousers folded them across the back of
a chair, as Henri always did: 'and now,' she thought,
'I had better get my case ready just in case the sirens
go.' She put the case on the table and folded her mink
coat over it so that only the shiny part of the satin lining
showed.

Sitting at her dressing-table she brushed her lovely
dark hair, and from time to time she would look up to
inspect the reflexion of the man in the mirror. He was
fair with strong shoulders, but he had gentle hands, and
she thought he looked very graceful as he slept. She
supposed he was about thirty, but one never could tell
with a fair-haired man. Henri, at this hour of the night,
would have the rough black stubble of a stevedore. She
put some cream on her neck, massaging from the bottom
upwards according to the instructions. Every now and
again she made resolutions to start beauty treatment
young. To start when it was not yet necessary, that
was the secret, but in the early hours of the morning
after being on her high heels all night, running up and
down the stairs, when finally her work was finished she
was generally too tired to massage her neck.

Besides, she was only twenty-two and had years and
years in front of her, and when, as it would have to
happen, she lost her beauty would she not have plenty
of money, an hotel on the Riviera, and Henri to look
after her?

'One can get a lot of wear out of real beauty,' she
reflected. 'It's like a good cloth.'

As she slipped noiselessly into bed the man opened
his eyes and looked at her. He seemed puzzled by her
youth and gentleness and, after considering her for a
few moments, drew her towards him. She responded

with the same loyal affection that she always gave to Henri, but there was something in the touch of his hands that put her into an agitation that she had not experienced until now. His warm, damp lips sought hers, and gradually she became aware of the thing hitherto unknown to her which her colleagues said that no woman can live without. It illuminated her lovely features, but she fought against uttering a cry or murmuring any soft word which might give away her secret. How could it be that she who was so experienced could feel so timid and ignorant in the face of this wonderful discovery, but perhaps it was a dream or some marvellous gift that heaven had sent on the night of her birthday, and if this was the case she might not experience it again: it would merely be a memory for always.

Henriette had no need to fear: she had met with the eternal wonder that is love, and she thought: 'If I had been married in a normal honest way to Henri, I might have gone all through life just missing it.'

When on Monday morning Clara came back to her mistress's flat she saw the officer's cap and his tunic with BELGIUM written on the shoulders. Henriette was not particularly gracious with her maid. The girls from Conduit Street and George Street had all been ringing up to know what was the matter with her.

'Are you ill, Henriette?'

'No.'

'Well, what are you doing?'

'I'm having my summer holidays. Aren't I entitled to a rest?'

'Yes, *ma petite*, but *à deux* it's not a rest. Watch your step, Henriette. Don't you go falling in love.'

She loved him as something she knew could never be hers. He told her nothing about himself, not even whether he was married. She could not discover his name. He treated her tenderly but with the superiority

with which men often treat us on the Continent when
they have had what they desire. He was not the sort
of man to allow realities to be affected by sentiment.
She was still what she had been on the pavement on
Saturday night and he might be a millionaire or the son
of a king. There was no encumbrance of pretence.
He was socially her superior and she, with equal Latin
common sense, was grateful to him for his gift.

He disappeared on Monday afternoon and she went
back to work with that cold determination for which she
had always been known. Her colleagues discussed her
between themselves, but did not speak to her much. She
was guilty of a breach of the rules, and nobody doubted
but that Henri would get to hear of it. Henriette did
not mind not being talked to, she had her secret, but
when she met the girl from Conduit Street with whom
she had gossiped on the steps of the church, she smiled
at her affectionately, for she thought:

'Suppose it had been she and not I who had met
him!'

Her breast beat with thankfulness that fortune had
taken a hand in the affair, sending the girl to Bond
Street while she had stood waiting by the church until
he came along.

The pace of the war was quickening and Henriette and
Clara turned over sums that would have surprised a city
broker. Now that the Americans were here everybody
knew what the outcome would be. The Americans,
therefore, brought hope and more money.

Henriette's Belgian, from some distant camp, used to
come and see her from time to time but the other French-
women showed growing hostility to Henriette. The
corporation abides fanatically by the rules and all the
women were on Henri's side, determined to safeguard
his property. They said meaningly:

'While the poor boy is risking his life in France the girl is having a good time.'

Henriette winced, for she feared them.

Her loyalty, however, was steadfast. The money she made was still for Henri, and indeed, influenced by talk from the Continent, she was taking new steps to safe-guard it. Agents who travelled backwards and forwards by secret means, told her how both the Germans and the French were putting their savings into gold coins. Gold was apparently the thing to have, and few people in this phlegmatic country where they were so busy prosecuting the war, had yet woken up to the dangers of less valuable money. The French girls rather liked the game and had no difficulty in obtaining what they wanted, for those people who subterraneously dealt in nylons and American nail polish quickly added napoleons and sovereigns to their wares, and so Henriette, feeling her loyalty to Henri grow stronger, amassed the little blood-red pieces which French peasants have always loved to handle.

Then, as she half expected, Henri, in the uniform of a French officer, arrived one day in her kitchen as if he had never left it. He had travelled in the mysterious way from France, less from patriotic motives than to join his Henriette. They embraced. She wept with joy, but he was so full of mannish resentment at the things he had heard that he released an avalanche of anger. He supposed that a man could never trust a woman when his back was turned: when he was in Paris she was making trouble in London, and now that he was in London his affairs in Paris were certain to go wrong. And now he was here, how did she think he would ever get back? He would thrash her, he would, just to show her what happens to a silly girl.

'But,' he said, his raised arm falling to his side, 'you are much thinner. You ought to weigh yourself, for when your cheeks become sallow your eyes look as if they are doped and that is terribly bad for business.'

'I haven't noticed any sign of it!' she answered angrily. 'But if I'm not pretty enough for you, go and find another girl!'

'I didn't mean that!' he said.

She smiled. He was noisy, but if he had come all the way from France to see what she was doing, it was undoubtedly a compliment. He had risked his life. He was actually taking part in the war for her sake, and it was better to be with him than with a man who might despise her as soon as she lost her looks. He loves me, she said to herself. We both love each other in our own way. We shall have our hotel on the Riviera—and I shall have my secret to look back on and dream about.

'I'll go and ask the butcher for a leg of lamb,' said Clara. 'Monsieur Henri must be hungry.'

She picked up her shopping-bag, and as she went downstairs she thought:

'Who warned Henri about madame? One of the girls certainly. I'd like to get my hands round her neck!'

Henriette was telling Henri about the money she had put aside. He was impressed by her astuteness, though being a man, he was a little vexed that a woman could manage so well.

The war was coming to an end and Henri was sent overseas. For Henriette's sake I felt a little sorry for him being trapped into this, though he proved braver than one might have supposed, and it was useful for him to see what was happening in the world. After the liberation he was in Paris and managed to send a letter to Henriette in which he told her to sell everything, collect her belongings, and join the women's section of

the French Army.   The big money now was in arbitrage.
Those gold sovereigns and napoleons must be brought
to Paris at all costs.   He knew that several other girls
were being told to do the same thing.

Henriette in uniform!   She thought it over and the
idea sounded fantastic.

'I!' she exclaimed to Clara, 'I in soldiers' boots!'

She laughed.   Was she not the very essence of the
illogical, untamable, ultra-feminine woman?   But after
all, the war was virtually over and it was really only a
method of returning quickly to France.

So one morning she was to be seen wearing lisle khaki
stockings and flat-heeled shoes, dragging a heavy kit-
bag, and not allowing anybody to help her put it on the
train.   She was with a small party of French women,
daughters of cooks, or typists at shipping offices who
had spent the war in khaki and were now being sent
back to France, dragging their poor clothes in grubby
kit-bags.

Henriette had rolled up her mink coat and placed it
in the bottom of this long, bulky, inelegant piece of
soldier's luggage.   She had folded her lovely silk lingerie
round hundreds of pieces of gold.   All this was covered
up with rough things.   Her features were nervous and
pinched and her lips were parched without lipstick.   She
had broken her beautiful long pointed nails tying a
mattress up with stout rope.   There was nothing in the
mattress; she would be able to open it out for the
customs people to see, and it might keep their minds
off the innocent kit-bag.   But it was no good trying to
get past on her charms, for they were not visible.   Her
hair was rolled up in a tight, ugly bun under her hat;
she looked alarmingly unattractive, but it was better so.
She had become the imitation man, she . . . yes, she who
had treated men with cold and bitter contempt.   She
was overcome with the gnawing fear that she might

never recover her feminine advantages. The thought was frightening. Perhaps she had not sufficiently realized her incomparable good fortune in being a beautiful young woman.

They had an officer who called out their names from a list. When Henriette heard her name she saluted. The thing was quite fantastic. What was the officer in private life?

On the boat the girls with their lifebelts and their kit queued up for tea, and by now Henriette, enjoying the excitement of this ship with its war aspect, the orders through the loud-speakers, the dangers of stray mines, and the anticipation of landing in France, was the gayest of them all. Going down the gangway, one of her companions inquired what she had in her kit-bag. 'Mine is full of woollies for the children, coffee, sugar, and soap,' she confessed. 'And yours?'

'I would rather they did not look,' answered Henriette, and she felt absurdly embarrassed like a girl at school caught hiding something from the mistress. But her companion, thinking of her own treasures, the woollies for small nieces, the coffee and soap for her sister in the provinces who had been drinking acorn coffee and washing her undies with cinders, said sweetly:

'I understand just what you feel, but stay close to me. I'll get you through. I know all the tricks. My trouble will be crossing Paris at night. There are no porters, no taxis, no buses. . . .'

'If you get me through the customs,' said Henriette, 'I'll take care of you when we reach Paris. My young man is coming to fetch me in a car. He'll drive you anywhere you want to go. I shall see to it.'

Her companion laughed.

'Very well,' she agreed. 'We'll stick together.'

Henriette wrote to me several times after her return

to Paris. She was to marry Henri and was now ready to start the second great adventure in her existence, to be a wife, a devoted little wife and—she hoped most of all—to have a baby. Oh! I think she would have wanted several. She had, which doesn't really surprise me, the maternal strain. We all have that at heart. We appear hard in some things, but fundamentally we are sentimental, and long for the joys of the home.

Alas, they never bought their hotel in the Midi. They met with a cruel accident on one of those white, poplar-lined roads along which young people drive too fast, and both, too young, were killed. I am not ashamed to say that I wept for Henriette. She had perhaps squandered the amazing beauty God had given her, but who could tell what she might have done with the rest of her life if only her dreams had been allowed to come true?

CHAPTER VIII

WHAT SORT of letters do people send a woman who writes books? I am surprised by the immense number of letters I receive from distant corners of the globe, and I am glad that even as a girl I was good at geography. I receive letters from the wives of tea-planters in India and Ceylon, from the wives of farmers in Australia who farm ten thousand acres, from the wives of prison governors in East Africa, from head mistresses of girls' schools in New Zealand, and from other women of this kind whose interests are so important and varied that the Commonwealth comes to me at breakfast time, all alive with colour and sunshine.

These women end by telling me of their lives. I admit that I am passionately interested in every detail. They could all, if they had the gift, write the most enthralling books: I prefer the vividness of truth to all the made-up stories in the world.

The new perspective, the forcing upon one of a new angle, is often what charms in a letter from overseas. One is tempted to consider the pageantry of royalty, for example, this royalty so bereft of power, to be a little senseless perhaps, even contradictory, in this democratic age, until one sees its light reflected in a mind thousands of miles away. For instance, in Cape Town there lives Ruby Tutt who one morning in the office pricked her finger with a pin.

Be with me in my kitchen off Piccadilly, having breakfast, and let us read her letter together:

78

Odeon Court,
Barnet Street,
Cape Town.

DEAR MRS. HENREY,

Perhaps I had better tell you about the accident first.

I was employed as a secretary in a local office, and I was busy typing some minutes of a board meeting when a coloured messenger brought me some papers. I asked him to put them down, and he placed them on the edge of my desk where they immediately rolled off on to the floor. As I was ambidextrous, I picked them up with my left hand, but as I did so the pin holding them together ran into my index finger.

No doubt you have pricked yourself many times. I know I have, and generally one thinks nothing of it, but this time I let out a yell and was unable to do any more work, busy as I was.

The finger was treated immediately (within two minutes of my pricking it) with hot-water fomentation and an application of iodine but without effect. For a month I applied poultices every two hours, night and day, but as this had no effect a surgeon operated, first on the finger, then several times on the hand, and later I suffered a major operation on the neck through the lung cavity and this affected my left eye. The last and most serious operation was on the spinal cord, and I would rather forget about the horrors of the weeks following that operation.

Since then my bad arm, the left one, jumps and dashes about of its own accord, bruising whatever part of my body it knocks, besides bruising itself. When the pain is most severe it jumps the most, and if anybody touches certain parts of my arm, just brushing me with their sleeve for instance, the pain is indescribable. It is like a tooth being permanently drilled, and so it is while I write to you.

This happened in August 1943. I was born in London, near Clapham Common, in 1904, and was brought up by my grandparents, but I loved travelling and used to save up my money to visit other countries, though not before I had visited every county in the British Isles. I did some cruising on the *Arandora Star*, and it was on this ship that I first heard of you, for one of the officers told me that you had been on it to the West Indies only a few weeks earlier. What a pity. I would have loved to meet you. I also travelled on the P. & O. and sailed in the *Viceroy of India* seven times. All this time I worked in a London office—shorthand, typing, secretarial work, the usual things we women do—but life was never dull, and what is more, it isn't now!

I must now tell you of my great and permanent interest —my love for the royal family. Dear old grandad was connected with the Guildhall and Mansion House. He used to take me to see these historic buildings and allow me, as a little girl, to hold the famous sword which is presented by the Lord Mayor for the Sovereign to touch on state visits to the city of London. Grandad told me a hundred stories, and I grew up with a deep feeling of regard for this truly royal family of ours.

At the time of the wedding of the Duke and Duchess of York, I stood in Bruton Street and watched a radiant bride drive off to become the smiling duchess beloved of all who saw her. She wore an ermine wrap over her shoulder and a veil, and smiled right into my eyes. A young be-medalled footman and a policeman in a dark blue helmet stood near by, and there was a nursemaid with a baby in a pram.

On the birth of our dear young queen I sent greetings to her mother. Since then I have sent greetings without cease. I had always hoped to see our royal family at close range, and this wish was granted in July 1939 when I went home on a visit. I was permitted to see the princesses at the palace, and it is a memory I shall cherish.

Then in 1948, when I returned for a short time to London in the hope of having treatment for my injured arm and hand, I had my greatest thrills. I had taken all my savings to pay for the journey in the belief that a final operation might put me right, but the doctors were of the opinion that it was better to leave me alone.

I had made one of those coloured woollen balls beloved of babies many years ago, and seldom seen to-day because they require so much wool. A friend had built me a wooden machine which I could hold between my knees, winding the wool round the disks with my sound hand. I had intended sending it to Princess Elizabeth after the birth of her baby, but in view of my visit to London I brought it with me, and wrote for permission to send it to the palace. The next day I received an invitation to bring it personally.

This was on the 1st July 1948, a Thursday. Everyone was most helpful and friendly, particularly the princess's lady-in-waiting. While I was waiting in the corridor to be presented, I saw a famous dress designer coming out, and then a small white Sealyham trotted into the corridor from the princess's apartment and I was informed that it was Johnny, Princess Margaret's dog which was being looked after by Princess Elizabeth. Her Royal Highness looked radiant and I shall never forget the charming informality with which I was received. Then something happened which I thought could never happen! I was received in audience at Marlborough House by that gracious lady Queen Mary. Whenever the pain seems unendurable I think of that wonderful half-hour. Queen Mary had sent me, all the way to South Africa, a piece of Princess Elizabeth's wedding cake and several autographed books which are a constant source of comfort. I was welcomed at Marlborough House by the

Dowager Countess of Airlie, and later by Lady Cynthia Colville, her ladies-in-waiting. Her Majesty was gracious beyond words, but so human and friendly. I have always held the beloved lady of Marlborough House in great affection, but I never dreamed she could be so wonderful.

That was the afternoon of the royal garden party at Buckingham Palace and I had been invited to attend that also. I was overwhelmed by the wonder of it all.

Knitting used to be one of my favourite occupations, as I believe it is yours, but I cannot knit any more and sewing is very awkward. I must stick the needle into something to thread it, and then place the material on paper, otherwise I would stitch right through my frock, but I do all the housework in my flat, and only send the sheets to the laundry. Everything else, including curtains and blankets, I wash myself.

I meant to tell you that before my accident what I liked best was dancing. Oh, how I loved those dances on the decks of liners, but now all that is over.

Good-bye, Mrs. Henrey,

RUBY TUTT.

I have not altered a word of her prose. You see how she rushes from Buckingham Palace to Marlborough House without so much as telling us what the future queen looked like and what words passed between them, but oh, the joy of it all, the richness of the day!

We go over to Ceylon now. Dorothy is the wife of a tea-planter, and she is about to come home on long leave. So let us learn what excitement this denotes in the lovely bungalow, a snapshot of which falls out of her letter:

My dear Mrs. Henrey,

What a business this going on leave is—strange people coming to act in one's absence, a search for friends to look after a golden retriever, an elderly dachs, and a tailless Siamese cat, and the handing over of childlike servants to another 'lady.' I have received a letter from my cook, a Travancorian, and his wife, typed in duplicate by his second cousin, twice removed, who is a clerk to an advocate in Batticaloa. My cook is a devout Roman Catholic and speaks five languages, cooks divinely, and drinks like a fish. When I ran in and told him the doleful news about the king's death he crossed himself and burst into tears. We heard the news at about a quarter to five in the midst of teatime music. The next day we had to go to Colombo, a hundred miles away, and were most impressed by the sincerity of every person we met from the ancient *ayah* who rings out bathing costumes at the swimming club to the loftiest Ceylonese. The sense of bereavement everywhere was incredible in such a place of political ferment as Ceylon is in these days. Practically everyone who wears European dress had managed to have a black tie even the day after the death, and in the Pettah (the native bazaar area, and a rough, tough place it is) every shop, *boutique*, and junk shack had its shutters or bits of planks up and a black flag dipped outside its door. I have come to the conclusion that all the world besides loving a baby, sympathizes with a bereaved woman, and that is almost surprising in a world that is in such a wicked mess.

Bless you for writing so sweetly. My great sorrow is that the tea I last sent you, straight out of our factory, although the very best grade was not so nice for drinking (we had the same for the household last month), and now my husband has had blended a really delicious drinking tea. I shall bring you some personally on my arrival in England.

Here is the letter from her cook:

My dear Madam,

I and my children thank you very much from the bottom of our hearts for the very kind present of a cake sent to us for the Christmas enjoyment. We also convey our kind thoughts to your partner, who is about to leave Ceylon with you on a furlough to your homeland. We pray for your welfare, health, during your journey to and from Ceylon. We also hope that both of you will get the blessings of His Almighty God during your absence from Ceylon, and arrive back quite safely.

Yours obediently,

Leon and Dora Pereira and their children.

Before you leave my breakfast table here is a long, oblong envelope with an air-mail tab from Texas, U.S.A. My address is neatly typed. I can tell you in advance from whom it comes. His name is Thomas F. Fortson, and he is interested in map-making. In his last letter he described how he had left the heat of Texas, with *The Little Madeleine* in his baggage for Homer, and he said:

'All my father's people are from North Louisiana, and both my grandfather's and great grandfather's old homes are still standing, the latter being built before the civil war, 1861–4. My main interest over there is my uncle, E. H. Fortson, a younger brother of my father. He and his wife have no children, and I have been going over there for visits since I was about five years old, and we have carried on a steady correspondence for several decades. We are both gun cranks, and while we have very different ideas about them and endless arguments, we have never come to blows. He and I built a duck "blind" on a big lake near by some years ago, and I usually go over for some shooting when the season opens in November—and he most always comes to Texas right afterward for the deer season. Three years ago my uncle had a contractor build a dam across a small stream on a farm he owns just west of town, and he now has a private pond of several acres. It is heavily wooded and quite pretty. My uncle stocked it with several varieties of fish which are now big enough to catch, and on my last visit we spent a good part of each day fishing and shooting at targets. It chagrins me to admit that at seventy-seven he is still a better shot than I. In my uncle's bedroom there is a gun-case next to the mantel, which contains on an average a dozen guns, and the first thing I do on a visit is to see what's new—and try it out. He is not so strong as he was. Fortunately he is rather well off, and his business of abstracters of land titles is in good hands and requires no attention from him. With my mother eighty-three and extremely feeble, my uncle seventy-seven, and my dog Snazzy ten years old this summer, I will soon be quite alone.'

Well, it was his dog Snazzy who left him first. He was so broken hearted that I wept in sympathy and asked him to tell me how it all happened. Here then is the letter in which he will give me this sad information. Let us open it together.

Oak Lawn Avenue,
Dallas 4, Texas,
U.S.A.

Dear Mrs. Henrey,

Snazzy belonged to the Ben McCleskeys who were our neighbours from 1941 till 1947, when they moved to the outskirts of Dallas some eight miles away. I had observed the dog without much interest from the time he was a pup until two years old, frequently passing him on the walk and sometimes attempting to pet him, but he was shy of strangers and would not let me touch him. Nothing could have concerned me less. I had observed one thing about him, however, that pleased me greatly, and that was the fact that he was able to enjoy life fully without barking. For that reason I was kindly disposed to him as our nights were usually made miserable by neighbours' dogs which barked at anything.

In the spring of 1944, when Snazzy was about two and I was working for the Army Air Force as a civilian employee, I stood on a nearby corner waiting for a bus one rainy morning when Snazzy strolled by and stopped a few yards away. I spoke to him and called him by name, getting the usual aloof and haughty stare for my trouble, and being somewhat peeved I told him to run away, but to my amazement he came over in a most friendly manner and let me pat his head. That did it! We immediately became friends and it was evident that he wanted to be my dog. Not wishing to offend the McCleskeys I asked them if they resented my interest in their dog, and was assured that it was quite agreeable with them.

Snazzy practically lived at our apartment. At first my mother objected to him being in the house, and was then determined that he should not be fed at the table; but she soon gave in and became more indulgent than myself. At table, if Snazzy had not been noticed for some time he would place his chin on my knee and bear down harder and harder until given something— but he was never rough. If he wanted to go out he would merely stand by the door until noticed. My bedroom had a rather shabby divan with a couple of ornamental pillows on which I used to stretch out for a nap. Sometimes Snazzy beat me to it. He would push a pillow into place with his muzzle, and then lie down with his head on it.

Americans, as you surely know, are ice-cream addicts.

Snazzy and I went for a long walk every night at nine. Our route sometimes varied, but we always ended up at a certain drug store for a dish of vanilla ice-cream. The flavour never changed as Snazzy liked nothing else. When we walked into the store he went ahead and sat at the side of the same stool, looking up impatiently until we were served, and after he had finished his share I would say: 'That's all,' whereupon he would walk out and wait for me. This routine attracted a lot of notice and one of the papers published a story about the ice-cream-eating dog. People still stop me and ask about him.

What pleased him most was to go to one of the nearby creeks where he swam or waded along the side of the bank looking for frogs. Our favourite creek was a clear, rock-bottomed stream with a good current and a few places deep enough for dogs and children to swim in. Few people knew of the place, and we seldom encountered anyone there. The dog always knew where we were going before we arrived, and showed his pleasure.

Snazzy slept on the floor of my bedroom. In real cold weather I kept a large sheet rolled up at the foot of my bed, and then he would come and whine slightly, waking me, and I would pull this top sheet over the bed and let him lie on it. This was dog heaven to him. If he got too warm during the night he did not jump off the bed, but would ease over to the edge and slide off slowly so as not to wake me. During our terrible summers, the heat of which you cannot imagine, Snazzy spent most of the time asleep on the tile floor of our bath-room, the coolest place in the house. This annoyed my mother at times, especially after the tiles had been freshly mopped, and she frequently made the dog go elsewhere. His efforts to outwit her were amusing and usually successful. On one occasion, when she was asleep in her bedroom, the dog started to the bath-room to sleep, but encountered a large sheet of brown paper in which a bundle of laundry had been wrapped. He knew the noise of the paper crackling would awaken my mother and she would see him, so he very deliberately reached out with one foot and felt for a 'solid' spot that did not crackle. He crossed this paper in that manner gingerly feeling his way across it without a sound, all the while keeping a sharp look-out at my mother. I watched all this from the living-room without Snazzy knowing it, and I laughed until it hurt.

During all this time I was on the best of terms with the McCleskeys. The dog spent some time with them and then came back to me. They seemed quite happy with the arrangement, but in the fall of 1947 they sold their house and moved to the country. I tried to buy Snazzy from them, but they declined, instead offering to share him with me. From that time he divided his time between us, sometimes over week-ends and at times for months.

Last October I took Snazzy back to the country, thinking it would be better to give him a change. I went to see Snazzy every Sunday and sometimes for a few minutes during the week. For a while I was without a car and took the bus. This meant walking a mile to the house which I did not mind, and when half-way there I blew a small whistle which the dog would hear and recognize. Running out into the road, he would wait till I waved my arm and then run all the way to meet me.

If the weather was at all nice, we went for a walk in the nearby fields and along a creek before I returned. When it was time for me to go, the McCleskeys would offer to drive me to the bus, which I always declined, for Snazzy would accompany me on this walk, staying with me at the bus stop until I got on. After paying my fare I usually went to the back window and waved at him while he stood at the side of the road and wagged his tail in reply. When he got almost too small to be seen he would turn round and start a slow trot home.

On 6th January I went out as usual, and he came back with me to the bus stop and waved good-bye, apparently for ever.

Most sincerely,

THOMAS FORTSON.

CHAPTER IX

ON THE FIRST day of the Easter holidays, having joined the band of mothers meeting their children at Charing Cross station, I discover mine and carry him off to a waiting cab. We sail the same night for Le Havre, and the following morning the Le Havre–Caen motor-coach leaves us at the side of the road with our luggage a quarter of a mile from my farm in Normandy.

The trees are not yet in bud, but yellow and red-brown wallflowers daub the gardens. A cold wind blows in from the sea and it is dry underfoot. Our harness-maker owns the house and water-mill at the corner of the lane leading to my farm, and as our bags are too heavy, we borrow the harness-maker's wheelbarrow and, putting our belongings into it, make our way democratically down one hill and up another to our orchard home.

At last we see the half-timbered house in the hollow. Farm noises rise above the sound of the creaking wheelbarrow, and cocks and hens wander at will through the grass between the apple-trees. The air is sweet with country smells, and I feel suddenly uncomfortable in my coat and skirt and town hat. I look critically at lopped hedges and newly planted trees, and unconsciously I am changing from the London woman to the Norman housewife who soon will be matching her brains against those of the peasants who for the last few days have been eagerly expecting her arrival.

Easter Day. Immediately after breakfast, in the quiet of my own room, I switched on the radio for the French Protestant service. The clergyman, in his short sermon, told us of his immense personal faith in the miracle of the resurrection and yet, he said, his heart was heavy because only a few hours earlier he had accompanied his father, a clergyman like himself, to the grave, where the family through its tears sang the hymn chosen by the loved one before going to meet his God. The beauty of this unexpected sermon moved me so much on this Easter morning that I was soon crying myself, weeping with all my heart.

The weather was truly springlike.

My young son was with his grandmother in the kitchen, making an Easter cake with eight eggs and half a pound of butter. We had slaughtered no lamb for this Easter Day, and the cocks and hens were free to enjoy the young grass and the sunshine.

Every morning now, from my bedroom window, I could see the lilac opening out and during the last few days the pear-trees were in full blossom. Cascades of white flowers billowing over the leafless branches, spread with such speed that I sometimes had the impression of a canopy of lace being hung even as I watched by fairy fingers across every orchard. The previous evening, while the house was asleep and I was taking advantage of its quietness to write my letters, the prettiest ladybird walked across the note-paper and started to climb up my hand. How dainty she was! Her beautiful round back shimmered, black stars on a red surface. She was so inquisitive, so light on her feet, that I knew she was a woman. She was in no hurry, delighted, I felt sure, by the wonders surrounding her in the course of this

D

nocturnal walk by electric light. Thus the pleasures of a long day were being prolonged for this young woman who, like myself, quite certainly had her little head filled with the most delightful feminine dreams. From my hand she jumped lightly on to the photograph of the Begum Aga Khan, the one that shows this lovely princess with a bouquet of red roses, standing beside her husband the Aga Khan. My ladybird, having made their acquaintance, returned to my writing-pad and inspected with new interest the letter which, by a coincidence, I was writing to the lady of the roses whom I knew to be very worried. For the last few weeks she had been nursing her distinguished husband night and day with utter disregard for her own health. During a visit to India he had suffered a serious heart attack and was brought back to Cannes in a specially chartered aeroplane. I decided to tell the Begum something gay. I would tell her that a ladybird had been walking up and down her photograph: this must surely be an excellent omen.

The ladybird was now rubbing her delicate legs against each other. Then she unfolded her wings to form a crinoline and flew on my finger where she looked down into the depths of my rings, examining her reflection in pools of diamond and sapphire. She was gone! Where would she go? Outside the wind was blowing; the flowers were asleep. I felt terribly alone, with no desire to go to bed. The immense stillness of the country kept me awake as so often, in London, does the incessant traffic in Piccadilly.

The days went by but the fine weather continued. On Low Sunday I had just been putting up my hair which I had allowed to grow almost to my waist, using at least twenty hairpins, when the telephone rang. This was the Russian Easter, a week later than our own. The radio said that the churches in Moscow were full.

Would to God the announcer spoke the truth! I ran down to the low room and lifted the receiver.

'Will madame take a personal call from Cannes?' asked the operator.

'Madeleine? It is I—Yvette, the Begum Aga Khan. I have just received your sweet letter. I am so ashamed not to have wished you a happy Easter.'

'But you are not late,' I exclaimed. 'It is the Russian Easter . . . the Greek Easter, so you see that you are not late at all.'

She said that my letter had given her all the pleasure I hoped it would. Her mother, who was eighty and who also lived at Cannes, was only just recovering from congestion of a lung. The prince, also, was much better and had walked half a mile. She was tired but happy.

'I saw in the papers that you had sent for my friend Dr. Bourne,' I exclaimed. 'It said he had flown specially to Cannes. He and his wife were guests of Wilfrid de Glehn when I went to his place near Salisbury to have my portrait done.'

'Dr. Bourne was wonderful,' the Begum answered. 'But he was so tired out when he arrived that for a moment I expected to have three patients instead of two to nurse. And then, he is so terribly cut up about the death of his brilliant wife——'

'The beautiful Margherita, with her dark, affectionate look? Is it possible?' I exclaimed.

I closed my eyes and saw again the scene by the river, and heard in imagination the sound of the croquet balls on the lawn. There was that evening when De Glehn had played Beethoven, and the little comedy at breakfast the next morning. And now two of us were gone—the painter and Margherita.

'The weather here is quite marvellous,' the Begum was saying. 'I am wearing a white dress, and the orange-trees are in blossom. It is paradise.'

'Here in Normandy,' I answered, 'the pear-trees are heavy with blossom. Our orchards are bedecked with bridal veils.'

'Then between us,' laughed the Begum, 'we could crown many a bride, you with your pear-blossom, I with my orange-blossom.'

She spoke about Simba the Blue Persian kitten. She had been afraid her husband would be angry when she first brought it back to the hotel because he only understood large animals, horses and elephants, but he quickly fell in love with the kitten, said it was a Persian like himself, and allowed it to sleep on their bed.

She asked about the cats on my farm—Miquette, who had lost a leg in a poacher's gin, and another black as night. She planned, if the prince was well enough, to fly to London the following week. 'We might go to the races together,' she said.

What a delightful number of subjects we managed to discuss over six hundred miles of wire! She is like some lovely flower always ready to open out its petals and expose its heart. As she hates to compose a letter she waits till she has a hundred things to tell me and then, from wherever she is, a hundred or a thousand miles away, takes up the telephone.

Friendships are indeed curious. Different friends mark different phases. When I was a little girl, soon to become a young woman, my first high-heeled shoes were given me by that exquisite Didine whose story I told in *The Little Madeleine*. My first evening-bag was the gift of that delightful woman whose hands I tended in her suite at the Savoy: she was anxious for it to bring me good luck. Yvette Begum Aga Khan, on her return from a fabulous ball at Venice, handed me a package done up in tissue-paper in which were two silk petticoats, one white, the other pink.

'I ran from shop to shop to find something small

enough,' she laughed. 'They are both embroidered by hand.'

During the war I knew an American woman whose mink coat was one of the loveliest I have ever seen, but she also owned a doe-skin golfing jacket whose colour had faded with sun and wind. She said to me one day:

'See how the skin is supple and how warm it is! I really cannot wear it any more, but it breaks my heart to give it to some woman who will judge it merely on its faded colour. If only I could persuade you to take it to your farm?'

So when the March winds blow or it snows, I put on the golfing jacket and think of my friend in California or in Florida, clad in shantung, sipping a tall mint-julep; and thus, also, Sonia was telling me the other day that her friends continue to congratulate her when she wears some silly thing I gave her fifteen years ago.

CHAPTER X

SITTING AT THE kitchen table was Émile, whose long moustaches are shaped like a milk-maid's yoke. He reminds me of a picture of Clovis, king of the Franks, that delighted me in my history book when I was a little girl. At my approach he removed his cap and got up. Then he sat down again and arranged his cap on his knees, saying: 'I came along to pay my respects to madame.'

Émile is exactly my mother's age. They must have been born within a few hours of each other. Émile is a Norman peasant rooted in the soil, but he specializes in horses. Nothing, as far as I can tell, distinguishes Émile from what a French peasant was a hundred years ago. He speaks very slowly and his language has the wealth of the soil he tills. Noble words no longer in common usage leap out from each phrase to startle and be remembered. He has a proud politeness with women and treats me with the deference shown by his for-bears, I imagine, to the lady of the manor. I who have come to think of myself, by acclimatization, as a Londoner, am often surprised on my return to the land of William the Conqueror to find these sturdy vestiges of a former way of living. Émile is not seriously aware of the radio, the aeroplane, or television. He sleeps on a bed of hay and his calm features mirror a soul that is tranquil, wise, and without cupidity.

I once met a French-Canadian twenty miles from

Quebec, tapping his maples for sap, who had never had the inquisitiveness to look at the sea.

'Madame,' said Émile, smiling, 'it needed the great panic of 1940 to teach me that there are other parts of France as lovely as our own.'

Why yes, of course, the whole of France and Belgium were on the move during what became known as the 'Exodus.' People ran away from their homes, leaving the doors wide open, anxious to put an increasing number of miles between themselves and the enemy, not realizing that soon the invader would be everywhere.

I looked down at Émile and smiled. I had a hundred things to do, for I was returning to London the following day, but Émile wanted to tell me his story, and Émile is a man. Therefore, clearly, as a woman it was my duty to smile at him and make him feel that I wanted desperately to hear his story.

'Émile,' I said, putting a hand on his shoulder, 'please tell us all about it.'

For my mother was also in the room. We sat on either side of him, gazing expectantly into his eyes.

'I was looking after the horses,' he said, 'at the farm known as The Prairie. Our mistress'—he used the feudal term, *nôtre maîtresse*, for the lady who owned the farm and whom he served, this appellation of respect and affection having, each time he pronounced it, an extraordinarily sweet sound—'our mistress had two children, Jacqueline, then about fifteen, and little Daniel who was only two.

'"Émile," she said to me that morning, "go and harness the mare. We must be off like all the others."

'She made bundles of what she needed for the journey, but Jacqueline, who had been given a bicycle for passing her school certificate, refused to take her place in the trap. "No," she declared, "I cannot leave my bicycle behind. I would rather be killed on the way." Our mistress pleaded with her. Then Jacqueline had an idea. She said to her mother: "With you, mother, and Daniel, and Émile, and all the bundles in the trap, the mare will go no faster than I on my bicycle. Therefore I shall ride beside you, or if necessary behind."

'Thus it was done. The little girl was right. We travelled slowly, for from time to time I had to rest the mare, and there were so many people on the roads, most of them with mattresses on the roofs of their cars, but as everybody knows about these things, the less I say about them the better.

'I drove the mare, while the mistress sat beside me with her baby in her arms. We travelled south for several days trying not to think of the poor cows we had left behind with nobody to milk them, so that with their inflated udders they would die miserably. The hens were free in the orchard and the watch-dogs were unleashed. And what for? To allow us to drive on like this, day after day, not even knowing whither we were bound? Surely that is a thing we cannot forgive those who make wars?

'Then one morning, with the sun hotter than ever, we came upon a wide river. Jacqueline, who had been at school, unable to tell us the name of the river, was sulking as she pedalled at our side, but from my place in the trap, holding the reins, I could only see the top of her head and her knees going up and down like a spinning-wheel.

'"Mistress," I queried, "supposing this river turned out to be the Loire?"

'"The Loire!" said my mistress.

'"The Loire!" echoed Jacqueline. "But of course. Why did we not think of it before?"

'We crossed a wide bridge, and here right under my mare was the Loire. I felt a good deal of pride seeing this famous river for the first time, but it just showed what a long way we were from home, and the sun shone,

as you will remember it did that terrible summer, and
little Daniel was teething. I thought it high time our
mistress should find a bed to spend the night in. I drove
till evening. The birds were flying low, and the corn
was ripening, and when I saw a woman with her children
at her cottage door I said to myself: "There is still
happiness on earth." I thought of our own farm with
the animals let loose, and then from my high seat I would
look over walls and see green lettuces in kitchen gardens,
and peaches ripening on trees.

'We came in this way to a great farm. There were
sheep, and a dog barked. I pulled up the mare and,
jumping down from the trap, tied her to a tree. Jacqueline put her bicycle in the ditch, and having climbed into
the back of the trap, curled up and went fast to sleep.
Then, with my whip round my neck I walked straight to
the farm.

'Oh, it was a fine place. Indeed, I have seldom seen
a finer one. There were two heavy doors in the form
of a pointed arch, and a heavy bell chain with the handle
in the likeness of a stirrup upon which I pulled heartily,
for, said I to myself gruffly: "Émile, you are no thief,
but an honest man in search of a bed for a woman and
her children." There was the sound as of a monastery
bell, and one of the doors opened. A youth, who was
neither a boy nor quite a man, asked me my business
and when I told him he turned and called out: "Mama!
Mama!" and a woman arrived wearing a fine apron and
a gold chain with a cross.

'I said: "I have money to pay, ma'am," but she
answered:

'"My good man, pray come in and do not bother
about the money."

'"No," I objected. "I have left our mistress with
her two children asleep in the trap, and the mare is tied
to a tree."

*D

'"Then, in heaven's name," cried the woman, "go quickly and fetch your mistress and her children, my man."

'When I returned driving the trap both doors had been opened, and the farmer, the farmer's wife, their son, and an old servant were waiting to welcome us as if we had been visiting relatives. The old servant helped me to unharness the mare and led me to the beautiful stables, giving the mare so much to eat that I said: "Not too much, my friend, for she has starved these three days, and spent herself, and too good a meal would do her harm."

'When we had rubbed her down and given her water and set her up for the night, Father Simon said to me:

'"Except when I am expecting a foal, on which occasions I curl up in a shepherd's cloak and sleep in the box where I have just put your mare, I spend the night in the grange. I have been here sixty years and my quarters are snug. I shall be honoured if you will join me."

'Thus, thought I, the master and the mistress are entertaining my mistress and her children, while the servant entertains me. How simple it is!

'They were all in the big farm room where cheeses hung in baskets from the ceiling. The furniture was rich and heavy. There were benches on either side of the long table; but at each end was a large wicker chair. The farmer's wife was cutting bread into a soup tureen. Flop ... flop ... the bread fell into the soup, slice by slice. The farmer's wife looked very cool and homely with her long, thin knife cutting the bread, and she was talking to our mistress about our Norman orchards where the grass is always so damp and green, and about our cows whose milk is so creamy. I listened while the two women spoke, perhaps for an hour or longer, exchanging information. We ate cheese and drank wine: I had seen the vineyards stretching down to the Loire.

'"My poor Émile," said our mistress suddenly, "your head is nodding. I do believe you are half asleep."

'I went off to spend the night with Father Simon in the grange, but at five I was already up and about thinking about the mare and wondering how I could make myself useful. The farm was even more beautiful than I had supposed. I followed Father Simon, admiring his horses, his cows, his sheep, his pigs, and his goats; and in the big farm room there were bowls for milk, or glasses for white wine, and big loaves of bread, and the farmer's wife asked me, laughing, if I had slept as well in my bed as I had done at supper, and I blushed, for I am not bold with women. I soon fell to helping her with one thing and another and I had no need to be told what to do, noticing at once where the faggots were kept and where they drew the water and the wine.

'On Sunday morning I harnessed the mare and drove our mistress to church. The farmer, his wife, and their son had gone in front, taking Jacqueline with them. We sat all together in the family pew, but Paris had fallen and everybody knew that France had lost the war. Oh, what a melancholy service! The priest broke down in the middle of his sermon and wept.

'Father Simon had gone to an early mass: on our return from church he was waiting for us in the *patio*. He had set out a long table under two elms with several bottles of white wine, some bread, a goose *pâté*, and several kinds of cheese. This was the custom each Sunday morning, the master pouring out the wine himself, but he insisted that every person under his roof should first attend mass.

'While the master cut the bread he told us that, by order of the mayor, farm workers from other parts of France, those who had taken part in the exodus, should in return for their services be lodged and fed and paid forty francs a day.

'"Thus," he said, turning to me, "I will pay you the agreed wage, just as it will be paid to your mistress. Even Mademoiselle Jacqueline will have something, according to her age and the work she does. You do not need to thank me.

'I was put to minding the horses, and soon we gathered in the harvest. A harvest is a harvest anywhere and there is little difference between a hayfield by the Loire and one in Normandy. I did not worry about the money: quite apart from the old age pension I knew that our mistress would look after me as long as I lived.

'In due course we learned that the Germans were willing for us to go home, and then our mistress showed as much impatience to return to Normandy as she had been in a hurry to leave; she made up her bundles and ordered the trap to be ready early the next morning.

'"My brave Émile," said the farmer as he came into the yard to bid us good-bye. "My horses have greatly prospered since you have been with us. If ever you wish to come back I will gladly send you the expenses of the journey."

'He handed me my wages and, peering into the trap in which our mistress and Jacqueline were already seated, added:

'"Now let me have a look at your belongings. I wouldn't like anything to happen to you on the way back. For instance, my poor Émile, you will have to leave your gun behind."

'"My gun?" said I. "But I have had it for more than forty years. I would feel lost without it."

'"I know," said the farmer. "A man hates to be parted from his gun, but you will have to trust me. I will hide it with my own and with Father Simon's."

'I had taken it up and was stroking the barrel.   I loved the feel of it, and it hurt me to hand it over.

'"You don't need to bother," I answered suddenly, "there are far too many weapons in the world as it is."

'And with a quick movement I broke it in half over my knee.

'Thus, our mistress, Jacqueline, and I set off once more, but this time we knew where we were going.   Many others were returning home and traffic on the bridges over the Loire was terribly congested.   Soldiers in *feldgrau* with bayonets searched each vehicle.   It was not a pretty sight but, thank goodness, we had nothing to hide.   A farmer who was travelling in a buggy just ahead of us had his rifle confiscated, but as the soldiers did not even speak to him, and as there were plenty of others in the same predicament, he took courage and even said, laughing, that they would doubtless merely make him pay a fine.

'Then suddenly this unhappy man and all those from whom the soldiers had taken firearms, were led to the river bank, lined up, and mown down with a machine-gun.   Mown down without a trial, without a chance to explain.   For the first time in my life I nearly fainted. How I thanked God that the master had been so strict with me!

'After this the bridge was opened and we were allowed to pass through.

'It was lovely to see our own farm again.   Neighbours had fed the chickens and milked the cows, and the apple-trees were heavy with fruit.   The kitchen garden, of course, was full of weeds and it was too late in the year to plant anything.   I slept above the stables, under the beams, climbing up to my bedroom each night by a ladder placed against the wall.   And so it went on, season after season, with the Germans all round us, though for

my part I had no occasion to speak to them and I kept
to myself, for I had not forgotten the lesson of my gun.

'Then one night during the battle of Caen, having
climbed up my ladder to bed, I threw myself exhausted
on the hay, but it seemed to be arranged differently.
I thought that an animal, a cat perhaps, had slipped in,
but on reflection this was not possible, for there was no
window and the door of the loft was always closed.
There was no moon, so in spite of a few cracks in the
half-timbering it was quite dark, and I never troubled
to bring a lantern.

'Suddenly I felt something move beside me. A hand
closed over my moustaches, and a voice whispered:
"Hush!" I guessed at once that it was a parachutist.
He explained with a good deal of difficulty that he was
English. He mentioned London several times. Somebody had brought him here and he would have to remain
hidden in the hay till somebody else came to fetch him.
He had a friend who had also dropped in the neighbour-
hood. I was to go to sleep and he would keep watch.

'For more than two weeks, ma'am, I had them both
hidden in my hay under the beams, the one who placed
his hand over my moustaches to warn me not to make a
sound, and his companion who was brought in later by
one of those who made it their business to hide the
English. I don't pretend I was very brave, but it's a
great deal easier to break a gun over one's knee than to
get rid of two embarrassing guests. I shared my supper
with them and brought them a little tobacco, and then
on the fifteenth evening, just as I was ready to go to
bed, I noticed that the ladder, instead of being placed
as usual against the half-timbering rested against the
door of the loft.

'"That's the end!" I murmured. "They've been
caught!"

'I knew how interminable the hours of daylight must

have seemed to them, hiding in the hay, afraid to talk
above a whisper.   They were always so happy when I
arrived, for it meant that we could close the door and
smoke, and when there was no moon I would send them
down into the kitchen garden for some exercise.

'I took a lantern this time and climbed the ladder—
having changed its position back to the half-timbering—
very slowly in case I was being watched.   I opened the
door and looked around.   What remained of the provisions were neatly put together, and there was a piece
of paper on which was scrawled: "Merci bien, from two
London boys."   So my guests had flown away in safety.
Between ourselves, it was high time; a few days more
and all three of us would have been shot!'

CHAPTER XI

ON THE FIRST of May our village, with the sea shimmering at the bottom of the street, was countrified with lilies of the valley picked by children in the woods. Frenchmen, according to tradition, buy these flowers for their women on May morning.

The holidays were over and we were to sail from Le Havre that night. While we waited for the coach from Caen a great commotion took place: the fire siren had just sounded, and the tradesmen who belonged to the fire brigade were rushing to the town hall to put their helmets on. I had been talking to the headmistress of the girls' school, but when she caught sight of a bevy of her pupils dashing in joyously amongst the firemen, many of whom were fathers or brothers, she decided, thinking that their presence might impede the preparations of the brave men, to pull them back: 'Everybody on the pavement!' she ordered. 'And keep calm!' Then looking back at me, she smiled attractively. Now a man, running and out of breath, announced that the fire had gone out by itself. The firemen looked pained. How charming was our village, and what a pity to leave it!

The coach arrived, and I entered cautiously because of my basket of eggs—I was bringing nearly a hundred back to London. All the other women had farm produce of one kind or another, and most of them had armfuls of white and mauve lilac as well as their tiny

bouquets of lilies of the valley. The steel coach rever-
berated heat, but I love these journeys that take peasants
from one village or town to another. The men joke
amongst themselves; I soon found myself drawn into
conversation by the women. Our route was through
Deauville, Trouville, Honfleur, and by ferry across the
estuary of the Seine. Hens cackled on the floor. The
whole thing was an enchantment.

Though it was past seven when we reached Le Havre
most of the shops were still open. We had dinner on
the terrace of a café, a succulent steak with fried potatoes,
and a muscatel. At the adjoining table a little boy with
dark, intelligent eyes was asking his father, the captain
of a ship, about his last voyage: 'Do you think I've
grown taller, dad? And you know, dad, at school we
all used to listen after the news to the movement of
liners. We knew when you left Pernambuco and when
you reached Dakar. Was I proud of you, dad!'

The sea captain looked at the little man who had drunk
rather too deeply in his mother's glass, and I examined
the wife. She was very young. The face was oval,
but dark eyes were full of admiration for husband and
son. Her thick hair was piled up at the back of her
head so that she put one in mind of a schoolgirl who,
in short dress and white socks, folds her hair in a bun
to look like mummy. And to think that she was
already the mother of a little boy whose thoughts
were turning to the sea! The lad was doing all the
talking.

'Don't you think, mother,' asked my son with a touch
of jealousy, 'that he is putting on airs?'

But he added quickly:

'I would like to know the name of his father's ship.'

However, the boy's success was of short duration.
He upset the coffee, which made him blush. Then he
yawned, and soon his head drooped against his mother's

shoulder, the little mother with her mass of black hair
gathered up at the back of her head.

And now my son, in turn, was beginning to yawn.

How poignant the building of a new city on the ashes
of an old one! Here at Le Havre the cafés that line the
wide avenue which leads from the docks to the centre
of the town, have built-in terraces, heated in winter by
tall porcelain stoves, and so filled with bright flowers in
pots that they look like conservatories. When spring
comes, the glass is taken away and the terraces opened
up. Farmers bring their dairy produce to this avenue
and place it on stalls, so that it becomes a huge market-
place. The restaurants are remarkable, for the inhabitants of Le Havre brighten their tragedy with good wine
and excellently grilled steaks.

The harbour itself seems full of romance. One can
wander from dock to dock right up to the sides of the
ships. Here are mail-packets from Far Eastern ports;
here are white-painted evocations of African sunshine
with awnings in their decks and crates of bananas. The
magic of foreign lands is not hidden behind high walls.
Here, being towed in gently by tugs, is a cargo ship
from the Argentine. Spanish words float gently across
the night, and squat men with dark lashes smile at the
woman in high heels who holds her child by the hand.

When I wake the next morning I look through the
port-hole at Southampton where the *Queen Elizabeth* is
in dock. But though I spend much time each year in
travelling, I remain eternally anxious. There are the
bags to count, my face that needs powdering, and the
child who might catch cold. I feel like an uneasy
tigress.

This morning the customs men were charming, even
greeting me by name, as if they were glad to see me

back in England, and the boat train, drawn up in the shed, was waiting obediently to take us to London. I looked for a quiet compartment. Out of a first-class window leaned a nun. I smiled at her. A nun, a mother, and a child. We shall compose a gentle picture. She made as if to welcome me, and I took the seat opposite hers.

She sat down, and my eyes turned to her heavy black shoes, the sort schoolchildren wear. Her feet, possibly well shaped, had ceased to take any notice of the pleasures of the world, and had become feet without sex. From time to time I could see the coarse black laces, but not the colour of the stockings.

A very light, brown valise, made of fibre, stood end-up between us, and on this my companion had placed a moleskin bag with the mouth wide open, so that one could see, protruding from it, a smaller one of black serge, probably containing her passport and her money. A fat prayer book, with the cover protected by another piece of black serge embroidered with three small crosses in red cotton, also peeped out of the moleskin bag. I wondered what the three crosses stood for: were they a symbol of the Trinity, or merely some mark to distinguish her belongings from those of her sisters in the convent?

While I was still turning this matter over in my mind, she took out from a pocket a limply bound brochure of foreign aspect which might easily have passed, in the possession of another person, for something quite gay, a novel, for instance, but I soon distinguished Latin words printed on the cover, and from a slight movement of her lids, it was clear that the reader was trying to learn passages by heart, but curiously enough her eyelids, not her lips, appeared to move.

Behind narrow, gold-rimmed spectacles, her eyes were dark and lively, but age drew her skin tightly across her bones. The soft lines had gone, but an admirable sculpture remained. Her nose was truly aquiline, and her mouth, with its lips the colour of a tea-rose, was still charming. The oval of her face produced by the wimple was very effective. This severe head-dress which hides the charms of the pretty novice, also hides the wrinkled neck, part of the cheeks, the telltale chin, the greying or whitening hair of the older nun. As with eastern women, in the days when they were veiled, the wimple is the triumph of eyes and nose. My companion's face was seemingly drained of blood. The nose did not shine, the cheeks appeared impervious to heat or cold, and during all this time the eyelids beat to the rhythm of the Latin phrases she was committing to memory.

Her hand, of the same parchment as her face, held the book reverently, and on the third finger shone the heavy ring binding her to our Saviour. The symbol of marriage against the blackness of the dress was magnificent. She would never be a widow. Hers was a tie that nothing could break. Was she the Mother Superior of her community? Doubtless. Vainly one would search for the slightest speck of dust about her person. How do they perform the miracle of travelling long distances, perhaps all the way from Rome, without creasing their fragile black, without spoiling the impeccable white of their wimples?

I started to unwind a skein of wool slowly, this occupation allowing me to continue observing my companion without fixing her.

She closed her brochure and placed it beside her prayer book in the moleskin bag. She looked at me, and seeing me unwinding my wool, smiled, a smile that without in any way inviting conversation was yet friendly.

She now made an almost imperceptible movement, and her hands quite disappeared beneath her robes like a child folding itself to sleep after too much exertion. Her figure, because of her luggage, had slanted a little, and her legs relaxed though her feet remained close together, the black shoes just visible as they looked out from the black folds. What grace in this languid pose! How elegant this feminity hidden beneath the long black veils! My curiosity was great. Even though as a little girl I had gone to convent, I still wondered how the becoming wimple was removed from head, cheeks, and neck. And all these skirts and underskirts! Their putting on and taking off remain a secret to those who have not made their vows. I felt rather absurd, almost self-conscious, with my short skirt and varnished nails, frivolous little woman enslaved to the dictates of the fashion papers, eternally preoccupied with her waist-line, her hair, her vitamins, her make-up, and her shining nose.

My companion slept as calmly and as gracefully as an angel. Even in her unconscious state she gave the impression of being aware of her dignity. Dignified in sleep, she would wake up with equal dignity. If ever I allowed myself to doze off thus in a train, my eye-black and my lipstick would be almost certain to run.

Who was my companion? Had she, as a young woman, been tragically in love? Her expression was so peaceful that it was hard to believe that she had suffered the cruel disappointments of the world, and yet as her limbs, in sleep, became increasingly languid, the whole body became nobly, resplendently feminine.

Knitting in my corner, I seemed to be watching over her.

At Winchester the train stopped. The sleeping nun and the child at the other end of the compartment at first kept away newcomers, but at last the door was cautiously opened and a man entered. He smiled at me and took his seat gingerly by the side of the nun. He was Adonis! He was Satan! He was of an age, so attractive to romantic young women, when a man's hair turns slightly grey above the temples. Tall, good-looking, impeccably dressed, a light suit, and an ivory-coloured shirt of pure silk—such were first impressions. His cuffs, without links, were so beautifully fresh and neat that they joined in elegant abandon. His shoes were obviously hand made.

Taking a sheaf of documents from an attaché-case, he began to run down a line of figures with a gold pencil held delicately in white fingers. Then he took out a pass-book and seemed to compare the figures he found in it with those on the sheet. One felt that he was thus passing in review impressive sums.

The nun continued to sleep, and I went on knitting the tight little garment that I would wear on chilly days under the jacket of my coat and skirt. Nobody took the slightest notice of me; the City man, if such he was, had his head full of figures, and the nun was far away.

Suddenly I caught sight of the Palace of Westminster. How quickly the journey had passed! Still the nun slept. I would be obliged to wake her up. What a pity! She must have greatly needed the rest. I felt increasingly sure she had gone to Rome on important business. I began to feel agitated. We were arriving. I powdered my face and put my lipstick to my lips. Inspecting my features in the tiny mirror I could see that I wore my anxious expression, the expression of a little woman arriving somewhere. I looked over the top of my mirror at the sleeping nun. She was beginning to move, but the City man had already stuffed his documents into his attaché-case and was making for the corridor. The nun opened her eyes. She would never know that she had slept soundly beside a rich and good-looking man. Her expression was perfectly calm. Yes, sister, you slept deep and well. She gave me a great smile full of tender affection, and asked:

'I think I slept a good deal?'

'Yes, sister, you slept well.'

'I do hope I didn't talk in my sleep,' she exclaimed. 'They tell me it does sometimes happen, and it is so very embarrassing.'

'No, sister, have no fear.   You said nothing.'

I only wished she had.

She took her valise and stepped down.   Nobody was waiting for her at the station.   The black figure merged with the crowd as it glided quickly away.

CHAPTER XII

THIS MORNING I changed the sheets. This occupation has its reward, for this evening I shall slip into a cool bed. I had a friend whose dream of being rich was to own sufficient pure linen sheets to sleep in fresh ones every night. The war has done away with all this, and we have been robbed of our most feminine satisfactions, for in the days when a woman had a house and a family to look after, the linen cupboard with lavender sachets was amongst her most treasured possessions. Now, my only friends who own any linen to speak of are those who once lived in a large house, then in a single wing of their house, then in the lodge or above the garage, and finally in a small flat in town. They have inherited their linen from themselves, from their former splendour. There are no guest rooms now, no servants' quarters.

As a young married woman, I kept the cheque my mother-in-law invariably gave me at Christmas until the White Sales. I then bought two pairs of Irish linen sheets with their accompanying pillow-cases for fifty shillings a pair. With the money that remained, I bought large Turkish bath towels and neat piles of glass cloths. At the beginning of each week the laundry delivered the clean linen in an osier basket, and two days later called for the dirty. I can still hear the sound of the horse van at the door.

Now the laundry sends back my washing in a thin sheet of creased brown paper which, as often as not, is torn. The glass cloths are so badly ironed that the ends do not meet, and the pillow-cases are frayed. If as a girl I had ironed like that, my mother would have slapped me. On the other hand such a thing could not have happened. I was brought up to respect the work of others.

What is left in a home where the housewife has no sheets in her cupboard and no food in her larder? Anybody would think that as a sex we have become redundant. Are we all to wear trousers and smoke cigarettes? Happily, my body has its curves. It betrays me. I do not smoke, and my hair, now that I have let it grow again, reaches almost to my waist. Nobody shall take me for anything but a woman.

'Linen?' echoed Sonia on the telephone. 'I am hoping that my sheets will last till the end of the year, but my pillow-cases are in such a state that I am ashamed to send them to the laundry. I shall be reduced to washing them at home like you do, but then you like housework. I have so little time.'

She reflected a moment, and added:

'Of course, all women are not like us. Some have plenty of linen. Flora, for instance, when she was buying that house in Ireland, bought sheets by the dozen, bought them as we might have done when they cost fifty shillings a pair. The trouble with us is that we remember what they cost before. We would be better off to have no memory. The other evening I came across some table-cloths so large that I could almost use them as sheets. Do you remember those Christmas dinners on damask linen?'

'What made you mention Flora? Have you seen her lately?'

'Less than an hour ago,' answered Sonia. 'Having spent the whole morning at the hairdresser's she dropped in for a cup of coffee. She smelt delicious and, would you believe it, my dear, she was wearing £10,000 worth of jewellery! What surprised me was how little impression it made—a necklace, a bracelet, and a ring. £10,000, my dear! The very idea makes me gasp.'

'Why so?' I asked. 'You have spent more than that in your time.'

'Yes,' she agreed, 'but as I seldom put money aside, I cannot imagine having so much at once. Ten thousand pounds in notes might make a pile higher than a man. The funny thing is that I am beginning to find Flora almost beautiful.'

'Because of the jewels?'

'Perhaps. . . . The fact is that a woman must be beautiful for a man thus to bedeck her. Don't you think so?'

I would not be drawn into this argument, having learned to be careful with my friends. Sonia might need to be reassured. If Flora inspired such generosity, undoubtedly Flora had something. But I would not admit this to Sonia. I would not invite the criticism that £10,000 spent on jewels was immoral, for personally I did not believe a word of it. There could be nothing immoral, I thought, in a man spending £10,000 on a woman. Most men if they could make the money would think of themselves first. They might buy a motor-car, for instance.

'Where was Flora going?' I asked.

'To preside with her husband at some civic banquet,' Sonia answered. 'Apparently she does it to perfection.

'Where do they get the food from?' she asked inconsequently. 'Last week I had invited two friends to dinner. The butcher had nothing: he claimed to have received only a fifth of his allocation. This meat business is very queer. You and I must keep the little we do get for the Sunday joint; otherwise what shall we give our families over the week-end? But every day

the public-houses in the heart of London offer a choice
on their menus of roast beef, saddle of mutton, pork
chops, and a range of cold dishes like Virginia hams and
ox tongue. Where do the publicans find their meat?
No wonder husbands grow fat. When they leave their
wives in the morning they know that wherever they
choose to have lunch, in the public-house, the restaurant,
or the club, they will have a square meal. Who worries
about the woman who stays at home? She will get
no meat from the butcher; only one egg a week from the
grocer. For her the strong cup of tea and the cigarette,
but when it is a question of inviting two friends to dine,
tell me, what must she do?'

'A chicken?' I suggested.

'Too expensive,' snapped Sonia. 'As it happened
I saw some fillets of horsemeat steak in the Marylebone
Road. The meat was Irish. Flora says that Irish
farmers are killing off their horses because the farms
are being mechanized. Tractors are the thing. The
farmer sits at the wheel and takes things easy, but
when petrol fumes have poisoned the soil, he will
probably start calling out for horses again. I grilled
the fillets, sprinkled them with finely chopped parsley,
topped them with pats of fresh butter, and served them
piping hot. My two guests were delighted, and pestered
me for the name of my butcher. I didn't want to tell
them it was horseflesh. You know how fussy people
are. I tried to say that my butcher would be unlikely
to give them the same sort of meat they had for dinner.
"Why not?" they asked. "Do you bribe him?"'

Sonia laughed bitterly.

'That is what one gets,' she said, 'for trying to give a
friendly dinner party at home. I wouldn't be surprised
if at least one of my guests went to the police.'

Over the telephone wire I heard faintly the strains of
an old-fashioned waltz.

'What is that?' I asked.

'An organ-grinder in Grosvenor Square,' answered Sonia. 'Do you remember the tune? Do you remember how we used to say that we would never be able to live without dancing? Then suddenly, one ceases to dance altogether. By the way, Flora is going to slim.'

'Oh?' I queried hopefully.

'It will be expensive like everything she does,' said Sonia admiringly. 'Fifty guineas, but of course it will be under medical supervision.'

'At home?'

'No, in the country. Some Elizabethan family estate the owners could no longer afford to keep up. It has been turned into a clinic for slimming—twelve days on a strict diet of orange juice. I would try it myself if I had fifty guineas. I am growing fat.'

She paused and there was an uncomfortable silence on the wire.

'You must have noticed it?' Sonia asked after a moment, tremulously. 'When you came for tea the other day, did you not notice?'

'No,' I answered with extreme caution, 'I didn't notice anything.'

'You're trying to be polite,' she pleaded. 'That's not a friendly thing to do. Between friends one should tell the truth, even if it hurts.'

'I did not notice anything,' I repeated stubbornly.

'Constance thinks I may have put on a little weight,' she insinuated. 'It wouldn't do me any harm to slim, would it?'

'It never hurts anybody,' I said prudently, 'to lose a little weight.'

'Then you admit I'm fat!' she cried. 'You admit I am much too fat! Oh, how can you be so cruel?'

CHAPTER XIII

THE WINDOWS of my ground-floor flat, overlooking the courtyard, witness every Friday a great exodus of tenants bound for the country in their motor-cars. One hears the rattle of golf clubs and the thud of car doors being slammed. Then reigns a great silence until the return on Sunday night or Monday morning.

I wash. I iron. I join battle with my electric sewing-machine. The bedroom is strewn with materials, thread, knitting-wool, and cosmetics. Great plans fill my head. I use the week-ends to work.

But where do these people go who make such a noise with their cars? Can they really still afford to keep up country houses, and how can they say anything if their employees start looking at the clock on Friday mornings? Already, during the middle of the week, in a number of our great stores, the assistants are busy covering their stands up with holland a few minutes before five. The shops in Regent Street that organize one late night a week give us, so much have we become accustomed to a tightly shuttered West End, the impression of doing something quite brazen. How nice if Piccadilly could feel a little jealous and keep open, not once a week till eight, but every night till ten, with all the lights blazing and special shifts of well-paid assistants to smile at the customers who from all over the world would come to visit the heart of the empire! Down Haymarket would be restaurants and oyster bars open till two in the morning, as in the nights of Augustus Sala who described them a century ago, pointing out how pleasant it was for theatre folk, coming out of the Theatre Royal, to have a good meal before going home to bed. What is there about the Englishman's present-day character that makes him more of a Puritan than the Victorian ancestor he so loves to laugh at? Is the new Elizabethan reign to be stuffier than Cromwell's commonwealth? No steaks. No shops open after six. No jostling on brilliantly lit pavements. No gay theatre suppers. No chance for the gay young woman to let her laughter ripple unchecked.

I have invented my own theatre.

My bedroom window swings open on a pivot. I keep it ajar as if the tall glass were a door, and all in front of it, within the room, are rose-trees and fuchsias growing in pots—and right in the middle of them a large loaf of bread sliced in half along its full length.

From six in the morning till eight at night an endless stream of sparrows fly through the open window on to the sill. As long as they enter the room I am within the law. My visitors cannot be accused of sullying the very pretty tiles that form the façade of our smart modern building. Neither do they attract pigeons which bring damage to a house. The pigeon is too fat a bird to squeeze through my glass door and, in fact, has never made the attempt.

The sparrows swoop down from a great height above Piccadilly and perch for a moment on a shrub in the courtyard opposite the window. They then queue up, just as our present government teaches us to do, on the outer sill waiting to enter. The first comes in, hops on the loaf and guzzles. He then cleans his beak on the nearest rose-pot and the next in the queue comes in. Sometimes three or four will come in together: more often a mother will bring her children, who line up on a stout book called *The Girlhood of Mary Queen of Scots* whilst, with beaks wide open, downy feathers fluffed out, they wait for mother to feed them with bread and milk.

Why do the children not hop on the bread themselves? Are their beaks still too soft to dig out the damp crumb, or does mother merely enjoy the fun of feeding them? They make the sweetest picture, perched in a row looking at mother first satisfying her own hunger. Then she turns and feeds them from left to right, patiently, even though it may take her six or seven minutes, and all this time the children set up such a clamour that I am afraid of being reported to the company.

Off goes mother; off fly the children. Whither? To the Green Park, I fancy. Grown-up birds take their place and soon they have scooped out all the inside of the loaf leaving only the crust, so that it resembles a bath into which they disappear entirely. I am glad to think that the government subsidizes bread, for at least I get back part of my income tax. I only hope that the agene in our modern flour does not kill the birds who have such faith in me.

Occasionally the parent birds fight, and then the children, frightened by the quarrel, panic, and instead of escaping by the window fly into the interior of the room. Generally, if I remain motionless, they quickly regain their sense of direction, but the other morning a baby threw himself against the mirrored wall of my built-in cupboards, mistaking the reflection of the open window for the window itself, and then fell stunned to the floor. I picked him up and felt his little heart beating violently, and when he reopened his eyes, his sharp, beady eyes, he looked at me with as much interest as fear. I let him out, thinking that after this frightening adventure I should not see him again, but within half an hour he was back with his mother to finish the interrupted meal.

What surprises me is that the children seem almost as

large as their parents. Only their soft feathers which
rustle like a warm wind in the trees, their plaintive throat
noises, and their open mouths show them to be children.
I am not even certain to what extent they are incapable
of feeding themselves, for occasionally they jump on the
loaf and themselves peck at the bread, but if this happens,
the mother is soon jealous and tempts them with the
softest pieces.

How long does a sparrow live? Will the babies of
this year bring their own babies next spring? A taxi-
cab turning in the courtyard does not frighten them in
the least, nor do people passing to and fro, but other
things which I am not even aware of, send them all
scurrying away and for a few moments there will not be
a bird on the sill.

My garden restaurant has its rush hours. Three in the
afternoon is probably the busiest time, and then at about
seven just before they go to bed. Sunday sees my
largest attendance. Is this because there are no office
workers to feed them during the lunch hour? They
come to me instead.

Though they seem to know me I cannot persuade
them to come to the foot of my bed as did Mme George
Sand at her home at Nohant. Mme Sand, of course,
was a charmer and neither bird nor child could resist her.
Her contemporaries declare that nobody was cleverer
than she at cutting and sewing dresses for the characters
in her son's puppet show. What a delightfully long time
people took in those days to plan their winter evening
pastimes! One member of the family would write the
play, the others carve the dolls, paint their faces, design
their dresses, learn to manipulate their arms and legs.
Imagine a puppet show with George Sand to write the
dialogue and Chopin to compose and play the music!

Nowadays we all need university degrees to fit us to
listen to the radio or watch television. Before I sent

him to school my son invented the cleverest amusements. At eight he wrote sketches and painted minute cinema strips that became animated when moved across a screen. School, excellent for his health, robbed him of creative power. The trouble is that in our role as parents we are not brave enough to teach our children from the age of six to be actors, dancers, painters, singers—so afraid are we to see them depart from the general pattern. The oddity of upbringing will soon become a thing of the past. If, instead of my picturesque girlhood, I had been to Roedean or the Cheltenham Ladies' College, which would have been delightful, wanting nothing, having my head compressed into the same shape as that of other girls, my imagination, which always has an element of revolt about it, might have suffered. Preserve us from an agene-fed, mass-educated nation that talks in clichés, submits to queues, and limits its aspirations to the pools.

What imagination grandmothers have! When my son was small he much preferred to listen to my mother than to me. The games she played with him required infinite patience, and her stories had a witch-like character that filled his mind with strange, magical happenings. Brought up without toys, her games had mostly a direct relationship to her needle, for she sewed almost from babyhood. There was a game she used to teach me that had to do with pins. Each little girl, with immense care, made a paper pincushion (this operation alone taking a long time). A number of pins were then placed in the centre of the ring of players and covered over with sand or garden earth: upon this mound each little girl, in turn, threw a pebble, and the pins thus brought to light were hers to stick into her pincushion. This innocent game taught me the value of a pin. When I make a dress or a skirt every pin is carefully retrieved.

The most curious thing about superstitions is that their

E

opposites are true on either side of the Channel. Thus, whereas May is not propitious for weddings in England, in France, on the contrary, June is thought unfavourable. Dreams and the art of telling a person's fortune in a pack of playing-cards are also full of opposing interpretations. In spite of this, clubs are everywhere the sign of good luck, while in both countries the darkest calamities take the form of the sinister spade.

In both countries also the heart remains the same— the magical thing beyond discussion. Diamonds signify hesitation, doubt, betrayal, delay, or infidelity. Diamonds next to hearts spell uncertainty in love: next to spades, they delay bad news; next to clubs, they minimize good luck. In short, they act as a brake in every prediction. Thanks to them, calamities lose their sting. They play an important role in telling us what to expect of the good-looking young man at the office, or the too pretty, over-painted managing director's private secretary who is either the queen of spades or the queen of hearts, according to whether we are a young woman or a young man.

All my life I have sailed over an ocean of dreams, playing-cards, and other forms of superstition which has never prevented me from being deeply religious. The agnostic alone puzzles me and makes me feel terribly sad. A distinguished and erudite critic to whom I sent my respectful thanks for a sparkling dissection of *Madeleine Grown Up* (though the brilliant fellow is clearly suspicious of women), wrote in his answer: 'Your powers of delineation exceed anything of which I am capable. I can claim to resemble you only in my respect for truth, but at present I have no faith whatsoever, and I hope to die—fairly soon—without surrendering to superstition.'

Because I respect him and admire him so much, these words tore at my heart. He believes in nothing; I,

though a believer, am superstitious which is a great sin.
Yet I consult the cards and kneel beside my bed to pray.
I take care when a new book is on the point of coming
out not to walk under ladders, and if I dream of cats
fighting, dirty water, or mice, I am overcome with fear.
The cats are the critics, the dirty water represents dreadful
failure, and the mice are a sign that I have slipped back
into the poverty of my girlhood.

I often dream that I am living once more in a one-
roomed flat in which there is no running water, and
where a stale smell of cooking (one's own and that of
the neighbours) hangs about the furniture and curtains.
There is only one thing to be done about dreams of this
kind—at least, as far as I am concerned—to sew, to write,
and every time one wants to spend some money, to put
it off. I knew an ambassador who when he had written
a letter locked it up for a week in a drawer, knowing
that when he read it again he would almost certainly
decide not to send it at all.

Dreams, in fact, are a healthy deterrent to one's follies.
I fear them but I feel that I could not do without them.
They have knocked pride out of my system. Nobody
is less sure of herself.

I have dreamed the most fantastic things. In 1940
I made a long speech in German to a Nazi officer who
wanted to requisition a hare that I was jugging in
claret. I argued in favour of my hare like a modern
Portia. It was an absurd dream for a woman who had
just abandoned a house with everything in it to the
advancing armies. But it was a dream, and dreams are
absurd.

The most wonderful thing that can happen to me is to
dream of flowers. That spells success. Never have I
known the portent to fail. At twenty I often dreamed
of flowers, and as in those days my desires were more
modest, they were granted, I fancy, more easily. I liked

to be complimented when I went to dance at a very un-
pretentious club facing the Middlesex Hospital.   Generally my blonde hair earned me this pleasure, but once
an Italian called Pietro whispered in my ear that he liked
to dance with me because, under my waistless dress,
which was then the fashion, he could feel that I had a
natural and delicious waistline!   He added that for him
this had proved the most marvellous surprise.   He
appeared so very serious.   It was no silly compliment
but something he obviously felt keenly.   I got more
pleasure out of it than a bouquet of red roses.   Pietro
became a waiter in a London restaurant and occasionally
later, when I was a married woman and went out with
my husband to dine, Pietro would look at me archly
and say: 'Good evening, madame!' remembering how
he had once pinched my waist and made me blush, but
determined now that the secret should remain inviolable
between us.

What else do I dream?

Here is one of the most curious which befell me a
week ago.   I was having tea with my husband's great-
grandmother.   She appeared to me as a charming
dowager seated very erect in an arm-chair.   Her black
dress fell in graceful folds round her feet, and I had a
glimpse of a satin shoe ornamented with a diamond
buckle.   The diamonds were rather yellow, set in silver,
and I was fascinated by this elegant shoe, so precious
and fragile.   I watched it treading thick Persian carpets.
I even saw it mount the step of a carriage against a
background of coachman, footman, and a pair of
horses.   My interest was such that I quickly ceased to
be afraid, but there is no doubt that at the beginning
I had felt very nervous.   Beautiful things intimidate
me.   A fine piece of prose, an old master, hand-made
lace, a rich dress, draw my tears, and that makes me
happy; what spoils my pleasure is that people hate

a woman who cries. They like her to ape man's
insensibility.

At all events I began to address the old lady, telling
her all about myself. Nothing seemed to surprise her:
after all, she must have known all about me by watching
me from heaven where she had been for the best part of
a century. She must have seen me when I was a little
girl playing in the streets of Paris pulling other little
girls' plaited hair. Tea arrived, but with an effrontery
quite unlike me, I suggested champagne to toast our
acquaintanceship, and in my enthusiasm I invited her
to come to see me at my flat in Piccadilly. 'It is
very modest,' I said, 'very small and dark, but you
will see a charming portrait of your daughter, Lady
Blanche Lindsay, which is said to be the best thing
G. F. Watts ever did. I had it removed from the Tate
Gallery.'

'What!' she cried. 'A portrait of my daughter! A
portrait by Watts! I know nothing about that.'

'Of course not,' I answered. 'He painted her twenty
years after your death; on the other hand, did you not
look down from above? I should have thought you
would have been interested.'

At this point I woke up, but the dream made a strange
impression on me. She, the dowager, with the diamond-
buckled shoes, her daughter Blanche, and I, look out of
our gilt frames at one another in my London flat which,
in truth, is very small and dark. And here at a table
am I, still alive, detached from my portrait as if I were
its double, writing these words which perhaps will live
after me, at which time another woman will presumably
own the three portraits in my room.

For several mornings a temperature of a hundred
vaguely alarmed me, but if the doctor had not come on
a routine call, I should not have worried him. These

temperatures in a volatile person come and go without valid reason.

While he was examining me the room was full of sparrows flying amongst the rose-trees and the fuchsias or perched on the sides of the scooped-out loaf. A mother fed her little ones. To my surprise, the doctor suddenly stopped what he was doing and gazed at them in admiration.

After a while he exclaimed:

'Let us come back to you. How are you sleeping?'

'Not very well. Instead of dreams I have nightmares.'

'What sort of nightmares?'

'The most horrible kind. Last night I dreamed I had a cancer in the throat. I was in terrible pain and called for you.'

He was sitting at the foot of the bed, quite relaxed because of the birds which amused him, looking at me with patience and understanding.

'I also have nightmares,' he said, 'but mine do not end when I wake up. This morning, for instance, though it's only eleven o'clock, this morning has already been long enough to shatter me for the day: a cancer in the throat (no, not a dream one like yours that daylight can disperse), another in a kidney, a third in the stomach; a fourth that we had not even suspected but that we brought to light while looking for something else. That's a balance sheet for half a morning!'

'Do you tell them?' I asked. 'Must they know?'

'Yes, one must tell them. At least I do. They become cunning and end by finding out, and then they would no longer have confidence in you.'

'Happily,' I said, 'you must be so accustomed to these dreadful tragedies that they leave you indifferent.'

'Oh no!' he exclaimed with emphasis. 'When I have looked after a patient for years, when I happen to be the family doctor, I am terribly unhappy. Consider, for example, one of the cases I mentioned—a man in a very high position, still in the early forties, a young pretty wife and two adorable children, a lovely house, an expensive car. Everybody would envy them. This morning, for once seeing more than I could bear, I hurried to hospital where yesterday I had helped to bring a baby into the world. I needed desperately to set eyes on something tender and beautiful, something that had never been touched by illness. My baby in hospital . . . your baby birds feeding on the window-sill . . .'

I had never seen him thus. Generally his manners were rather rough. He had run army hospitals in Burma, but suddenly he was almost unnerved. He placed the tips of his fingers on the loaf that I had moistened with warm milk for the baby birds whose beaks were not yet hard.

'Sometimes,' he said, 'I wonder how I shall finish myself, what illness will get the better of me. One cannot help thinking about it, and the years pass. I suppose, seeing so much death round me, that I should be wary of making plans, but on the contrary, I'm always starting things. I worry terribly. This insane income tax stifles one. My wife is brilliant and earns also herself. We sometimes wonder if we ought not to divorce and live in sin. That would cut down the tax considerably. These governments are mad and we are mad to obey them. I should be putting you on a diet of grilled steak, but with no meat about that would be an absurdity.'

He laughed and went on:

'You are right to have growing plants in your bed-room, roses that grow in pots. And these French moss roses are delightful. More and more I dislike complicated cross-breedings. I loathe gigantic chrysanthemums that look like lavatory mops. As if nature did not know best. I also detest vegetables that are forced to an unreasonable size with artificial manures. Our stomachs are being slowly poisoned by synthetic foods, just as our lungs are being burned up by the fumes from motor-car exhausts and cigarette smoke.   I must run.   It has done me good to talk to you: I am not sure that you were not the doctor and I the patient.   Take things easily for a day or two, if you can, and give me a ring if the temperature doesn't go down.

CHAPTER XIV

I N PICCADILLY I met Prunella, a young woman who only a few months ago was fashionably married in white satin, with orange-blossom, a bevy of bridesmaids, the Mendelssohn march, and photographers from the society magazines.

One is always a little surprised that fashionable weddings have been able to survive the fierce attacks against our English social system. The lovely débutante is presented to the queen, becomes a bride, is photographed, and goes off on her honeymoon. What happens to her then? Where does she toil? Just as empire builders were supposed eventually to meet in the Strand, society people are at some time or other irresistibly drawn to that part of Piccadilly between Hatchards and Fortnum & Mason. This short pavement is their club, their illusion that nothing has changed in a traditional, aristocratic world.

Prunella was now in tweeds: a shapeless coat flapped against her ankles; her short-clipped hair suggested that she might be recovering from typhoid; in flat-heeled shoes resembling a man's bedroom slippers, with a leather bag slung over a shoulder, her lips unevenly painted, she strode along, jostling the passers-by.

'I'm up for a day's shopping,' she exclaimed. 'Doesn't London smell good?'

I smiled, for inwardly I was comparing her with her

mother, who was always so very neat in dark tailor-mades and a little hat perched on carefully groomed hair. But at least her daughter was married. That made Marion glad.

There was a son called Duggy who, with his pretty wife Iris, owned a farm. Duggy, after leaving the Guards, had wondered a good deal what to do with himself.

Happily he met Iris. There was a little money on both sides. Duggy had a few thousand pounds, the tail-end of a family fortune, while Iris received, as a wedding present, a similar amount from her father, who was giving his children their shares early to escape death duties.

At Marion's suggestion they used the money to buy a farm. Thus husband and wife became partners, not merely in bed but also in business. They bought some furniture and patched up the farm buildings that were falling to pieces. Marion said that her son had never worked so hard. His ancestors would have jumped out of their picture frames. Like Adam turned out of the garden of Eden, he earned his bread by the sweat of his brow. When a sow was about to have a litter, Duggy sat up all night. His wife had her children on the health scheme.

'When I think,' said Marion, 'of the money it cost us to send him to Eton, nearly £2,000 in fees, as much again in unnecessary clothes, and a specialist when he had mumps and measles. Then all the paraphernalia for the Guards. This amazing education to become a farmer. Still, they eat—that's the important thing. You see, at heart he's an awfully sweet boy, like most of the boys that come out of Eton. Too nice, perhaps, for this modern world. They get lost in so much unkindness. For the Guards, of course, it's wonderful—to march up and down outside the palace, and even to get killed in dangerous places. But since Duggy has had his farm, his wife,

his children, his pigs, and his dogs, he has become quite
a different boy. Thank goodness he didn't fritter his
money away, because now that we haven't got an empire
any longer, with India gone, and South Africa not
wanting us, and no jobs for Old Etonians in the Foreign
Office, I don't suppose there'll ever be any more capital
again. When we've spent what we have, we'll just
come to an end.

'Their first child was a boy,' Marion continued. 'I
asked him if he was putting him down for Eton. "But,
mother, you're mad," he answered. "Supposing we
were to have three sons . . . four sons? How could I
afford it?" So I suppose they will go to board school
and look after the pigs.

'Of course,' his mother went on, 'it's a little strange.
I mean, it's hard for me to get used to. My husband
did such wonderful things at Singapore, in Delhi, but
then I suppose it wasn't as right as we thought it was.
One would need to be Russian, if you know what I
mean. They, at least, seem all out for expansion.
They are not ashamed of having imperialist designs.'

Her face suddenly brightened.

'At first I imagined that Duggy was an exception, but
now Prunella is doing the same thing.'

So having come up against Prunella in Piccadilly,
I said:

'Yes, London does smell good, but do tell me what
you are doing with yourself.'

'We live in a tiny cottage on a family estate,' she
answered. 'The place belongs to Lord X who was at
Eton with my husband. It's too large for him to keep
up by himself, and so he has hit on a wonderful idea.
My husband and he run a pig farm, and now they are
busy fixing up a cottage for a third school friend. They
hope to make it a sort of Old Etonian *kolkhos*. The

important thing is that they will all be gentlemen together. If ever Lord X needs to take back one of his cottages, he feels he could ask the tenant to go in a gentlemanly way. You know how things are these days. The laws are so idiotic that once you get people in a cottage you can't ever get rid of them, neither them, nor their children, nor their children's children, even though they have ceased to work on the estate! Being solely amongst people of one's own class should make things easier.'

'It might for the men,' I said, 'as long as they are content to breed pigs. Men have so little ambition these days. But when I was a young married woman nothing in the world seemed beyond my reach. The hours on a pig farm might have seemed rather long.'

'Oh no,' she exclaimed. 'I know what you are thinking about. The shepherdess who dreamed of marrying the prince, and all that sort of rot. But that's terribly out of date. It's the prince who wants to keep pigs. And for the women it's not so bad. Take me, for instance. I look after the chickens and the soft fruit, and take them to market. I send eggs to my women friends who, in return, send me nail varnish and nylons from London where they starve. We go dancing from cottage to cottage. One doesn't fear to meet the wrong people as one does in town. The aristocracy are all down on the farm. And life is much cheaper. There are no appearances to keep up.'

'If you think that is an advantage,' I answered, fascinated by her strange get-up.

'Well, so long!' she said.

I was on my way to Jermyn Street.

There is a shop with the old-fashioned name of Floris that has a restful air about it. There are no extravagant lights, no cubist designs. It is a real shop. A delightful smell pervades it, a perfume of long ago, of what is excellent now and in the future, amber, chypre, and benzoin, aromatic shrubs and resins in their natural state. The shop is long and narrow with show cases hiding the walls. There are framed mirrors too, and real tortoise-shell combs, from the handworked tall Spanish kind to those which Victorian ladies placed in their long hair, some in blonde shell, others in dark; one feels they have slept there undisturbed since the First World War. There are tortoise-shell slides, nail polishers, and silk brushes. What woman now polishes her nails to bring up the rosy glow?

I want a comb, an ornament for my hair which has become almost Edwardian. I have decided never to cut it again. I have no heart, at my age, when one knows that one's physical charms must before long abandon one, to make the sacrifice of this precious possession.

What patience I have needed during the last year! At first my hair was too long for short hair. All my hats became unwearable. I experimented with every known way of doing it. Then came the bun, which refused to stay up because my hair was still too short to be worn long. At important moments the edifice collapsed with a wreckage of hairpins. I blushed and had to do it up again in public.

Victory came at last and now when I am naked I look like a painting by Degas. There is that upwards curve in the nape. I could step very easily into an Edwardian dress. When my hair is down it reaches almost to the waist; when it is up, it stays up. A bird could nest in it.

After my bath in the morning, I do as I so often watched my mother doing in Paris—I brush, I tug, I make grimaces; in the evening when I unroll my hair I make a bet with myself as to how many pins I shall find in it. Generally there are fifteen; my record is seventeen. I am aware that I need exactly half an hour to do my hair in the morning. Some say I look older;

others say it suits me.   Happily there is no hairdresser
to influence me, for I no longer go to one.   I always do
my hair.   It is a point of honour with me like making
my dresses, and the money I save can go into furs or
jewels.

My shampoos have become long and difficult; on the
other hand, my hair does not need to be set.   I simply
hang my hair down my back against a towel and wait
for it to dry.   Afterwards there is the business of comb-
ing it, which is often painful.   One must expect to
suffer a little.

My son, who at the age of ten was already wonder-
struck by the golden plaits of the little girls in the Tyrol,
has championed me all along.   He used to bathe in the
lake at Thiersee; as the little girls emerged, dripping
with water, they would tress their hair like nymphs, and
I think this, for him, was the first dazzling manifestation
of the difference between the sexes.

Mrs. Terry, whose advice I asked, answered:
'I love long hair.   My mother's was so long she could
sit on it.'

Then I remembered hearing in Vienna about the
morning ceremony of the lovely Empress Elizabeth
whose day was quite spoiled for her if she lost so much
as a single hair while it was being brushed.

The beautiful tortoise-shell combs at Floris sank their
long blonde teeth deep into my hair, tightly moulding the
bun, and crowning me with different magnificently
sculptured designs.   With a hand mirror outstretched,
I tried each in turn, delighted to find a young saleswoman who was not merely patient but as interested as
myself.   She gave her advice intelligently, knowing, I
suspect, that I would not leave the shop without falling
in love with one of the combs.   I chose almost the
largest.   It would serve the same purpose as a hat.   I
meant that it should gloriously dress my hair.   It was

truly beautiful and I was certain that this comb would
have cost an Edwardian lady a great deal more than the
relatively modest sum I was asked for it. I was delighted. The blonde shell had not been in my hair a
moment before it seemed alive. Warm life was running
through it.

I paid with a cheque and the pretty young saleswoman
said to me with a deep blush:

'I hope it will give you as much pleasure, Mrs.
Henrey, as your lovely books give us.'

I blushed dreadfully in turn, not finding the right
words to repay elegantly the smile and the pretty speech.
To my mind the compliment of a young woman is the
most precious of all. Could she guess how happy she
would make me for the rest of the day? The comb
and the compliment went to my head, and it was almost
awkwardly that I crossed Piccadilly into Bond Street.

CHAPTER XV

I HAVE KNOWN tidy women in all strata of society. To be neat has nothing to do with being wealthy, or even with the way one is brought up. One is born tidy, as one is born intelligent or stupid, ugly or beautiful, and tidiness with one's possessions about the house is virtually synonymous with neatness about one's person. Alas, these are no qualities of mine, but I admit they can turn a not very pretty woman into an extremely elegant one.

My cousin Rolande was like this. As a very little girl she would not have gone to bed without putting away her toys and folding her clothes, though nobody had ever taught her to do so. She had no sooner learned to trot about the house than she picked up her mother's duster: she could not bear the sight of a speck of dust. When, much later, she went to the sanatorium at Groslay her corner, her bed, were models of tidiness. She carefully ironed her dresses even though she could not wear them. On Mondays she would go through her cupboards, in spite of the effort which was almost more than she could bear. Every Tuesday she went to the hairdresser, and when she was back at home she put aside a morning every week to check the house linen, clean the silver, and tidy her work-basket. On the eve of her death she had her hair permanently waved and sent for her dressmaker to have something new made, a bright, cool dress, saying that she was going on her holidays.

Death found her surrounded by orderliness, her person well groomed and neat. She had a piece of sewing in her hands: the needles were so fine that none she used was ever straight. When, some months after her death, her things were still as she had left them in my uncle's house at Versailles, my mother going to stay with him, used to find my cousin's needles stuck neatly into flannel, like well-brought-up little girls waiting for permission to go out and play. They were all tidy but all bent. The reels of cotton and silk, the ribbons for lingerie, were beautifully put away, waiting for somebody to wake them from their slumber. My mother later told me that she was heart-broken upon discovering these treasures belonging to her niece, but she had not been able to resist comparing Rolande's orderliness with my untidiness.

An American woman from one of the southern states who lived in our block of flats during the war was immaculate, whether going out or at home, yet she had no maid. She resembled one of those highly coloured drawings in a woman's magazine. When she tidied her cupboards she wore a special blouse and a turban. The blouse was elegantly cut, the turban draped in such a way that it protected every wisp of hair. When she made up her face she wore another ensemble, never powdered herself until she had put on her dress, and always left herself plenty of time so as not to be flustered at the last moment. Everything was calculated in advance. The bag she would take with her was waiting on the dressing-table with the perfumed handkerchief, the lipstick, the compact, her keys, and a square of white silk which, on entering a taxi, she unfolded and placed under her on the seat for fear that there might be something on the leather to stain her coat or the skirt of her tailor-made. She sometimes got on my nerves, but I admired her. Though she smoked, a habit I detest in women, one never found a trace of ash on her clothes or furniture. I spent agonizing moments in her apartment trying to be as careful as herself. I hardly dared move. I felt as if I ought to be continually washing my hands. Everything was so very clean, each garment brushed and carefully put away. My natural exuberance dried up. Conversation was stilted. I became horribly timid.

'Look!' she exclaimed one day as she slipped on a well-cut jacket of shantung to protect her blouse as she did her face in the mirror, 'my little Madeleine, I will give you the skirt of this two-piece. Then in six months' time I will give you the jacket. I don't wear the skirt any more, but the jacket will be useful for keeping the powder off my blouse when I make up. I hate to give it away, but I must. I make it a rule to change the whole of my wardrobe every so many years. I find it excellent for the morale—and then again, it prevents one from the shock of noticing how one grows fatter here, or thinner there, as one grows older. For example, I am going to sell my mink coat, my beaver, and my astrakhan, and when in six months' time I go back to America, I shall wear my three-quarters Canadian mink which is handy for travelling, perfect for slipping on over a coat and skirt. In New York I shall buy a new Russian mink. The sleeves will be more fashionable, the collar differently cut. Mink coats in New York go out of fashion as quickly as hats in Paris.'

Yes, though she rubbed me up the wrong way, I admired her. She was rich but, after all, she was not a Rockefeller. She was merely American, and American women love change. When, in whatever southern state she came from, she had the walls of her house repainted, she changed the curtains, the carpets—everything was bought new to have the joy of an entirely different colour scheme. From green she would pass to rose, from rose to blue. At college American girls already learn how many thousand dollars they will need first to exist, and then to live in plenitude. What is more, they appear to get what they want. They achieve each ambition, one after the other. I have come to the conclusion that we European women know practically nothing about this art, and that we need to rub up against women from the two Americas, north and south, to understand not merely the meaning of luxury, but even more, the strength of will and the orderliness of mind that are necessary first to obtain it, and then to keep it.

'But,' said I, continuing, 'won't you be at all sorry to sell your coats and all your dresses?'

'Not at all,' she answered. 'Do I not intend to replace them with new and more beautiful ones? I could not be happy moving about with my friends in New York or Palm Beach wearing a mink coat with bishop's sleeves when the fashion is for sleeves to be cut like those of the Emperor of China.... Come! It simply could not be!'

I admire her but I am jealous. It is all very fine for me to be a woman of letters, a literary woman, the mother of a charming son, but something tells me I shall never have, at least all at once, a Canadian mink, a beaver, and an astrakhan. I fancy this disappointment shows a little on my face. As for a full-length Russian mink with the sleeves of a bishop or an Emperor of China, that, to my mind, is the visible sign of success, and who would dare say to that woman that she was not the richest, the most loved, and the most spoiled in the world! I can see myself pushing through the swing doors of a luxury hotel thus attired, though it suits a tall woman better than a small one. But even if I were to tire of it and cut it up, I would at least have possessed it once in my life.

With these thoughts, I rose. I had merely called on my friend to exchange a bag of sugar for a bag of

Caroline rice. My reflection in her triple mirrors shows me in a pullover of many colours, made of bits and pieces of left-over wool, and a grey flannel skirt that has gone so often to the dry cleaners that I have spent more on it than it is worth. Indeed my skirt and pullover together would not fetch a pound at a jumble sale.

She lit an American cigarette and, closing her eyes, inhaled deeply, sensuously. This gleam of pleasure, filtering through her long lashes, made her look pretty. This was almost her only weakness. Then, reopening her eyes, she looked me up and down, and after a moment said rather harshly:

'All the same, Madeleine, if only you knew how I envy your "chic" in that cheap skirt and that home-made sweater. My dear, if I were to dress like that people would take me for a factory girl or a laundress— and your hands! What wouldn't I give to have hands like yours!'

Was it possible, I wondered, that this smart American woman could find anything in me to be envious of? The whole affair was bewildering. A few days later she telephoned down to say that there were ants in her kitchen. I could hardly believe her. How could these pests have passed through the formidable barrage of her orderliness?

'I am out of mind,' she spluttered. 'Fancy this happening to me!'

After inquiry it was discovered that they were in other flats also, having apparently been brought over in food parcels from America.

'The reason I am so shaken,' she explained, 'is that one is convinced that one can prevent certain things. But no, there are things one cannot prevent, like bombs and microbes—and ants.'

Thus ants marched into her kitchen, just as microbes

of a deadly kind killed my cousin Rolande in spite of her
tidiness.

In Paris one day I took my son to lunch with a French
friend in the avenue Foch.

'You are going to meet one of the richest women in
Paris,' I explained.   'I hope you will like her.'

He gripped my hand, for he was still very small.   A
very dark little woman with immense eyes was waiting
for us, and because we had been separated by the
Channel during the long years of war, she was seeing
him for the first time, and now, half Spanish, broke into
a torrent of words, determined to conquer the affection
of the little man.   I perceived this clearly and it amused
me, but what intrigued me even more was to see how
the young mind was enchanted.

She placed him at lunch on her right hand but, experienced hostess, instead of talking down to him,
allowed him to eat and drink and take an interest in
the general conversation.   Afterwards, during coffee,
her husband having gone off to his business, their
daughter Jacqueline being present, we talked dresses and
hats.   On such occasions, my friend Juliette is surprising.
She really scintillates, but then Jacqueline's blouse caught
her eye: the bow needed something done to it.   Quickly
her fingers repaired the equilibrium.

'Which reminds me, she exclaimed, addressing her
pretty daughter severely, 'that when I went up last
evening to kiss you good night and found you already
asleep, your watch was not put away in its case and the
collar of your blouse was not cleaned.   You must learn
to be tidy, my little girl, for otherwise, in spite of being
rich you will never be elegant.   I have never given a
blouse with a dirty collar to my maid to clean.   I have
always cleaned it myself, sponging it with a cloth dipped
in benzine.   It's my modesty, a little thing that soon

becomes second nature. Thus, when I travel I don't
need anybody's help to remain neat.'

I remembered how before the war Juliette used to
come to London. We used to spend the afternoons
shopping and then go to her apartment at the Savoy for
tea, but she would never open a parcel, however excited
we might be, till she had first brushed her coat and hung
it up, ironed the dress she intended to wear at dinner,
and put what she needed in her evening bag. Then
she would turn to her parcels, but without cutting a
piece of string. Patiently, with agile fingers covered
with diamonds, she would untie all the knots and roll
the various pieces of string into bundles. Then the
tissue-paper was folded and packed away in her
trunk.

'I was one of three girls,' she explained, 'and whenever we came home from a ball, our mother would make
us put away our cloaks and shoes and hang up our dresses.
However tired we might be, everything must be neat and
tidy before we slipped into bed.

'"And what would the maid think in the morning,"
asked our mother, "if she found your things in a heap,
or thrown over the back of a chair? You will sleep all
the better for having a clear conscience."

'Now that I am grown up and no longer have my
mother, her counsels prevail. Believe me, it wouldn't
help to have all the jewels in the Tower of London if
you were to go about in a soiled blouse, a dress that was
not freshly ironed, or a creased skirt. You would never
be elegant.'

'But of course there was Camilla,' said my mother as
we were discussing this question one day round the
kitchen table, shelling peas.

'I never knew Camilla well,' I answered.

'I bring up her name,' said my mother, 'to show that,

as in the case of Rolande, neat women are found in a diversity of worlds.'

Camilla's world was, indeed, very special.

'Go on!' I urged, anxious to make my mother talk about the extraordinary Camilla.

'Curiously enough,' said my mother, 'though she walked the streets of Paris while we were living in Clichy, it was not there but in London that I first came to know her. We were more or less the same age. Our young womanhood was spent under the same political climate, but while she amused herself and was loved, love being her profession, I fought against penury and to bring you up: then later, when I might have had a little respite, I still fought to keep alive, though in Soho instead of in Clichy; while she, in Bond Street instead of in Paris, continued to practise the art of love.

'Well, anyway, she was rather a nice girl. There is always something pleasant, looking back, about girls of one's own age. One thinks of them as a mirror of oneself; afterwards it is comforting to see that they grow old in the same way.

'And Camilla was not beautiful, no, not even when one saw her for the first time. In fact, she was almost ugly. What was extraordinary was that she was impeccable in everything and in every circumstance. Yet when she talked to one about her childhood, the ghastliness of it was enough to make one's hair stand up on end, but Camille always said:

'"You know, Mme Gal, even in a pigsty I would have found a way to make myself a nice clean corner and then, every day, I would have enlarged my corner until in the end the whole place would have shone like a new pin. That's how I'm made, Mme Gal. A speck of dust, something not put away, and I'm perfectly miserable. I find myself wishing I could walk about with a duster and a broom, and yet there are people who would say that because I'm generous with my favours . . . well, after all, it's my profession, isn't it, Mme Gal?"

'Of course,' explained my mother, 'she was always talking about herself. Every other phrase began with "I." Intellectually she remained until her death what she had always been; on the other hand, she never tried to show off. She was a simple girl, neither very good nor very bad. When she really fell in love, it seldom fell short of a devouring passion. My! How some of those women can love! But through it all she remained meticulously tidy. Nana, her maid from Brussels, used to say:

'"Imagine, Mme Gal, that we no sooner move into some furnished apartment than madame sets about the furniture with such a will, polishing, polishing, though there isn't a stick worth sixpence, that the chairs and table shine like mirrors! Of course, I am obliged to join in. I assure you that Mme Camilla knows as much about keeping a place clean and tidy as I do myself. It's no use trying to take things easy when she's about."

'One Sunday,' my mother continued, 'I had gone along to Camilla's place to make some alterations in one or two of her dresses. The maid was out. We were alone, Camilla and I—she in a cotton dressing-gown, a newspaper tied round her head because she had taken advantage of Sunday to dye her hair with henna, rubbing for all she was worth at the furniture, I stitching at a dress. She was without make-up, resting her skin, no powder, no lipstick, giving even the muscles of her face a chance to relax. Her cheeks shone like those of a little girl at convent school. She radiated health, but I must admit that with her cotton dressing-gown and the newspaper round her head she cut a fantastic figure. A chicken was roasting in the oven and there was asparagus.

'"Mme Gal," she said, "as Nana is spending the day

at Pimlico, you will give me the pleasure of your company for lunch."

'So there we were, putting aside our work, settling down to a fine meal. She was very friendly, having nothing to hide from me, even taking a certain satisfaction in discussing her qualities and defects.

'"You know," she said, "I'm rather glad now that I was never pretty, for those I was most jealous of have lost their bloom by this time whereas I, with no claims to beauty, have remained just as I was. Change is always fatal to a woman. Thank goodness I simply don't know the meaning of the word. I merely remain 'I'! And as you see me to-day, Mme Gal, take it from me, I have been madly loved. Yes, indeed!" she repeated, shaking her head surrounded by newspaper so that she looked like a magician in a medieval play.

'"And who was your first love?" I asked.

'Camilla laughed.

'"I begin to wonder," she answered, "if there ever was a first love. From the time when as kids at school we used to play at being pregnant, tying a cushion round our waists, to . . . well, to all the rest. Honestly, I don't remember. And what difference would it make? Those things are all very well for provincial young ladies, young ladies who become brides in white. All the same, I should have liked to be married in a white lace veil. When I come to think of it, my mother was not married in white, nor were my aunts. Were you married in white, Mme Gal?"

'"No, indeed," I answered. "There was neither time nor money for that, and nor were my sisters Marguerite and Marie-Thérèse."

'"There!" cried Camilla in triumph. "See what I told you. It must be very rare to be married in white!"'

My mother at this point interrupted her story to exclaim, looking at me:

'And you, Madeleine, were you married in white? And your cousin Rolande, was she married in white? You see! You see! Yet here in Normandy all the girls are married in white, all the village girls. Camilla knew what she was talking about.'

She gave me a look of great satisfaction, and continued:

'The roast chicken and asparagus, and the red wine, had made Camilla more expansive than ever. She went on: "Well, you know what sort of woman I am. It has been that way as long as I remember. In Paris, when I was quite young, I had my work and also, distinct from my work, a small, comfortable apartment in a most respectable building where I used to meet a young man who really adored me. Louis was always beautifully dressed, never a spot of dust, never a wrong crease. His clothes were exactly right, his shirts soft and clean and freshly ironed, and he was not merely neat about his person. I rather think his neatness first endeared him to me. I approved his habits; then loved him. He was neat in everything he did, and served me better than any lady's maid, for he wouldn't have a servant in the place, not a lady's maid, nor a housemaid, nor a cook. He used to brush my things, iron them, and put them away, but what was extraordinary was his passion for polishing my boots, for, as you will remember, Mme Gal, it was the fashion in those days for elegant young women to wear laced boots that were cut out at the top in the form of a heart. The poor boy was appallingly jealous, and while he polished my boots, he wept so continuously that great tears of anger and jealousy fell upon them. I believe that it was because of his tears that there was always such a shine on them. I was extremely fond of him, though I knew quite well that I would soon forget him if he were to disappear out of my life; and he guessed as much and used to say: 'You'll lead me to suicide, Camilla!' Wickedly I would kiss him, laughing, just for the fun of seeing him cling to my kiss like a drowning man, trying to make it last a moment longer. No, poor lad, Louis's love was not of the gay sort. His jealousy made him morose, and you know how it is with jealous men, they make one so angry that one ends by baiting them. I used to come back from work and tell him of the men who had loved me. He would turn white, and his head would go round like it does when one is pregnant. Honest! It's amazing how wicked I was to him! I often wonder if the devil wasn't in me. He used to answer, rubbing my boots: 'Cruel Camilla. I love you so much that I haven't even got it in me to hope that your turn will come to suffer, to suffer as I am suffering now.' He used to cry again, and I would realize that I had gone a bit too far.

"'We were still in Montmartre when war broke out in 1914. What worried him was that he was still just as much in love with me. He used to say that if he had been given a few years longer, his love might have burned out. Then he would not have felt so badly about going to the front. As it was, he merely allowed himself to be killed. I suppose it was better than if he had come back blind or gassed. I was genuinely sad. One cannot help being moved by a great love even if at times it gets on one's nerves. Then the years pass and one thinks back regretfully. I thought more often about him. He was so tidy. He really had a host of good points. For quite a long time I used to come across bits of paper on which he had written: 'Adorable Camilla! Why the hell do I love you so much?' My name was scribbled everywhere—on the kitchen walls, roughly cut with a diamond ring on the window-panes. On the sitting-room window, for instance, he had written his name and mine in a heart, the idea being in his jealous mind that if ever I sent him away, I should either have to call a glazier or

get involved in some awkward explanations with whoever had replaced him in my affection.

"'After a while I felt I had cried enough; and then
there was the rent to pay. The month was October,
Mme Gal. The air was crisp and the Paris streets were
very animated. I sat down at the terrace of a café beside
an oyster stall where a man was busy opening Portuguese
oysters, and I ordered coffee with hot milk in a tall glass,
and I watched the people hurrying along the pavement,
women going to work, *midinettes* with boxes under their
arms. I began wondering what I would do before it was
time to start work, whether I would go and have lunch
with another girl. There was no hurry. I found it very
pleasant watching the people in the street; after a while
smarter women made their appearance, and they were
all wearing their first autumn hats, mostly velvets of
autumnal colours, not so much of copper or red leaves
as of ripe plums, grapes, and pomegranates, and under
these immense hats the wearers seemed to have tiny
heads.

"'Suddenly I exclaimed: 'What's the matter with me,
sitting here with my out-of-date hat?' You ought to
have seen me get up and leave that café terrace, Mme
Gal! The waiter must have thought I was mad. He
could hardly guess that what I desperately needed at that
moment was a big velvet hat. I wondered how I had
existed so long without one. A really lovely new hat
is the most invigorating sensation in the world. There
were some nice shops in the rue de Rome, but most of
the girls preferred adjoining streets where we could
more easily hear the latest gossip about our friends.
Before finally choosing a hat we liked to hear what the
others had just bought. It generally started like this:
'Not on your life! No mauve for me if you tell me
that Aline has bought a mauve hat.' Then, on reflection:
'Yes, but if Aline is as pretty as you say in mauve there's

no reason why mauve should not suit me as well!'
I suppose we shall always be the same. We can't do
without one another. We are not happy unless we are
together, being jealous of one another, stealing our men,
talking about love.

"'I knew a little hat shop, rather dark, but from inside
one could see who was passing along the street. An
old woman wearing a sky-blue Balaclava sold newspapers
on the pavement. The modiste was one of ourselves,
retired from business, and we felt at ease with her. We
did not have to pretend; she knew exactly what each of
us needed. Her hair was grey and sparse and her bust
ample, but she did not need to worry any longer about
her looks and was contentedly married to a man of her
own age who mostly sat in the back room tallying up
the accounts. They had quite a clever technique which
used to catch us every time. She used to make us try
on the prettiest hat in the shop; then softly she would
call her husband, and with her hands on her hips would
exclaim: 'George, just take a look at Mme Camilla, and
tell us what you think of her in that hat!' George, his
face pale with the pallor of a man who merely leaves the
back room of a shop to play billiards in a café bar, would
say good day and then look at the customer, who would
immediately feel herself being judged as if she were a
slave in a slave market. I know that I, for one, always
felt a trifle embarrassed. Then George would lift a
plump white hand, a diamond flashing on his little finger,
and rounding his lips he would emit a long whistle of
admiration. The fact is that he had such a reputation,
he had been such a terror in his time with the girls, that
though this form of flattery was obviously a trick, we
could not help being impressed. After all he was a man.
He had such a way with him that he would have convinced us we looked becoming in a flower-pot!'"

My mother interpolated:

'Camilla, with the newspaper round her head, paused a moment then went on:

'"They sold me the prettiest velvet hat, but as you know, Mme Gal, nothing requires so much attention as a velvet hat. I left the shop and walked out wearing it, into the Place Clichy, and looking at my reflection in the plate-glass window of the chemist's shop could not resist feeling rather pleased with myself. And I wasn't the only one to appreciate the new hat apparently. The chemist's window showed me the reflection of another hat, but not a velvet hat; this one, the cap of a young American officer. He smiled, fine youthful teeth, and because I am not severe I allowed him to take me by the arm. We walked a little way along the avenue de Clichy. It was delightful. Had my new hat gone to my head? Was it due to its claret colour? We lunched. We ate oysters and drank Chablis. He made love to me and we agreed to meet the next day. He was young, he was good looking, he was rich and he loved me, and for the time being I loved him. Life was marvellous.

'"Yes, but I had my work to do. As soon as he had left me I tidied up my apartment and inspected my new hat. How pleased I was to have bought it! My hat and my new lover's face seemed as one. They merged into each other, but now that night was falling I must go out into the street. I put my hat on again and ran down the stairs.

'"Everything went well for a while; then suddenly there was a police whistle. I found myself caught up in one of those periodical raids that the Paris police organize to catch us, and in a matter of seconds I was bundled with a dozen other girls in a Black Maria bound for St. Lazare. Oh, we knew the way all right. The others shouted and swore: I said nothing. I took my hat off and held it gingerly on my knees so that nothing should happen to it. We arrived: the door was opened and we were taken before the usual officer, a beast of a man, by far the cruellest in Montmartre; and so there were all of us, seated on benches, waiting to be taken to the women's prison. One waits hours. I hung my hat on a nail on the wall where it would come to no harm. It was near the door and I could keep an eye on it. Then I went back to my place and started to tell the girl next to me that I had pains. I claimed, every few minutes, that they were getting worse. 'It's my old salpingitis!' I moaned realistically. 'Oh, the agony!' I had to be rather careful because amongst the girls there were some who were not my friends, but I went on moaning and after a while I lay down on the bench which some of my companions had cleared for me, and I started to writhe in imagined torture, being careful to rub off secretly the rouge from my cheeks and my lips so that my face would look horrible. My eyeblack also ran, making rivulets down my face, and amongst the other girls so beautifully made up I was the ugly exception. Yes, indeed, Mme Gal, I must have looked the picture of a woman in pain, but from time to time I looked across to the door at my new hat hanging on the wall, just to see that it was safe. At last even the girls who had no reason to like me showed signs of pity, and both they and my friends began to strike the floor with their heels and insult the policeman guarding us, saying that we were not criminals, and that anybody could see that I was in pain. They made such a noise that a door opened and an inspector came out. For a moment I was afraid he would have me sent to hospital, but he looked rather nervous, frightened by all these women shouting 'Down with the police!' and after questioning me, he called a policeman and said:

""'You had better take this girl home.'

"'And to me:

""'You know, Camilla, if this is just an act you're

putting on, I warn you that we shall take it out of you next time.'

'"In spite of my joy, I went on pretending I was in pain. I got up. A girl went to fetch my new hat which I took from her carefully, and the next moment I was being driven home in a car! I was careful not to cease playing my part even when they dropped me at my front door. They watched me going up the stairs, suspicious till the end. But when at last I was in my flat, the door securely locked, I ran to my bedroom, and who do you suppose, Mme Gal, was lying on the bed waiting for me? My young American officer!"'

'Alas,' said my mother, 'such romances are merely incidental. When Camilla went out again she found that the police had their eye on her. She therefore came to London, but though Camilla was extremely successful here, finding things easier than in Paris, money more plentiful, the police much kinder to deal with, she quickly became involved in a new and much more serious love affair which made her suffer as poor Louis had once suffered at her hands. For it was she this time who loved: he who was unfaithful.

'She was at the height of this entanglement that Sunday when I was altering her dresses.

'So there she was,' said my mother, 'with the newspaper fastened round her head, suddenly in tears, twisting a dish-cloth between her fingers, saying between gulps:

'"Oh, Mme Gal! How I love him! How I love him!"'

'I began crying myself,' said my mother. 'Camilla looked so miserable. She described how only a few days earlier he had come back, saying:

'"'It's a wonder I am here at all, Camilla. I have just spent the evening with the prettiest girl.'"'

'You see,' cried my mother, 'he was doing to her

exactly what Louis had hoped might not happen, Louis who was so much in love that he had never wanted her to suffer. That's how the world goes round. We all end by getting our deserts.

'She was in a terrible state,' my mother went on. 'As it was Sunday Camilla supposed that her lover had gone to the races at Longchamp, for just now he was in Paris. "Amusing himself with other women!" she exclaimed. "Leaving me alone in London. Oh, why was I so wicked to Louis! But supposing he is not at Longchamp, Mme Gal? Supposing he is, at this very moment, hurrying back to London to spend the evening with me? There is a train due in at Victoria at any moment. Supposing he were on it? Oh, I must do my hair." Suddenly she ripped off her paper bonnet. "Oh!" she exclaimed, looking at herself in the mirror, "how ugly I am!"'

My mother combed Camilla's hair. Then Camilla put on one of her loveliest dresses and made up her face, and as she did so her courage returned. 'No wonder!' my mother commented. 'The transformation was extraordinary. She became more than beautiful!'

But the hours passed and her lover did not come. She tried to concentrate on the furniture, frantically polishing the wood, but her features which had been momentarily lit up with hope drooped. When at last it was too late now for her man to arrive, she said to my mother:

'"The worst of it is, Mme Gal, that I have no longer any interest in making money. To give you an example: one evening last week I was hurrying along the street, pondering over my man's wickedness and unfaithfulness, when a little man came up asking permission to accompany me back to my flat. Consider, Mme Gal, what a state I must have been in for a man to have time to accost me before I accosted him! "How much money

F

have you?" I asked roughly. "Twenty pounds," the
man answered humbly, as if he thought the sum in-
sufficient. I brought him home, but though he covered
me with compliments, I was neither interested in his love
nor in his money. I wanted my own man. On his
way down a door opened and Georgette invited him
into her flat. She must have heard me insulting him,
but it was not right of her to call him in."

"'As you did not want him yourself?'" queried my
mother.

"'That is not a sufficient reason," answered Camilla.
"She was not correct, for we are friends and I often lend
her my saucepans. When my man returns from Paris
I shall have him speak to her."

'Midnight struck,' said my mother; 'there were no
more trains for Paris. Camilla's hair, the henna dye, her
lovely dress, her make-up—nothing mattered any more.
She sank down into a chair and wept.

'I gathered up my sewing and said:

"'I would willingly spend the night with you, Mme
Camilla. I could lie down easily enough on Nana's
couch, but my cat has not eaten all day, and I have
wrapped up the remains of your excellent chicken in this
newspaper so that she shall not go hungry to bed.
I have been stitching, stitching since nine this morning.
The poor animal will have been very lonely."

"'You are right," said Camille. "How lucky you are
not to have anything but a cat to worry about. Life is
so complicated when one has love affairs."

"'Complicated?" said my mother. "Do you think
so? If you ask my opinion, you are very lucky. At
least you live. I merely exist.'"

CHAPTER XVI

FRIDAY MORNING, and the weather is close and damp—Friday the thirteenth! I foresee trouble, for although yesterday all my bus tickets had a 7 in them, I have just dealt a hand of cards and find it full of spades. The horoscope in my weekly women's paper advises me to wear mauve to-day, but this colour is so forgotten, so Edwardian, that I am surprised that the editress who is generally so up to date should have allowed her seer to counsel such a thing.

I continue to have the most extraordinary nightmares. This morning, for instance, I dreamed that on arriving in my Normandy village somebody told me that my charwoman's son (the young man who is training to be a schoolmaster) had killed himself. I went off to comfort her, but though she and her husband were very sad, they were sensible, and finished off all their phrases by saying:

'You must understand, Madame Henrey, that it no longer has the slightest importance because by next year we shall be at war.'

She gave me a small guinea-pig that talked. This animal said to me:

'Take me away with you. I love you and will obey you.'

Charmed, I took it in my arms but it chose this moment to forget itself on my dress, and I began taking frantic pains to hide this misdemeanour from my charwoman to prevent her from feeling vexed, but the guinea-pig continued:

'Trust me, and I shall not misbehave myself again. It was the emotion of seeing them cry so much when they learned of the death of their son.'

I am sorry the guinea-pig was only a dream.

I once knew a beautiful woman who loved a hunchback, and as he was ugly one might have supposed that she was doing him a favour, but she said that of all the men she had charmed, this one was the most difficult. It is, of course, our business in life to please, and this woman drove herself quite ill trying to discover ways of being agreeable to her hunchback, but she soon noticed that nobody found grace in his eyes. He thought himself so very superior. The guinea-pig in my dream, though only a guinea-pig, said that he loved me, and that in itself was a lovely compliment.

I am disappointed because the postman has brought me no letter from my son who is on the eve of a difficult week. On Monday and Tuesday he sits for his common entrance examination, and on Thursday he goes to the London clinic for a throat operation. Thus my nightmares continue, even after daylight.

The second post brings me a small package from a reader in New Zealand who likes me to call her 'Torch' Campbell. The parcel contains a tiny cream jug of Royal Crown Derby and a sachet of lavender to put in my lingerie.

This is what she says:

105 Wai-iti Road,
Timaru,
New Zealand.

DEAR MRS. HENREY,

The lavender I picked on Boxing Day, and will perhaps bring some fragrance from my garden into your lingerie drawer. The shoulder-strap ribbon is from France. I saw it the other day and bought some to put away in a trunk in which I keep various odds and ends dear to the heart of a sewing woman. Whenever anything is wanted, my sisters and I lift the lid and usually find a scrap of lace, a piece of ribbon, a snippet of material, a flower, a button, a skein of wool or silk.

This trunk has a curious history. Mother bought it for me at the Lost Property Office in the Strand when we were in London in 1934: a new trunk made of fibre with strong wood battens, brass corners, and two locks. It cost 14s. and the man who charged us 1s. 6d. to paint my name on the lid in black, delivered it to our hotel a week before we sailed for India. To-day its many labels tell of my long journey—London, Bombay, Agra, Delhi, Melbourne, Sydney, Wellington, Timaru. It accompanied me to another city where I worked as a companion help to an old couple. The woman was terribly inquisitive and I was glad of the two locks to keep safe from her prying fingers my letters and my bank book. Next it became a glory-box to store my trousseau while I was engaged to an English naval officer during the war. What treasures I put in it! Bed linen, table linen, tea-towels and cosies, lingerie, nighties, and all the other things that a girl lovingly collects when she plans to be married. Alas, wars do cruel things, and my glory-box was never used because the naval officer married another girl, but some of its contents swelled the trousseaux of my friends.

Now it is partly a work-box and partly a treasure chest.

The rustle of dry autumn leaves accompanies my pen as I sit in the garden where the acrid scent of tawny chrysanthemums comes from the flower-beds, and frost nips my fingers.

Yours sincerely,
'TORCH' CAMPBELL.

A quite young peer who has four daughters confessed to me at a small lunch party that he hoped the Queen would revive the splendour of pre-war courts for débutantes. There was every reason, I suppose, for this lovely ceremony to be abandoned during the war, but none, except class friction, for doing away with the feathers, trains, white gloves, and nocturnal visits to Bond Street photographers, when courts were held again. It is sad that a girl, on one of the most exciting days of her life, should be robbed of the pageantry.

'As each of my daughters came into the world,' said the young peer, 'I consoled myself for not having an heir by the thought of what pretty débutantes they would make in their feathers!'

We often say that England is a land of tradition when in fact every year men cut down the ceremonies they love best. The Queen alone, thank God, remains, and because she is young and beautiful she blossoms as a young flower on a sturdy tree. But even in fairy-tales young queens are attended by a great number of lovely maidens, and it would be nice to see the young women of England brought out once in their lives in a magical setting.

Men have become terribly selfish. They enjoy the tussle of politics and the masochistic satisfaction of doing without things. Besides, they have more than enough for their needs. Their political party, the ministry to which they belong or some giant firm gives them a motor-car, a priority berth on the Paris night ferry and pocket-money for their pipe tobacco. What more do they want? But consider the joy of trying on one's first ball dress! Do you remember those scenes in the Mall when débutantes before the war sat in their lighted cars waiting to drive into the palace? Each great capital likes to spoil its more fortunate young women. In Paris no girl is so poor that she is not made to feel the excitement of turning into a woman. I was never

jealous of a lovely material or a beautiful dress.   I merely
put it into my head that heaven would give it to me.
There has been of late in London a furious tendency on
the part of men to take glamour out of the lives of
women.   As it is no sacrifice on the part of politicians
to go without nylon stockings, lipstick, and nail varnish,
he smugly creates shortages and smacks on taxes.   He
is a far more cruel ogre than the ones in Grimms' fairy-
tales, for there is no Jack to climb up the beanstalk to
kill him.   His wordy speeches about the need of arma-
ments and exports do not take into account the years
that so quickly rob us of our beauty.   What will a girl
of seventeen do with a favourable trade balance in ten
years' time?   In her place I would prefer a new hat!

The peer at this lunch party had been to the reunion
party of his old school.   He told us about the top-hats
and the traffic down the High Street.

'Is it true,' asked our young married hostess, 'that
several of this season's débutantes, in order to earn a little
pocket-money, work as charwomen in a foreign embassy, scrubbing the floors before breakfast?'

'Oh yes, indeed!' came the answer.   'One seventeen-
year-old débutante has earned herself £5 for washing up
all night at a London hotel.   She found it rough on her
hands, but what surprised her most, apart from the excellent pay, were the cockroaches.'

I laughed rather bitterly.

My short time stepfather was a London chef and
there is little I do not know about the seamy side of
kitchens.   The cockroaches are less frightening than the
rats.   But seriously, I think it scandalous that the parents
of well-brought-up young women should allow them to
wash up dishes in an hotel.   I would not have done it
myself at the time my mother and I were nearly starving.
Young women of seventeen are formed in the loveliness
of angels, and my heart bleeds to think that something

so crazy has happened to English society that nobody
shakes down the building when the prettiest girls in the
land do jobs that the commonest men keep safely out of.
When society cracks from the top, aristocratic parents
countenance crimes against young womanhood that poor
people would never stand for.

CHAPTER XVII

GEORGE MARMIN, a Londoner by adoption, had for some months been telling me about his brother Paul who is a leading citizen of Boulogne-sur-Mer.

Everybody knows Boulogne because of the Channel crossing. One is for ever passing through it. Then, of course, there were the day trips that were a music-hall joke when they only cost a few shillings, but towards the end of the Second World War the Allies warned the population to evacuate their town, and Boulogne was almost completely razed to the ground. The Germans, in leaving, added to the destruction. Port, fishing-fleet, harbour station, bridges, post office, hotels, shopping centre—all these and much more were blown to pieces.

Paul Marmin, amongst his other activities, used to own the Brasserie Liégeoise or Grand Café and Hotel. As a young married woman I think I once went there, but in those days, of course, I knew nothing about Paul Marmin. What I liked to see were the fisher-girls in their white lace head-dresses and the old women in black. Then I took to going to Paris by air and I saw much less of Boulogne than I would have liked.

'My brother Paul,' said George Marmin, 'has rebuilt the Brasserie Liégeoise and, indeed, a new Boulogne has risen on the ruins of the old. There is to be a family party and we wondered if you would join us? We could go over on the steamer on Saturday morning and be back on Sunday night.'

So off we went to Boulogne.

Both brothers were born in this French fishing port from above which Napoleon once looked down on the assembled ships that were to take his army to invade England.   Sophie Gay says that Napoleon had a tiff with his admiral and that some of the boats were swamped. She tells the story in her contemporary book on the Paris *salons* and both she and her lovely daughter Delphine were well informed.   The brothers Marmin had a French father and an English mother.   The father had something to do with the casino and was very gallant with women.   The mother, in a fit of jealousy, came back to England where George eventually married an Englishwoman.   Paul, on the other hand, after working in Northumberland Avenue as a chef returned to Boulogne and married a woman from north-east France. Mme Paul is one of those women who make one proud to be of her sex.   She is infinitely more efficient than any man but also extremely tender.   When her husband, appalled by the disaster, fell ill in 1945, she first made him strong again and then inspired him with the necessary courage to start life all over again and rebuild the Brasserie Liégeoise.

As soon as the steamer docked we were greeted by a little man with clever, humorous eyes who obviously was beloved by everybody: the police, the customs men, the dock hands, the porters with whom he spoke indifferently in French and in English, they being as fluent in this language as himself, for it was clear that here was a section of people who for generations past had practised their own interpretation of the *entente cordiale*.

Walking straight past the train for Paris, he led us to his car and we drove into the town.

Everywhere on this Saturday morning men were putting up buildings, mixing cement, digging, hammering, climbing up poles, laying telephone wires, singing

and shouting at one another.   After all, it is the government that pays, or pays at least the biggest share.   The
town shimmers with the whiteness of new houses.   Even
the humbler ones were being fitted with central heating
plants run on heavy oil to take the place of those archaic
black furnaces so difficult to stoke, so capricious, that
they invariably end by turning the sweetest little housewife, however courageous and loving, into a tired,
ill-tempered drudge.

The Brasserie Liégeoise was just off the main street in
a part of the town where there remained great empty
holes.   But there was the theatre, sweetly evocative of
the very early 1900's, that had escaped by a miracle and
was being used as a temporary casino whilst the new one
was being built.   Paul Marmin stepped out of the car
and, with a sweep of his hand towards the new hotel,
cried: 'There you are!'

The entrance is through the brasserie: how little these
French cafés change!   How easily one recaptures the
spirit of the past!   There are the same leather seats
running lengthways from end to end, back to back,
topped by shining copper rails, but the leather seats are
well stuffed and bright red in colour, much more fun
than those tired black ones to which, in Paris cafés, my
bare legs used to stick when I was a little girl.   On one
side of the copper rails and ferns is the restaurant; on
the other the café with the telephones and the Bottins.
All the tables in the restaurant had spotless linen, and
the waiters had freshly laundered white jackets and white
aprons.   There were great quantities of flowers growing
in pots, especially hydrangeas blue as a summer sky, and
on a table on the restaurant side a plate with freshly
cooked lobsters and prawns.

What strikes me most in France since the war are
flowers, flowers everywhere, plants of every kind, lovingly
watered.   I had noticed them in cafés along that new

avenue at Le Havre which is rising from the harbour to the centre of the town.   When in winter the café terraces are enclosed in glass, like hothouses, the plants remind one of the glass-houses at Kew Gardens.   One lunches or drinks one's apéritif, or dines in tropical beauty; when in summer the café terraces are open again to the warm air, the plants continue to thrive.

There is something singularly gracious in these flowers that grow all round one, breathing the same air, seemingly saying: 'It's pretty here, isn't it?   You are certain to eat well.   They will look after you as they look after us. We are watered every morning and put in our pots for an hour or two in the sun like children in their prams. We sniff the town air, listening to the noises of the street, and the Channel steamers letting off their sirens, and the swish of the fishing boats going out to sea. Have no fear.   You will eat well here.'

And here is Mme Paul!   She smiles the sweetest welcome; her features in repose are clever and thoughtful, and her hair, impeccably waved, is a dignified length. A woman like Mme Paul in a religious community, in a hospital, in a business, would be bound to succeed.   One feels that she knows absolutely everything about her Grand Café and Hotel.   I immediately engaged her in conversation.   She answered the most complicated questions in a few words with delightful clarity, but when some question happened to fall outside her scope, she threw up her short, plump arms to the height of her very becoming bust and said serenely: 'I know nothing about the matter, or at least not sufficient to discuss it.'

Yes, indeed, one does not waste one's time with Mme Paul.   She gets up every morning at the same hour, and donning a useful but elegant blue overall, inspects her tall new building from attic to cellar.   My housewifely instincts warmed to her.   She it is who checks the merchandise: the same farmers have served her for twenty years, bringing in their farm butter, their eggs, and their thick cream. I had not until this brief week-end realized the beauty or the richness of the pasture-land within ten miles of Boulogne. One speeds too often in a boat train through what appears from our corner seat dull flat country. I did not know that there were thick woods and grass as luscious in places as in Normandy, where the shire horses graze beside the cows.

'And you know, madame'—she was old-fashionedly formal in her politeness—'fresh food should not remain too long in refrigeration. Things should come in often and be served when they are still fresh, at the precise moment when nature has brought them to maturity. This evening you will eat strawberries that are being picked this afternoon. I shall serve them in the simplest way with fresh cream. There will still be strawberries next week, but if the weather stays fine cherries will take pride of place. Then there is the fish. The fishing-boats come in and we eat the fish within a matter of hours—turbot, soles, lobsters.'

I trot round beside her, our high heels echoing on the stone floor of the airy basement. There is a corridor with rooms on either side, giving the impression of a liner's lower deck, white and air-conditioned. Paul stood by the refrigeration chambers and proudly un-locked the doors like a schoolboy showing off something new, a lamb, a side of beef, fillet and minute steaks, and veal as white as milk; a sucking-pig, too, whose roast outside will crackle under the teeth when it is served, a delicacy so much appreciated in England during Shakespearian times.

'It looks nice, doesn't it?' exclaimed Paul, closing the door behind him. 'But of course it's expensive.'

'Yes,' said Mme Paul, 'it is all very expensive, but, my friend, what is excellent, what is of the very finest quality, has always been expensive. We have some difficulty in explaining this simple fact just now to people who come over from England. They will ask, for instance, for a lemonade. The waiter takes a fresh lemon and squeezes it in front of them into a tumbler and he puts a bowl of sugar on the table. This modest drink is therefore expensive because the ingredients are real. The lemon comes from Spain or North Africa, the castor sugar from the West Indies. The English customer believes I am over-charging him because in England you have acquired the habit of satisfying your thirst with mass-produced drinks. That may be all very well for schoolboys, but I do not like to see it in a person of mature discernment. Even bread is expensive when there is no subsidy and when the wheat supplied to the miller is of the highest grade. It would not be right for bread to be so cheap that people did not realize what a lovely and precious thing it is. A loaf of bread represents a great deal of work in spite of modern machinery in the fields, at the mills, and at the bakery. The European has understood during the last few years that he must not argue about the price of food. He knows the price of everything because he also receives a high wage. Our builder was continually exceeding his estimates to put up this hotel; when he comes in for a meal he is not surprised if the food is expensive. He knows that if he wants to eat well it cannot be otherwise. Nobody obliges you to order a steak worth ten shillings, but on the other hand nobody obliges me to sell it to you for half its value. The real price is the price. The simplicity of this statement occasionally causes surprise. The farmer who fattens the beef is prosperous, the butcher is prosperous, and I who own a restaurant have nothing to grumble about. If the European these days wants to eat well, he must work hard and well. If you own a shop in the main street where people are passing all the time, and close your shop at five in the evening and all day Saturdays and Sundays, you must not grumble if you cannot afford to eat as well as the man who keeps open all the time. And above all, you must not expect me to pity you, for if I only worked five days a week I would be in debt to-morrow.'

We went ino the café for an aperitif.

After leaving Paul downstairs, Mme Paul and I had inspected one or two bedrooms on each floor. The chintzes were gay, the mattresses made of real wool, and each bedroom had its bathroom and shower. Now where had I read that the food was good in France but the plumbing dreadful? It is amazing how the world thrives on clichés.

The two brothers, George and Paul, discussed business: the two sisters-in-law, the Frenchwoman and the Englishwoman, discussed their homes. Mme Paul had offered us one of those excellent light ports that people on the Continent drink before a meal: it was known in the brasserie as her own vintage. She had it shipped from Portugal, and she told me that for twenty years she had made it a habit to have a small glass once a day, and she added with that preciseness which was so much part of her:

'I drink wine with extreme moderation, and have quite given up spirits. One must curb oneself if one wishes to remain in good health. I have no time for indispositions and headaches. We have so many more responsibilities than men.'

She said all this very seriously and authoritatively, and I kept on thinking what a pity it was that she had no daughter: how I should have loved to be trained in so many housewifely matters by a mother who knew all the secrets of the linen-room, the kitchen, the cellar, and the store-room. Of course, from my own mother I had learned how to sew and wash and iron, but to have a

big establishment must be lovely also for a woman, and
to have been shown from girlhood how exactly each
thing must be done. From time to time Paul would
brandish a menu, and we the guests would all busy ourselves choosing complicated dishes we had not tasted
since the war. I wondered how the unfortunate *maître
d'hôtel*, who never said anything, who never took a note,
would remember it all. We would then return to our
interrupted discussions. I learned the most interesting
things, that whereas Mme George, representing the
English viewpoint, was enthusiastic about modern
washing-machines and old-fashioned grate fires, Mme
Paul considered that grate fires gave off more smoke
than heat, and that her experience of washing-machines
was that their usefulness was greatly exaggerated. I took
this opportunity of questioning Mme Paul about the
linen.

'Oh!' she exclaimed. 'This is the decision I have
reluctantly come to. I replace the whole lot every two
years. In this way the restaurant customer has spotless
napkins, the hotel guest new sheets, and I—well, I have
none of the trouble of employing women to darn and to
mend as I used to before the war. The old system was
excellent: it was the right system, but now it has become
too difficult. One can no longer find women to spend
hours mending a sheet or a napkin. It is an art that I
fear will die out. But as I was telling you just now, the
customer has got into the habit of paying a right price,
and that helps us to give him better service. We can
afford to change all the linen every two years and in the
long run this is to everybody's advantage, for though
we, the owners, make less money because of taxation
than we used to, the staff is better paid, and in one way
or another we have contributed to all the welfare schemes.
Yes, we pay lots of money to the government, but we
don't mind about that as long as it is understood that

they don't interfere in our business or prevent us from increasing our turnover. That is the way we see it in France. They must not prevent us from working. Thus my cashier—there she is, sitting at the end of the room—bought herself a bar of gold. Anybody can walk into a bank and buy a bar of gold. So my cashier made no secret of her gold. She and the chef, the cellarmen, and the waiters all discuss their investments over lunch. But the other day the cashier decided to sell her gold. She said she was tired of having something so unproductive. She sold it with a small profit and has bought herself several acres of pasture-land which she rents out to a farmer for a yearly return. He is the farmer who supplies me with butter, so you see that everybody is interested in everybody else's work.

'Personally I am delighted. Instead of having employees who hate me because they are envious, they are already owners of something or other. They own gold or land or a house or a shop in the town. They break less. They steal less. They are more polite with the customers.'

'Madame,' said the *maître d'hôtel*, 'lunch is ready.'

'Then,' asked Mme Paul, looking round at us, 'shall we move across to the restaurant?'

She added slyly:

'As a matter of fact, you are none of you going to have what you ordered. I let Paul have his way. He likes to look grand with the menu, but I know what just now is best and tenderest. After all, I am the mistress of the house!'

She smiled maternally:

'You will have a steak and fried potatoes . . . and lots of strawberries and cream. Am I forgiven?'

CHAPTER XVIII

WE WERE SHOWN to a long, narrow table against the low flower-banked partition between restaurant and café, and this was agreeable because a long, narrow table allows those sitting on either side of one to join in any conversation one is having with the person opposite. I do not know of any better way of seating people at a meal. I have often found it tiresome to be primly confined to a neighbour especially if, as sometimes happens, I quickly clash with his ideas, or if he unwittingly begins by putting me on the defensive.

Mme Paul directed the operations of the meal: her husband looked after the wines. The wines were excellent and one felt immediately that nobody would have too much, but that towards the end of the meal our hearts would warm and our conversation become more animated.

Mme Paul talked about cooking. She said that of course men remained the grand masters of this difficult art, but that one of the reasons for their success was that they never counted the cost.

'For instance,' she said, 'unless a woman is very rich, she should never send her husband out to do the shopping. It is his nature to buy expensive luxuries.'

Paul, who in his young days was himself a famous chef working side by side with Latry, who later made quite a name for himself when he went to the Savoy in London, protested, and I took this opportunity to say:

'M. Paul, I have come to be rather proud of my omelets, but it too often happens that while I am folding them they split, which makes me unhappy!'

Husband and wife answered in one breath:

'They are overdone. That's why they break!'

Paul then began to tell his brother the secret of the famous Mère Poulard omelet at Mont St. Michel, and I, turning to Mme Paul, whispered:

'Your husband, madame, must be a wonderful cook!'

'Yes,' she agreed, 'he is good, but between ourselves there is nothing he does that I cannot do as well, but you know how it is with men. One must always make them believe they are cleverer!'

During the afternoon we drove to the cliff to see their newly constructed villa where in due course they hope to retire: no other part of France tempts them. Boulogne is where they have their heart.

I thought the villa delightful and I liked the magnificent central heating. Wide windows and comfortable balconies looked out to sea. Below us lay the harbour with the cross-Channel steamer that was to leave for Folkestone that evening. When they live here they will regulate their lives, I am sure, by these fascinating mail-steamers, watching anxiously for the one due each morning, speculating about its passage in storm and fog.

There is also the fishing-fleet. The little ships, said Mme Paul, when homeward bound from long journeys let off their sirens in view of the statue of the Virgin, greeting her—though some people claim it is merely to warn their wives to get dinner ready!

Standing on the balcony we watched the immense activity of this Saturday afternoon, the pastry-cook shops doing a fine business, café terraces crowded. Everything was warm, gay, and frantically busy. Here was

life, picturesque and vital. Small cars brought house-
wives and little girls from Lille, Calais, or Abbeville to
buy fresh lobsters or prawns perhaps. No shop was
closed; the shopkeepers' idea of a happy week-end would
be counting the till at night.

The villa was of blinding cement built against the
higher part of the cliff. Mme Paul and I stood together.
I liked her. We understood each other even in our
silences. We were women, glad to be women, sure of
our own strength. Both of us could dispense with unnecessary words. The crowd moved below us in the
still unfinished street. 'It must be as good as a comedy
to be behind the scenes in this Anglo-French town, and
watch the airs and graces of some of its sojourners. Are
you tired, Isabel?'

What a capacity I have for storing up phrases like this
from books that have influenced me as a writer! Why
yes, of course, that is another reason why I love Boulogne.
Mrs. Henry Wood made Mr. Carlyle take his Lady Isabel
to Boulogne from East Lynne. They arrived by the
Folkestone packet and proceeded to the Hôtel des Bains,
but Isabel objected to the bustling hotel and Mr. Carlyle
found excellent rooms in the rue de l'Écu near the
port.

'Where is the rue de l'Écu, madame?' I asked Mme
Paul.

'Just in front of you, madame,' she answered.

Boulogne is razed to the ground but Mrs. Henry
Wood's characters still move like living people along the
rue de l'Écu. They were amused with the scenes of the
busy town. Now I am amused by it. This Anglo-
French town, as the authoress puts it, as if it were
English first and French afterwards—but then, whether
we like it or not, are our two countries not inextricably
mixed up in history, in tastes, in literature?

And what other picture have I stored up of Boulogne?

Why, of course, Elizabeth Bowen must have been here to describe those poignant scenes in *The House in Paris*. So I look down from this balcony on the scenes from English literature superimposed by women writers.

'You should come and see the garage, madame,' said Mme Paul.

Our French politeness is still delightfully formal. We are not for calling each other after ten minutes by our Christian names. The Channel is still very wide in spite of those fast Channel steamers and the aeroplanes that from time to time roar across the sky. For women like Mme Paul and myself, a trifle old-fashioned perhaps, yet very much in tune with all around us, the sound of 'madame' is very agreeable to the ear. It gives us a sense of dignity, of warm and pleasant pride.

Thus we went down to the garage.

We entered it from a downstairs room, as if it had been just another room, and it was warm and snug, warmed with the same central heating. Here, indeed, through another door was the central heating plant worked by heavy oil and a laundry with modern machines.

On our return to the Brasserie we were met with the news that workmen digging the foundations for a new building in the same area had gone through some underground power cables, with the result that there was no power in the Marmin domain. The lifts had stopped, the refrigerators had ceased to function, but M. Paul took the news most calmly, for it appeared that when everybody in a town is digging, hammering, riveting, this sort of accident is frequent. For instance, M. Paul said, the poles carrying some overhead cables between his place and the casino were so lightly stuck into the loose soil beside a bomb-hole that they might collapse at any moment. 'And that would be tiresome,' he added, 'because they would probably fall across the hotel.'

He smiled in a way that showed me there was really no danger, and hurried off to put a spare dynamo into action.

'We'll move you from the top floor to the first,' said Mme Paul, 'in case my husband does not get the lift working. We don't need to worry about dinner. We cook with every sort of heating, always ready to shift from one to the other. That is being modern, never being too dependent on any particular form of modern invention!'

She went about her business and I was left alone.

I went for a walk in the town. One climbs steeply to the old walled-in city, and here and there some old streets, old ramparts, gaunt old doors, seventeenth-century buildings, remain to give one a picture of the past. I was anxious to visit the cathedral of Nôtre Dame that has a dome like St. Paul's, and is so tall and noble that it is visible from far out at sea.

The cathedral contains a statue of the Virgin, about which there is a charming legend as important to the English as to the French. One day in 633, just after the Northumbrians' victories over the Celts, when no king had yet made himself master of England, the inhabitants of the tiny place that was Boulogne (Caligula had named it thus after Bologna), saw a fishing-boat riding towards them over the waves in which, instead of fishermen, was a statue of the Virgin between two angels. Some verses embroidered on a medieval tapestry that once hung in the cathedral, began:

Comme la Vierge à Boulogne arriva
Dans un bateau que la mer apporta
En l'an de grâce ainsi que l'on comptoit
Pour lors, au vrai, six cens et trente-trois.

By the thirteenth century the most distinguished pilgrims were visiting the statue, amongst whom were

Winchester-born King Henry III, Louis IX, or St. Louis, of France, and Cardinal Foucaud who, when he became Pope, took the sanctuary of Nôtre Dame under his protection; and it was here that Edward II of England married his French wife Isabella, daughter of Philip the Fair, in a ceremony which grouped five kings or future kings, four queens, and fourteen sons of kings round the statue which seven centuries earlier sailed in so prettily from over the sea.

Henry VIII held Boulogne for a time, but I am glad to note that his Protestant soldiers did no harm. The town was liberated by France's Henri II; it was then, alas, that French Calvinists seized the statue, tried unsuccessfully to burn it (the wood was too hard), hid it under a dung-heap, and finally threw it down the well of a manor-house near Wimereux from which it was retrieved in 1607.

The statue held a heart aloft in her right hand: a heart became a symbol of the Boulogne Virgin. They were sold widely by the jewellers of the town and knights even took them on the Crusades. Some were even found in the Thames! Louis XI, a pious French king in the late fifteenth century, presented a heart of pure gold weighing $6\frac{1}{2}$ lb. (in those days 13 marcs) to the cathedral authorities, and ordering his successors to do the same, knelt humbly before the statue. Louis XIV renewed this gift in 1658.

The terrorists in the revolution of 1789 succeeded in doing what the Calvinists had failed to do—they burned the statue, all but one hand, which you may still see to-day. Pilgrims kneel and humbly kiss it. Thus the kissing of a woman's hand is not merely a pretty society custom in France: the poorest fisherman kisses the hand of the Virgin Mary. I admit that as I left the cathedral I felt even prouder than usual of being a woman.

I think it is good to lose oneself for a moment amongst

these pretty beliefs in an age when, for my sex at any
rate, there is so little of interest in most modern in-
ventions.   The more terrible the present becomes, the
more we cling to what is left of the past.

George Marmin had arranged a surprise for me on
Sunday morning.   He said that I must not go back to
London without seeing something of the countryside,
and he had therefore hired a car.   I like men who are
so proud of the province in which they were born that
they must at all costs make others love it, and in this
case I had never suspected the amazing beauty of villages
only ten miles from Boulogne.

One came upon them nestling amidst enchanting valleys,
the houses with russet roofs, and in orchards and fields
one caught sight of the powerful white horses, the pride
of this part of France.

We stopped in the wide square of a village which I
thought the loveliest yet.   There were two little shops
as one would expect to see in a fairy-book, and next to
them, set amongst trees, the prettiest church into which
little girls were being led, dressed in bridal white.   On
the other side of the square was a manor-house.   Ducks
waddled on the grass fringe.   A wood was visible
distantly.

'This is where many people still come from Boulogne
on Sundays,' said M. George, 'for a good bottle, a dish
of jugged hare, and—a great village speciality—a plum
flan with a wide and buttery brim, *la tarte à gros bord*,
as they call it.   Nowadays, of course, the younger people
prefer to go further afield.   Their fast cars take them
to Le Touquet in no time, but here we are in driving
distance for the horse and buggy.   The atmosphere is
of the nineties.

The little girls in bridal dresses with prayer books in
their hands, the little boys in new suits with a wide satin

bow on the arm, show us that a first communion is
taking place to-day. We shall see them at morning
service. I lead the way down the little path into the
church which was already so full that many men in
Sunday black stood on the steps, but as soon as I arrive,
as soon as they see a woman, they smile, and make a
passage and whisper that there will certainly be a chair
within, and so I enter the minute church and take my
place beside the sweetest little boy, who looks up wide-
eyed from his prayer book which his mother, a plump
farmer's wife, has bound for him in a black material on
which she has embroidered a design. As the church is
so small the chairs serve both to be sat upon and as
kneeling stools, with the result that every now and again
there is a great clatter as we all turn them round together.
The children who are taking part in their first communion service are in the choir stalls, the girls on one
side, the boys on the other. The priest with wide
tortoise-shell spectacles in white surplice is very young.
Towards the end of the service, he consults his wrist-
watch and says:

'Dearly beloved, I shall not give you a sermon to-day.
These children whose Sunday is beginning in so memor-
able a manner should spend the rest of the day in their
homes in the peaceful atmosphere of their families. Let
us pray for them. Let us also pray for the Countess
of X who has been gracious enough to give us to-day's
consecrated bread.'

While he spoke two choristers came down the altar
steps bearing large wicker baskets in which the
consecrated bread lay on lace napkins of the most beautifully home-made kind, and as the basket was handed to
me, I realized that this was not bread but *brioche*. Then
I remembered that when I was a little girl at Marais the
bread for the communion service was given each Sunday
by a different parishioner, the farmers bringing freshly

baked loaves but the lady of the manor giving this light, delicious buttery cake that in France we call *brioche*.

How better could we start our Sunday than in this God-fearing atmosphere? I reflected how simple are the things that make us happy, how difficult these simple joys are to discover now, and being a hopelessly sentimental woman I wept.

CHAPTER XIX

WHILE WAITING for the Sunday lunch we again joined the two families for what they affectionately called Mme Paul's aperitif, by which they meant a distribution of the port wine sent to her specially in cask from Oporto.

A young English couple were already lunching in the restaurant. Their car was drawn up outside the temporary casino, and as they had managed to lock all the doors and lose the key, M. Paul had gone to fetch some mechanics from a nearby garage who were trying to open the doors again without breaking anything. A little crowd of townspeople had gathered round the car offering advice. I could see their friendly, interested faces through the wide plate-glass windows of the café-restaurant. The port wine was very pleasant after the morning drive, and the head waiter was standing in front of us with a large menu.

'I have already ordered,' said Mme Paul, with a voice of authority, 'a leg of lamb, a traditional dish on first communion Sunday.'

We beam with satisfaction and M. Paul arrives to say that the mechanics have been successful in opening the doors of the English car. He sat down contentedly. The hotel was quite full. There was a famous general and, oh yes, a French couple who had brought their cat. . . .

'The cat is very sweet,' put in Mme Paul, 'but if I had been here when the couple arrived with it I should

certainly have not given them a room.' Then turning
to me: 'You must not think, madame, that I dislike cats.
No, on the contrary, but one can never trust their
owners. It's the same with dogs. Dog owners will
promise anything when they arrive, and it's very difficult to refuse some woman who looks at one with
appealing eyes and says: "My little dog is very well
trained, madame, and of course I shall keep it in the
bath-room," but I know perfectly well that the little dog,
who is so sweet and so well trained, will jump up on the
fresh cambric muslin arm-chairs, and even on the satin
bedspreads, and that in spite of the well-intentioned
lady accidents can happen, or the dog can have fleas,
and that is not fair on whoever takes the room afterwards. So I have to pretend that I am hard. Thus
when I saw the owners of the cat just now I was obliged
to scold them. I will not have cats about the place, not
unless it becomes necessary. As you have seen, madame,
everything in the hotel is new and brightly painted, even
downstairs where there are no dark corners as you will
find in an old house. A rat or a mouse would have to
be very clever to hide in the basement. Before the war,
in the old hotel, it was different and we had a cat, the
most extraordinary cat.'

'Yes, indeed,' put in M. Paul, 'a cat that was as
obedient to my wife as we all are. He came to us as a
kitten when the film *Snow White and the Seven Dwarfs*
was being shown at the local cinema. The whole of
France was under the spell of that charming picture:
grown-ups and children spoke of nothing else. My
niece Hélène, George's daughter, was then a very little
girl and she used to walk up and down the café holding
the kitten in her arms, kissing it, rocking it to sleep,
and the kitten would close its eyes and appear to be in
a perpetual ecstasy, so that Hélène, who had seen the film,
called her pet Dopey.

'Dopey grew up and divided his time between the kitchen and the store-room, and when my wife suspected a mouse or a rat she would go round all the corners with an electric torch until she discovered a hole. Then she raised her voice and called:

'"Come and sit in front of this hole, Dopey!"

'And Dopey would not move till he had caught the rat or the mouse.

'He stayed with us during the war, but right at the end, when we had to evacuate Boulogne, Dopey was not to be found. The British and Americans sent over waves of bombers; the Germans, before retreating, were making arrangements to blow up the harbour. Unable to wait for Dopey we hurried to Paris, leaving the hotel and all our possessions behind. Dopey, we learned afterwards, returning from some adventure and finding the hotel empty, made his way to a brothel near the harbour where the women were packing up their things to go to a villa in the country owned by their "madame." They would spend the next few weeks playing cards and going for walks in the country. The holiday would be good for their looks. One of the women took pity on Dopey and packed him in the cart with the crimson plush arm-chairs, the mattresses, the mirrors, and the dresses and lingerie. Dopey was delighted; he also was making his first trip to the country. The "madame" wrote to us in Paris saying that her young ladies had adopted Dopey, who was charming but lazy.

'We returned to find the hotel in ruins, and then I fell ill and nearly died, but Mme Paul with her habitual courage started a temporary café in an army hut half-way up to the cathedral. The building was too hot in summer, too cold in winter, and we were cramped for space. Meanwhile the "madame's" ladies had also returned to town, but though like ourselves they were obliged to live in a hut, they brought back with them

their comfortable wool mattresses and their crimson
plush arm-chairs.   Dopey was delighted to see us again.
He arched his back against our legs and took his meals
with us in the café-restaurant, but as we owned no easy-
chairs he left us after each meal to sleep with the young
women in their temporary brothel, and in this way he
spent meal times with us and nights with them.   We did
not discover his stratagem at once.   Then one day, after
Mme Paul had succeeded in making our private apartments a little more luxurious, she called Dopey and
showed him the divan and the new arm-chairs.   We had
just finished supper and Dopey had been preparing to
leave us, but when he saw the freshly upholstered room
with the soft cushions he jumped up, purred, put his
head between his outstretched paws and went fast asleep,
and from this moment he never returned to the ladies
of the brothel.   Poor Dopey, he was old, and two years
later he died in his favourite arm-chair.   Mme Paul still
has a very warm corner in her heart for him, so you
see, madame, though she is strict, she loves animals.'

This family lunch was delightful.   We were joined
first by General Koenig, the victor of Bir-Hakim, then
by some Marmin cousins who had come over from
Calais, and finally by a tall young man with close-cropped
dark hair, a very bright pullover, and shoes with thick
crêpe soles.   The new arrival was the brother of Hélène
Marmin's doctor husband.   The little Hélène, who used
to walk through the restaurant of the old hotel with
Dopey in her arms, was now a young mother nursing a
baby in arms.   They lived in Paris, and from Paris in a
sports car had come the brother-in-law, who was engaged
in some form of journalism.

Hélène had been educated in England.   She took up
fashion designing, and during a course of training in
Paris fell in love with Jean-Jacques Willard, a young

Frenchman who was just taking his degree to be a doctor. Brought up by the Thames, she would rear a family by the Seine, but Boulogne remained the rallying point where both branches, the English and the French, met to exchange news. The student doctor, who had just qualified, wanted to be a children's specialist, and everybody was anxious to help him, M. le docteur Jean-Jacques Willard, on with his career.

Our steamer returned to England at 6 p.m. and I wanted to buy some butter, a Guerlain lipstick and their new scent Atuana, so I slipped out alone in the streets. A group of little girls in their white first communion dresses, but without their long veils, were playing on the kerb waiting for vespers. A nun, leaning across her motor-cycle, was talking to two young women, and strange was the medieval costume against the machine.

I found a small store where groceries, fruit, and milk were sold, and though the place was temporary, there were magnificent refrigerators in which various sorts of butter were placed, butter freshly made by farmers' wives on their farms, and pasteurized butter whose neat, exact packages contrasted with the great mounds of farm butter enveloped in gauze. The owner and her husband were very definite about what sort of butter I should buy.

'You need butter that will travel,' the woman declared. 'Though England is not far away, just across the water, it is quite a journey all the same. England! Fancy, madame, not a day passes but we talk about England or the English, and yet I have never been there. What a lot of fine English boys I have seen tramping, tramping over the cobbles of the town—and wounded going back on stretchers after the battle of the Marne. Two world wars, madame! Is it not terrible in a lifetime?'

From the back came a young woman wearing a pretty hat, a young husband, and a well-behaved little girl.

'Yes,' continued the owner as she weighed the butter. 'These are our children, my daughter, her husband, and their little girl. Every Sunday afternoon they come to fetch us to take us to the cinema.'

'What is wonderful,' said the husband, 'is that at our age we were still young enough to lose our business and our home, and to build everything up a second time from nothing, but if there is a third war we shall be too old. Is there anything else, madame?'

'I should like some apricots,' I said, 'to make a tart when I get back to England.'

He served me, and the family locked the door and put up a notice saying 'BACK AT SIX,' and went off to the cinema. Then I turned in the direction of the market-place, having seen earlier a very pretty corner shop entirely devoted to scents and cosmetics.

There was a long glass counter in the form of an L, behind which were glass wall-cases filled to the ceiling with elegant bottles. At the far end of the shop sat two ladies and between them, on a chair with several cushions, a little dog called a Japanese.

One lady was clearly the owner of the shop, the other wore a hat. The owner was dark skinned and dark eyed. Her hair was white but her eyes twinkled and shone. Her tiny dog was white and black so that in colouring it resembled its mistress, and its eyes were as bright as hers. The two women were gossiping; the one wearing a hat was withered and dressed entirely in black.

The owner at my approach rose from her seat. A white overall, very beautifully cut, revealed through the artistry of drawn threads, a black satin dress. She was immensely gay and did not hide her admiration for all the lovely things in her shop. As she was much too old any longer to use cosmetics herself, she might well, I thought, have destroyed the illusion that her goods helped to keep one eternally young, but I was bound to admit that on the contrary she reconciled me to the idea of growing old. I said to myself: 'If when I grow old I can be as pleasant to look at, as neat about my person, as gay and bright-eyed, perhaps there is something to look forward to!' I asked her for an eau-de-Cologne that I have loved since I was a young married woman, and I exclaimed:

'Really, it's my favourite of all.'

Her eyes brightened.

'That's just what I think!' she exclaimed. 'And what is so strange about that?'

Why no, there was nothing strange in our having the same tastes, but it was charming to forget the shop and the owner of the shop, and simply to exchange confidences with another woman.

The little dog suddenly jumped up on the glass counter and ran towards us, lighter and more graceful even than a Pekinese.

'Well,' said I, laughing, 'I'll buy the dog as well.'

'No,' said the old lady, 'not for a million, nor even for a million and a half. I will not sell little Mitsou. When I had spent the million and a half I would neither have Mitsou nor the money.'

She took the little dog in her arms and covered it with kisses, saying:

'My little Mitsou!'

She then returned to where her companion all in black was sitting patiently with hands folded on her lap, and made a neat parcel of my eau-de-Cologne, my scent, and my lipstick, and when in the street I took a last look at them, the two old ladies were happily gossiping once more, with Mitsou on its cushioned arm-chair between them.

.   .   .   .   .

G

'Well,' asked M. Paul when I was back in the café, 'what have you been buying?'

'A lipstick,' I answered. 'Also some butter and a basket of apricots to make a tart when I am back home in London.'

M. Paul immediately plunged into what he considered the best way to make pastry, and in his excitement he mixed imaginary flour and butter, kneading the dough with his finger-tips, adding a little water, rolling the dough with a rolling-pin, imploring me to keep a little syrup from a few apricots boiled in a saucepan to pour over the flan after I had removed it from the oven.

'It will be delicious!' he exclaimed, and he closed his eyes, raising two fingers to his mouth in ecstasy so that I had the impression of really tasting his open apricot tart, warm and full of juice, crackling with sugar.

Now it was time to go to the steamer. Here was his brother George.

'Don't forget to turn the radio on when you are home,' said M. Paul to Mr. George. Then turning to me:

'There is a concert on the B.B.C. we listen to every Sunday night. George and his wife listen to it in London; my wife and I listen to it in Boulogne. While we, in our café, listen to the music, we think of George and his wife and wonder what they are doing, and they think of us. Then there are the tunes we used to hear in the London of Edward VII's reign when I was a chef in Northumberland Avenue.'

'I think I shall have to listen also,' I said. 'Then my thoughts will converge with yours.'

Across the harbour the Channel steamer sent its warning siren, and the heavy train from Paris rumbled over the cobbled street.

It was time to go back to England.

CHAPTER XX

THE POSTMAN this morning brought me a card from Brittany. The glossy side showed a medieval castle near Rennes; on the reverse my little coloured friend, Elizabeth, had written:

DEAR MADAM,

My masters are here until September when we shall go to Sologne for 'la chasse.' I am very happy, and often pray for you,

Votre dévouée,
ELIZABETH.

On reading these words my eyes dimmed with emotion, for if the meek and gentle inherit the kingdom of heaven, then Elizabeth will assuredly have great honour there.

She arrived here by ship during the great raids on London, with her few possessions in a small bundle. Her father (she thought) was Syrian; her mother half Ethiopian, half French Somaliland. Djibuti was her home, and there the nuns of a convent in which she had been brought up had placed her with a French general and his wife who by separate routes were travelling to England. Elizabeth had also come alone. Nobody had told her where she was going. Submarines pursued her ship. Bombs fell round her as she entered London where she knew not a soul and spoke no English, but her simple mind was filled with a complete trust in heaven—and her name was Elizabeth.

Perhaps we were destined to find each other. From my girlhood I have always loved women of this name. Was there not, to begin with, the wife of Zacharias whose baby, the future John the Baptist, leaped in her womb when her cousin, the Virgin Mary, already chosen to bear the Son of God, paid her a visit?

Then the royal Elizabeths. . . . Elizabeth of Valois, daughter of Henry II of France and Catherine de Medici, who, as a girl, played with Mary Queen of Scots, composing verses in Latin. Her wedding to Philip II of Spain (who had asked our own Elizabeth I to marry him) witnessed the mortal wounding of her father by Montgomery in a joust.

There was Elizabeth of Russia, daughter of Peter the Great and the Empress Elizabeth of Austria, wife of Francis Joseph, whose morbid dread was to become less beautiful as she grew older. I have read so much about her that when I entered the vault of the Hapsburgs under the Capuchin church in Vienna, I wept over her tomb as if for a friend.

Elizabeth of the Belgians, widow of King Albert, I met at her palace of Laeken. She had seen her country twice invaded, her son Leopold forced to abdicate. Compared with all these of course my Elizabeth was, by our worldly standards, nobody at all, a coloured servant thrown into the turmoil of London during the raids.

I was to follow her fortunes till several years after the peace celebrations. She became maid to the ambassador's wife, Mme Massigli, acted as nurse to her adopted daughter, Jacqueline, and laundered the ambassador's shirts. Ordinary servants seldom stay long in embassies. They probably become homesick. Mme Massigli once said: 'I don't know what I would do without my Elizabeth.' But in the end Pierre, the embassy butler, sent Elizabeth to his sister in Paris, telling her that she would never really get on well in life till she went to a country where she had not been known penniless. He was thinking of the way she had arrived with her bundle from Djibuti on the ship. Pierre's sister found Elizabeth new 'masters.' That explained my postcard from Brittany.

A strange meeting with the wife of the French general, her employer at that time, preceded, though it was not responsible for, my introduction to Elizabeth. One Sunday afternoon in July, early in the war, when it seemed that we must all be blown to pieces, my child, who had only just learned to walk, was standing on a chair leaning out of an open window overlooking the courtyard of my ground-floor flat in Shepherd Market.

A cab drew up and out of it stepped a woman who, instead of coming boldly into the house, looked at the façade, mounted one or two steps leading to the main entrance as if hoping for a porter to emerge, seeing none returned to the cab to interrogate with difficulty the driver, and finally, having given many more signs of bewilderment and hesitancy, made her way immediately to the low window where my child and I were intently watching her movements.

Her eyes, as she considered us, were charged with disappointment, helplessness, and anger. They were very dark eyes, deeply embedded in her features, and her skin, obviously burned and ravaged by a hot climate, was drawn tight. She seemed an authoritative woman, accustomed to being obeyed. Her clothes were sober and well cut; her hat was by no means inelegant.

In very slow but impeccable French, stressing each syllable in the hope that it would help me to understand, she asked if this was Carrington House.

'Yes, madame,' I answered in her own tongue.

Hurriedly she returned to the cab, and made signs to the driver to show that she had safely arrived at her desired destination, and without waiting for the man to help her, which he doubtless had no intention of doing, she pulled out one bag and then another from inside the cab with unbelievable strength and speed, and then, appealing once more to me, exclaimed:

'As, madame, you are the first person I have met since landing in England who speaks my language, will you continue to be my good angel and pay my cab, for I possess nothing but colonial francs, and it would appear that all my friends have abandoned me.'

I called to the cab driver who came to the window to be paid. I then opened my door to the stranger.

She sat down, but before saying anything more about herself, looked round and exclaimed:

'Well, this is a curious flat!'

'Yes,' I agreed, 'it is. I no longer replace pictures on the walls, for they are blown down every time there is a raid, and as you see the windows have no panes, but on the whole that is safer. . . .'

She made an impatient movement of her hand to show that she was not in the least interested in my explanation. She had merely recorded her first impression. That sufficed.

'To whom have I the honour of speaking?' she asked curtly.

I told her my name, and after making me spell it she repeated it and henceforth called me by it whenever urged to do so by politeness, but she also acquainted me with hers, and I immediately recognized in her the wife of a distinguished French colonial figure who, having recently arrived by sea, after being torpedoed, returned to his flat in our building punctually at a certain hour each night.

'Yes,' she said, 'I have come from Brazzaville to join

my husband, but he was not at the aerodrome, nor is he here.   I am extremely vexed.'

She had risen from her chair and was inspecting herself in a tall mirror against the wall, and I reflected how much older she looked than her husband who invariably, as he stepped out of his military car, waved to my little boy if he happened to be at the window.

'Would you like me to telephone to your husband's office to tell him you have arrived?' I asked.

She agreed, and after some trouble I was put through to an aide-de-camp who finally declared:

'The head porter has a duplicate key.   Tell him to let madame in to the general's flat.'

Mr. Crouch, our head porter, who by now had come down from the top of the building, opened the apartment which was next to my own and the lady, myself, my little boy, and our pekinese all went in.   My small family was delighted with the adventure, but we only stayed a moment, for almost immediately the general's wife dismissed us as if we had suddenly ceased to have any importance.

About a week later Mr. Crouch, tall and impressive in his uniform, came to my door with a tiny creature as dainty and timorous as a gazelle, whose shining white teeth shone in a face as swarthy as an Ethiopian's.

'Madame, it's your neighbour's maid, but she doesn't talk any English.   I thought you might take pity on her. She has been sent to do the shopping in the market.'

Almost ashamed of his audacity, he added:

'She looks harmless enough, madam.'

'Yes, of course, Mr. Crouch.   You are quite right. I'll do what I can.'

'Come in!' I said to the gazelle.

I led her to what the general's wife had called my curious room.   There was a large round table bought at a sale and on which we had our meals, several chairs partly broken in a raid, and a great pile of books on the floor. My son, who was playing with his teddy bear in a corner, looked with surprise at this black apparition in her white cotton dress.

'Won't you sit down?' I asked her.

'Oh no, madame!' she cried, as if this were too great an honour to accord a little black girl.

Her big eyes roved round the room. Suddenly she caught sight of my blond child and shouted:

'Oh, madame! The little boy . . . he looks just like Jesus!'

I took her by the hand and said gently:

'You are very welcome.'

She seemed to savour my words. Then she answered:

'I am so happy, so happy to have fallen amongst people whom I can understand! My name is Elizabeth.'

'Elizabeth is one of my favourite names . . . and what else after that?'

'Nothing else . . . just Elizabeth. Nothing else but Elizabeth. I have no family name, no passport, no papers. I am just Elizabeth. The nuns brought me up at Djibuti. I went into service with madame. She left. I followed. They put me in a troopship with soldiers.'

'And so you have just arrived?'

'Two days ago, madame. That is why I am still very embarrassed in the shops. Oh, not because of the shop-keepers, madame. They are all very kind to me. I would not have believed they would have been so kind to a . . . to a person from Djibuti, but, madame, I am shy. I don't understand a word.'

She smiled at me disarmingly and blurted out:

'If you could help me, just these first few days, madame, I would render you in return a number of small services. . . .'

She examined me to see if I was angry, and then added:

'For instance, I could watch over the little boy Jesus whenever you need to go out.'

'You must not call him that, Elizabeth. His name is Bobby.'

She smiled obediently, but explained:

'It is because of the doll in the crèche at Djibuti. In the convent, you understand?'

My son gaped with astonishment. Elizabeth delighted him, but he was afraid. He had the expression of the little girl in my favourite story-book by Mme Berquin, the little girl who, catching sight of a small chimney-sweep, imagined he was the devil. Their opinions of each other struck me as rather a frightening contrast.

Accompanied by Elizabeth gripping her shopping basket, Bobby holding my hand, the pekinese running ahead, I went into Shepherd Market. Elizabeth was right. She had nothing to fear from the shopkeepers. Old Bob at the vegetable shop was so charmed by the strange little person that, neglecting his other customers, he chose her the tenderest greens and called her 'Mam-zelle' in deference to his memories of the First World War. The butcher, looking very important in his striped waistcoat, gave her everything she needed. Soon her basket was full and we returned by the tradesmen's entrance, but on reaching my flat I discovered to my embarrassment that in the confusion of our departure I had left my keys behind. Happily, as none of my windows were ever closed, Mr. Crouch, to whom I confided my predicament, lifted Bobby up in his arms and swung him over the geraniums in the courtyard through the drawing-room window. A moment later we heard the child's feet pattering across the floor as he ran to open the door in the front hall.

*G

Thus we took leave of Elizabeth who went to cook her mistress's lunch whilst I did the same for the child and the dog.

From now on Elizabeth was always running in and out of my flat. She brought me the problems which her employer, the general's wife, was unable because of her ignorance of English to solve. Neither of them, for instance, could read the instructions on tinned foods. Then there were things she needed to borrow. She came to ask me for an iron, exclaiming:

'You understand, madame, I could never allow Mme la Générale to go out without first ironing her dress. I could not live down, madame, the shame of not making certain she was just right.'

Then confidentially:

'Officers' wives watch one another like hawks. The others would notice the least thing wrong, and then it would bring shame on the maid. We must take pride in our work, madame.'

It was not her pride but her humility that touched me. She added:

'Mme la Générale is going out at six, and as she is dining with friends, she will not be home till late. As soon as I have tidied up her flat I shall come to you. I notice that you have been washing your lingerie, and so to-night I shall iron it for you. It would never do to leave it till to-morrow. You would have to wash it all over again.'

Then, rolling her immense eyes, she declared sententiously:

'And to-morrow we shall have other work to do, so to-night I shall bring back your iron and iron your lingerie.'

'My sweet Elizabeth,' I exclaimed, 'you must not think that because you have borrowed my iron, I expect

you to work for me. I am not accustomed to being
helped.'

Her pretty face showed disappointment.

'I have never burned anything,' she pleaded. 'Is that
what you think? Nuns in a convent and officers' wives
have no pity for their maids. They don't allow us to
make a mistake.'

I smiled.

'Very well,' I agreed. 'Bring back my iron and spend
the evening with me. I shall be glad of your company.'

'Oh!' she cried as if I had done her an immense
favour. 'Thank you, madame! Thank you!'

One day Elizabeth brought me an invitation to take tea
with her mistress.

I thought the invitation to take tea with madame rather
formal. After all we were neighbours and we could
have seen each other without this excuse, but Elizabeth
said:

'Mme la Générale is like that. She loves to invite
people for tea or a glass of sherry with little cakes. In
fact, it is her passion. At Brazzaville and at Djibuti
she was famous for it.'

Formal calls were not my passion at all. I hardly
possessed an elegant dress. My ever open apartment
was like a railway station; people of varied nationalities,
from the most distant parts of the world, came without
warning to eat at my table, seeking the illusion of their
own homes that a woman and a baby gave them. I expect
they were tired of being solely amongst men.

As I could not leave the baby and the pekinese alone
in the flat, my entire circus arrived for tea, and instead
of bringing a pretty hand-bag I merely dangled the key
of my front door from an ungloved hand. Mme la
Générale, to my confusion, reclined on a Mme Récamier
sofa in a white satin housecoat. Her hair was beautifully
done; on her feet were the most charming embroidered

slippers. She excused herself for being in this recumbent position by alluding to the effect of colonial life on one's liver.

Helped by Elizabeth, who hovered round her like a slave, she poured out tea, deigning to address a few words to my child, but quite ignoring the impertinent presence of the pekinese. Her hands, as she spoke, darted here and there with the lightness of butterflies, and her conversation bewildered me by its brilliance. She described her long journey. The words tumbled from her lips, opening out like flowers, and one listened to them as one might listen in admiration and envy to a sonata by Beethoven. Gradually the music became softer and slower. Then she paused, sighed, and asked abruptly:

'Are you happy? Is your husband faithful to you?'

'I think I am happy,' I answered cautiously, not quite sure whether I was or not. 'The rest is in the hands of Allah.'

'How dare you invoke the name of Allah?' she cried. 'Elizabeth and I are making a novena to the Virgin. What would we become without our religion?'

Her eyes turned to the tips of her embroidered slippers. Her feet were pretty and small, and her eyes were large and luminous but she and Elizabeth, who was her slave, were making a novena to the Virgin. Elizabeth had gone into the kitchen to fetch more boiling water and she had been followed by my baby. Soon we heard their childish laughter; neither seemed grown up.

'Little coloured servants are not serious,' complained Mme la Générale. 'They are as irresponsible as sparrows.'

'But how faithful!' I broke in.

'One can never be certain of anybody!' she answered meaningly. 'Life itself betrays one.'

In an attempt to read further into her mind, I glanced

at a framed picture on a low table by her side. This
object was the only personal thing in a sublet flat. The
picture showed a fine woman in rich surroundings—a
Persian carpet, a profusion of flowers, damask curtains.

'Yes,' she said, following my gaze, 'it was in my house
in Saigon, a palace, and I was queen of it all. My first
husband was not merely important. He was very, very
distinguished. He spoke the most beautiful French I
have ever heard—and he tended me like a rare flower.'

Elizabeth came back from the kitchen and poured the
boiling water into the teapot; then slipping behind her
mistress, she took between her delicate black fingers a
curl decorating her mistress's complicated coiffure, and
rolling the curl up again round her index finger, dropped
it elegantly into place in the diadem formed by the
auburn hair. All this she did with the most touching
air of tenderness and humility. Perhaps Mme la Générale,
despite her apparent severity, was touched, for she looked
up at her little slave and said:

'The next time Mme Henrey comes, you must show
her my lovely lingerie.'

Then turning to me:

'Some of it was made in the various convents of our
colonial empire; other pieces are embroidered with lace
I made myself, for I would have you know that in my
own house I am never without a little piece of work to
do while I talk to my friends. There is nothing more
graceful for the hands; and then it helps when people
are anxious to confide in one. At the poignant moments
one looks intently at one's work. It's not nearly so
rude as puffing at them with a cigarette.

'You know, my dear, men adore looking at a woman
sewing. They imagine that to see a woman sewing her
lingerie is already to be intimate with her. I so much
prefer making useful things like lingerie than the more
genteel tapestry.

'But of course,' she went on without the slightest affectation, 'I was brought up in the various accomplishments—music, sewing, embroidery, knitting, and I am also a trained hospital nurse. It is all very agreeable, but the main thing is to have somebody to please.'

I gather about me my small family and take my leave, Elizabeth accompanying us to the flat as if it were already hers. Sweet soul, her heart is as free as the air, but she would like to marry to have a child like the Virgin Mary.

'Consider, madame, how the Virgin in church would look poor without the child Jesus in her arms! I often feel poor, madame. I do love people to love me a little. That is all I ask of them, madame. As for me, I love with all my heart. When I go back to Djibuti, I shall take presents for everybody.'

CHAPTER XXI

I HAD ALMOST come to imagine Elizabeth and
her mistress as inseparable, but at the end of the
war Mme la Générale went back to Paris alone.
I think her affairs had become too complicated to
burden herself with her devoted little slave, who
by now had taken a liking to England and refused to
return to Somaliland.

She was still without a surname or papers of any kind.
The sparrow lived on the crumbs that were thrown her.
Then she found work at the French consulate whose
officials, very hard pressed at this moment with returning
nationals, fixed her up with all the necessary documents
and gave her a room of her own and a bath-room that
Elizabeth described as 'nearly all mine.'

She was, of course, at everybody's beck and call, but
on the other hand she was becoming a person. She
dressed so much better that one day, when she came to
see me, I asked her if it would not be wise to put a little
money aside.

'Yes,' she agreed, laughing and showing her lovely
white teeth, 'but it's so lovely to buy new things. Up
till now I have depended on charity. Whatever I was
given was too small or too large. And now I just walk
into a shop and a lady comes along and calls me
"madame," and she asks me to sit down, and when I
want a pair of shoes, she kneels in front of me and tries

them on. So you see I have become like everybody
else. It's marvellous!'

And she laughed and laughed with the joy of discovering that she was somebody.

'Go on buying,' I conceded, 'but buy a little less,
and when you have put some money aside, you will see
that the bank manager will also call you "madame."'

'I had not thought of that,' she said gravely. 'I feel
so rich, being paid every week. It is like the widow's
cruse. When I come to the end of one week's pay,
another pay comes along.'

The winter of 1945 was extremely rigorous, and the
London parks were covered with snow. I was obliged
to visit my farm in Normandy and for several months
lost sight of Elizabeth. Then one afternoon in March
she arrived at my flat behind Piccadilly with a bag of
sweets for my child, and some sugar and butter for me.
Elizabeth's generosity towards those she loved was too
spontaneous to be checked, so though I blushed I
accepted with a guilty feeling the packages she pressed
into my hands.

She was very thin. My first impression was that she
had become more of a woman, but looking at her closely
I noticed that in spite of a little rouge on each cheek,
she looked far from well, and I exclaimed:

'You are pale, Elizabeth, dear!'

I took her by the shoulders to draw her towards me
and kiss her. Suddenly her eyes filled with huge tears,
and she gulped:

'Yes, madame, I expect I am. The truth is that I
have had pneumonia. I was in pain, great pain, but for
nearly a week nobody found out I was ill. It was not
their fault. I am not important enough to be missed.
Sometimes I work for one person, sometimes for another. When people see me they say: "Elizabeth, do

iron my dress!" or "Elizabeth, be a dear, and sew a button on my blouse!" but if they don't see me about, there is no reason at all why they should think of me. So I stayed unmissed in my room, too weak to call anybody. Of course, when at last they found out where I was they didn't know what to do to spoil me. And now, though I'm much better, they go on spoiling me.'

My own cheeks burned with shame. How careless I had been! Ought not something to have warned me that this simple soul, alone in the world, needed my help?

But with one of those changes characteristic of her, Elizabeth now gave the impression of releasing a great flood of sunshine stored up from her native Africa.

'Madame,' she cried, 'I have become quite crazy about dancing! On Saturday I went to a dance organized by the Swiss colony. One of the maids from the embassy took me. Oh, madame, I was so happy! I have been invited to go again next Saturday, but . . . it depends on you, madame, whether you will help me?'

'But how can I help you to go dancing, Elizabeth?'

She looked up at me, as excited as a child, and answered:

'I have been given a dress but it needs altering. It's here in this parcel, and so I have brought it to you because you love me.'

She added breathlessly:

'I need so much to dance . . . to dance. I'm getting old!'

'Old?' I laughed, but after all one is never too young to dance.

She clapped her little hands and cried:

'Oh, madame, I knew you would help me! Oh, madame, I am so, so happy!'

She was already stripping off the old dress, putting on

the new one. With our mouths full of pins, we pinched,
gathered, re-created, and finally I ran the seams up on
the baby Singer, explaining to her clearly what she still
needed to do. Her eyes, in this moment of excitement,
showed great expanses of white. Her legs, agitated by
secret music, moved up and down as they dangled from
her chair like those of a doll in a puppet show. She
clapped her hands in ecstasy and, unable to contain herself, ran across the room to smother my child with kisses.
Then, scarcely waiting to say good-bye, flew out of the
door and across the courtyard.

I do not know whether it was due to Elizabeth's social
activities, but not long after this she became an assistant
lady's maid to Mme Massigli, the elegant wife of the
French ambassador.

That summer I often met Elizabeth in the Green
Park with Jacqueline, the Massiglis' adopted daughter,
who was about the same age as my son. The children
played together whilst Elizabeth gave me many details
about her new and exalted position, and she even per-
suaded me to allow my son to accept an invitation from
Jacqueline, one afternoon when the ambassador and his
wife were absent, to visit her nursery at the embassy and
play with a new electric train from Switzerland.

My son had just finished his famous film role as the
son of an imaginary ambassador. He now accompanied
the little daughter of a real ambassador to her embassy,
which closely resembled the dummy one built at the
studios at Shepperton. There was the same impressive
hall with its ornamental staircase, and the French
tapestries with the woven fleurs-de-lis. Elizabeth and
I took tea while the children lay on the floor playing trains,
but I soon noticed that Jacqueline was already trying out
her powers of allurement on the little boy with whom she
was obviously in love. This was the apprenticeship of

a future pretty woman. She even stretched her imagination to the point of staging a slight attack of nerves, and I thought she looked delightful stamping her pretty feet as she faced him in her Scottish plaid skirt with its myriad pleats.

The dark-skinned gazelle at my side was also growing up. Just as she had become conscious of a personality the first day an English sales girl knelt down to help her try on a pair of shoes, so now her life was quite changed by the possession of a passport. She began, without entirely losing her simplicity, to note the things which surprised her, and even to judge her superiors. Not every woman, for instance, was like the general's wife who embroidered her lingerie or made lace. Some women had not learned to do anything with their hands but to hold a cigarette. She told me this as if she had made a most surprising discovery.

Thanks to me, she had learned to put money aside.

'I have a dowry,' she announced proudly, and when I repeated the word 'dowry' after her, she went on hurriedly: 'Oh, I do so want to get married, madame, but not to a man of my own race. I have a French passport. I should like to marry a Frenchman.'

It was this idea, I fancy, that made her suddenly leave her post at the embassy and strike out on her own. She had a little money, she owned a passport, she now spoke English as well as French, and she had a tremendous desire to add to the vividness of her impressions. Nevertheless she remained aghast at her own audacity.

'I am very sad to leave England,' she said to me almost miserably on the eve of her departure. 'I have been so happy here.'

'Perhaps you will come back, Elizabeth?'

'Oh no, madame. I cannot hope for that. I shall not forget you, madame.'

'I shall not forget you, Elizabeth.'

'But you have nothing to remember me by. I shall give you the Virgin of Brazzaville.'

She opened her bag and thrust her little black hand amongst a curious collection of objects.

'Here!' she cried.

The statuette was about two inches in height, rather heavy, painted gold with a good strong base. She had been given it by the nuns of Brazzaville, and in her mind this Virgin had the very special quality of rediscovering lost mothers.

During a severe air-raid in 1944, Elizabeth had found me in tears. I was thinking about my mother whom I had left in France, wondering if I would ever see her again. Elizabeth nestled against us and produced her Virgin of Brazzaville, which we set up on a table in the hall flanked by two tiny cacti in pots which played the role of candles, and when the bombs fell too close Elizabeth, my child, the pekinese, and I all crouched under the table.

'You see,' she now said, 'the Virgin of Brazzaville helped you to find your mother again.'

'Yes,' I agreed.

'Then,' said Elizabeth, 'take her, madame. She will remind you of your little friend from Djibuti.'

CHAPTER XXII

MY SON, WHO was at a preparatory school, was to have his tonsils removed at the London clinic. Though he was still young to sit for his common entrance, I had been asked to let him try if only for the experience it would give him. As soon as the attempt was disposed of, he came to town. Our first appointment was with a radiologist in Harley Street. On our way home for lunch I asked him if he had any hope of passing.

'I don't know,' he answered, but he took my arm and put his weight on it so that I knew he was more nervous than he cared to admit. The thought of going into hospital that evening added to his exasperation, and he exclaimed:

'Of course I'm only twelve.'

'Twelve is quite old,' I said, laughing. 'At eleven my father was already digging coal with grown men at the Grand' Combe, that sunburnt land in the Midi. You remember, I told you about the vines, the olive-trees, and the cicadas?'

He looked at me, surprised, a little hurt. How could I explain that at twelve not even I had been treated like a child? Now, what with schools, national service, and the university, boys remain children till they are well in their twenties!

We lunched very simply in the kitchen, after which I sent him to rest for half an hour. He looked quickly through his stamp collection, then, snatching his teddy bear, spoke to it roughly as if ashamed to need a toy that had been with him through babyhood, through two major operations, through the making of his films, and during long journeys across Germany, Austria, and France.

At five we walked through streets warm with June sunshine to the London clinic.

As soon as we were shown to the comfortable white room he went to bed, but I was shocked because though he tried politely to hide it, his only interest was in the test match.

'May I put the radio on and listen to the results?' he asked suddenly.

'Certainly.   Shall we first say prayers?'

We asked for courage for the night, and a few moments later, feeling very sad, I left him and walked back to Piccadilly.

It was Ascot week and the Begum Aga Khan was staying in London.   Every afternoon she was photographed in the royal enclosure wearing a beautiful Paris dress.   She and I did not meet on this occasion, but on my return home I was handed a very large box of chocolates with her compliments.   Ascot that afternoon had been superb, she said, but what had struck her most was the blue of the young Queen's eyes.   She would telephone the next day for news of my son.

Through my drawing-room windows I could see the untidy tangle of rich motor-cars bringing débutantes to a party, and it struck me that I would be wise to work, to wash, to iron, and perhaps to read.   I was too anxious about my son's operation to watch the outside scene with equanimity.   The dances, the supper parties, and the races I would not go to made me dislike the thought of them.   Perhaps I was neither quite young enough, nor quite old enough to be in tune with the noise and laughter round me.

Is it the lot of a woman never to be satisfied? Tears, laughter, alarms, desires, wishing to rest and wishing to dance, wishing to eat and wishing to slim, jealous of beautiful dresses but too thrifty to compete, anxious . . . yes, too anxious to think about anything.

I telephoned my son at nine the next morning but his voice, pathetically uncertain, reminded me of when he was very small. A nurse was arriving to take him up to the operating theatre and I was asked not to visit him till four.

I found him propped up against pillows and very drowsy. The surgeon was there, and having taken me into the corridor, he showed me a small bottle in which were the enucleated tonsils.

'I read how a Paris surgeon took yours out without an anaesthetic,' he said. 'So I thought you would like to see these.'

Unaccountably the sight of the blood and the memory of my own pain were too much and I fainted.

'There,' said a nurse, holding a bottle of sal volatile under my nose. 'One doesn't faint for so little.'

The surgeon looked surprised.

'I would never have guessed . . .' he began.

I excused myself on the plea that I was overtired, and to hide my confusion I asked the nurse how my son had spent his first night in hospital.

'He fell out of bed several times,' she answered briskly. 'Nightmares about some exam. . . .'

We talked about other things, and I was asked to come back in the morning.

On my return home the Begum rang up to ask about the operation, and I inquired about Ascot.

'A good day,' she answered, 'but I'm tired out. I

have been on my feet since ten, and to-morrow, my little Madeleine, after the last race I shall fly straight back to Cannes.'

I had hoped she would invite me to come and see her dresses, but she was obviously too busy and I was disappointed. I have a passion for looking at other people's dresses, to touch them, to admire them. I am not at all amused by dresses worn in fashion houses by mannequins. They have to belong to somebody I am fond of, who alters them, adapts them, and gives them life. In this way a dress becomes almost human.

We read that the queens of France used to invite courtiers to attend their toilet, but nowadays, of course, it scarcely takes a woman five minutes to change into an evening dress, and so it is impossible to make a ceremony of it.

When I was a little girl my mother, poor as she was, took hours to dress. She began by ironing the lace of her madapollam or Manchester longcloth camisole. She then threaded narrow black velvet ribbon through the holes, called *trou-trous*, in the corsage, so that the ribbon would be faintly visible under the transparent blouse. All this time she moved about the room in a petticoat of striped satin round whose pleated flounce ran a length of mauve. I passionately loved this petticoat, for we had bought it together at the Petit Louvre where it had hung with others on a sort of roundabout surrounded by excited shoppers. As eager hands unhooked these flounced petticoats from the roundabout, shaking them, they seemed alive and we were all overcome by the fevered desire of acquisition. I became on this occasion the willing accomplice to my mother's folly, for though she desperately desired a petticoat so great an expenditure was contrary to her thrifty nature, but because it was I who chose it, she succumbed. I, not she, was the culprit. She had dressed me from birth, imposing her

taste on my untrained mind, but now for the first time
I was revealing myself her adviser, capable of choosing
a petticoat.

'So you really think it will suit me?' she had asked.

Oh, that unforgettable moment when one is treated
for the first time like a grown-up!

Looking back across the years I saw her wearing this
petticoat and I even heard it rustle as she moved. She
put down her iron, and picking up the camisole fastened
it round her bust. Then bending her head she brushed
her flaming hair which cascaded down, even to the
carpet, like a river of fire. I used to watch her breathlessly, crouching in my corner, my doll in my arms.
Never have I been jealous of rich girls' nannies. Mother
and daughter, two women, talking dresses, hats, sewing,
ironing, threading ribbon—this, to my mind, was the
true picture of felicity.

Saturday morning. Must I admit it? My son was not
very affectionate in his welcome. Was he anxious? Did
his throat hurt? At Vienna when he was making his
German film we used to play cards.

'Would you like a game of bezique?'

He shook his head negatively.

I felt a pang of disillusion, as if this were just one
more memory hurled to the bottom of a childhood cupboard. I knitted, but after a few moments he looked
at me angrily as if I annoyed him with the clicking of the
needles. I thought: this is what comes of having a boy,
a son, a man. When my cousin Rolande was in hospital
and when my mother, my aunt Marie-Thérèse, and I
used to visit her, we eagerly discussed fashions, the
latest colours, sewing, knitting. Rolande would ask us
to hum the latest tune and then we would recount the
gossip of the street. Her eyes would shine and I think
we could have gone on talking all night. When the

bell rang in the wards for the visitors to go, the nurses had to tear us away.

Ascot was over and I looked forward to taking my son to Normandy for a week's holiday. The surgeon was entirely satisfied with his progress and I was to fetch him on Friday after lunch.

The nurses had dressed him and he was watching for me out of the window. He seemed taller but was pale and uncertain on his feet. There was a hydrangea on the table by his bed which I hated to leave knowing that it would be thrown away, so I put a newspaper round the pot and decided to take it to my farm. My son picked up his bag and we hailed a cab in Devonshire Place.

I sat with the hydrangea on my lap, reflecting that as it had watched over my son when he was ill, it was only right that it should enjoy life with other hydrangeas in my garden. Now, through its blue flowers, I watched my son who was demure and silent.

'My darling,' I said softly, 'I have something unpleasant to tell you.'

'Ah?' he queried.

'My darling, you have failed in your common entrance.'

He sidled nearer to me and, slipping his hand into mine, dropped his head on my shoulder. Tears filled his blue eyes.

'It's a pity,' he said, 'because I did my best. I shall have to work harder next time.'

CHAPTER XXIII

WHEN, FROM the aeroplane, Le Havre and the estuary of the Seine came into sight, the happiness on my son's face showed that he had altogether forgotten his troubles. He was in the front part of the cabin and I had been joined by a young woman of seventeen who was going to the Normandy Hotel at Deauville to work in the reception office to improve her knowledge of French. She had been there at Whitsun but came back to England because of her father's sudden death. She had been naïvely impressed by the splendours of Deauville as she had seen them during her first stay, the beautiful dresses, the wealth of jewels, and everything else that provided a direct contrast with the austerity of a puritan England. She had previously imagined that such luxury merely existed in the short stories of the more expensive magazines, and she said:

'I share the prettiest room with a French girl of my own age. I feel that this is the beginning of a new and more exciting life.'

She was born in Calcutta, but India for English people had ceased to be what it was, and her parents had been obliged to come home where her father, his health affected by the Indian climate, had died.

'I shall have to work hard,' she said, looking down at Deauville glittering below us, 'but I am not afraid of that.'

She spoke with the seriousness of a young person who had come to an important decision. One admired her quiet confidence and, glancing at my son, I prayed that he also in due course would know how to give the right turn to his life.

Our village is particularly animated on market-day, but as I walked between the stalls I noticed that there had been a rush for the local newspaper *Le Pays d'Auge* and that all my friends had formed themselves into groups, searching for something in the paper.

They were looking for the results of their children's examinations—the *brevet simple* and the *baccalauréat*. Our neighbours the Woolfs, related to the powerful widow Michelin, who had five girls and three boys were heart-broken because of three children who this term had sat for one or other of the examinations, not one passed. The father said bravely: 'They will try again in the autumn.' By contrast, the Vanniers, our butchers, were jubilant. Their daughter Mireille, who was only fifteen, had passed her *brevet* with eighteen months to spare. 'We are so happy,' said her mother at the cash-desk. 'The year started badly but now everything is going to be all right.'

It is the parents, not the children, who take the results of modern examinations to heart. Their prestige goes up or down accordingly.

Collette, the daughter of our coal merchant, who was seventeen had failed in her examination for the second time, and her father, after taking my order for a ton of Russian anthracite which by now had reached the price of £19, almost wept.

How beautiful were the roses in my garden, and what a paradise this was!

The kitchen garden was full of strawberries, and my

mother's farmyard was magnificent. The cocks and hens, born of English eggs, had improved our local breed. In fact, the cocks were ferocious and rushed to attack me.

I dug in the garden, I picked strawberries and cherries for market, I weeded paths, I clipped hedges, but although I was overworked I found it difficult to sleep at night. I was also vaguely worried about my son's future, and there sometimes ran through my mind a curious idea that a girl would have been easier to manage than a boy.

I liked to gossip with the woman who kept the local hairdresser's and beauty *salon*. As I have already pointed out I seldom went to a hairdresser myself, even in Paris or London. I was brought up not to be dependent on others. I made my own lingerie, my own dresses, I was my own manicurist, and invented my own hair styles, but I loved the atmosphere of perfumes and cosmetics, and would go to Mme Lebrun for my face-cream, eau-de Cologne, and lipsticks. She had everything that was new in Paris and we used to try out the samples together. The farmers' wives, though retaining their peasant background, came to have their hair washed and set, and Mme Lebrun's *salon* was therefore a charming meeting place.

Mme Lebrun and I were about the same age and she had a daughter, Francine, to whom she had devoted all her life.

She was one of the few women I have met who was both feminine and feminist. Feminine amongst her perfumes and lipsticks, she brought up her daughter to fend for herself like a man. Francine, as a little girl, was not allowed to cry, and fairy-stories were banned from her education. She was taught that life is cruel, and that if a girl wants to succeed she must not give way to sentiment.

At fifteen Francine, not to waste time in a plaid skirt

and flat-heeled shoes like other teen-agers who crammed for examinations and talked like Sartre, was made to leave school.   Her mother placed her with a beauty products firm that sent her to Algiers, where she showed such a flair for business that she was quickly singled out for advancement.   Francine learned English, German, and Spanish.   From Algiers she went to Tangier and from Tangier to Casablanca.   Soon she was writing to her mother from Singapore, and I remember Mme Lebrun pulling out of her hand-bag for my edification photographs of Francine, aged twenty, in shorts and a brassière, surrounded by Chinese, Japanese, and Indian admirers.   She was earning £70 a month and ran a motor-car, but announced that she was coming back to open a branch in Spain on an even larger salary.

Mme Lebrun felt immense pride in this daughter who was so brilliantly accomplishing all her own dreams. This was the ideal association between mother and daughter: two intelligent women with identical interests that bound them together in the most delightful way.

Francine's letters from Madrid, however, revealed a lessening of that strict attention to business that had hitherto been responsible for her rapid rise.   She described the wonders of the Prado.   She went increasingly to the theatre.   She danced all night.   She even began to slim.   At last came the sensational admission that she was madly in love.

'If only he had been rich!' exclaimed Mme Lebrun. 'A director of the firm, for instance.   But he earned less than she did!'

Anxious to hear the latest news about Francine, jealous perhaps that I had not a daughter as well as a son, I took my bicycle and rode down to the village.

'I am a grandmother!' announced Mme Lebrun.   'A beautiful baby boy!   Of course I'm delighted, though a little vexed, to think how little I knew my daughter.

The dear girl was a sham.   I imagined her to be a brilliant business woman.   She is nothing but a fussing, doting mother whose dream is to sit on the beach with her baby and her knitting.   She's far more maternal than I ever was.   I can't believe it.   She is not merely in love with her husband she is in love with marriage.   She wants half a dozen children.   It's no good even talking of the wonderful opportunities of a business career.   She dreams of putting on a frilly apron and cooking the lunch.   Why is it, Mme Henrey, that our children never turn out as we dream?'

The hydrangea that had watched over my son during his stay at the nursing home, took immediately in the rich soil at the foot of my vine.   Two rows of hydrangeas, many of them brought like this one from London, painted my garden blue and pink.

I continued to pick fruit, dig and hoe, but my nights brought me no rest.   We used to go upstairs soon after nine.   My son would say his prayers kneeling at my bedside, and then go to his room which was connected with mine by a narrow half-timbered opening through which I could keep an eye on him as he lay in bed, a passage like those one sees in Elizabethan houses.

He was soon asleep and I used to look forward to long hours of reading, but it often happened that soon after midnight I would droop from tiredness and put the light out.   Within a few minutes I was wide awake again. My apparent exhaustion was a mockery.   Sleep, like a mirage, remained at a distance, and for the first time in my life I found that even books lost their interest for me.

I listened to the sounds of the night.

There were owls, great numbers of them and of different sorts, but I loved their calls and learned to recognize them.   They lived in tall hollow trees in the hedges.   Though they filled the night with their hou . . .

hou . . . hou, there were other sounds just as easily dis-
tinguishable like the soft tread of our mother cats hunting
field-mice for their young, and if the kittens slept with
us, which was often the case, the mothers would call them
softly and then scratch at my door before dawn to bring
live field-mice to their offspring.

When the cows were in the home orchard (we put
them in various orchards in rotation) they would come
as close to my house as they could, and I could hear
them breathe and even cough. They were anxious for
human company and were for ever trying to knock
down the railings round my flower garden. I even
built, for added protection, a light barrier of hazel-staves
round the white railings. This I resorted to after a herd
had crashed into my garden, trampling the roses and
eating the peach-trees before settling comfortably at the
foot of my bedroom window.

At this season there were also the bats.

The soft whirring of their wings reminded me of rolls
of velvet being quickly unrolled. The flap of the wings
simulated the drop of the soft material on a shop counter.

I had been slow to understand the ways of the bats.
Each summer at dusk they flew low round the house,
but I did not guess that my house was their home as
well as mine. I had taken them as being merely things
of the night.

Both in my own bedroom and in that of my son there
were great medieval fire-places of Caen stone, the same
stone of which the pillars of Westminster Abbey are
made. I had the chimneys sealed up level with the
ceiling; the hearths became recesses in which I planned
at some future date to build book-cases.

I had noticed one summer that the hearth in my son's
fire-place was covered with droppings that might have
been those of mice. I knew, however, that this was
impossible. Kittens were continually brought up to our

rooms: there were field-mice in the garden, rats in the long avenue of stacked logs beyond the cowsheds, but no house mice. Like many women I was terrified of mice and I would have screamed my head off at the sight of one.

I then noticed that the upper part of my son's fire-place was inhabited by bats. This discovery, strangely enough, was not made by day. Bats had been flying into my room at night. They came in by the window at the left of my bed, circled once or twice, and then flew through the short passage. I went to investigate, and shining a torch into the upper part of the stone fire-place, saw several hanging like black velvet leaves.

I saw no reason to disturb them and went back to bed, but towards midnight, because of the moths and insects, I closed the window. Then as now I slept little, and I was more inclined to spend the night sewing or reading. At four-thirty, as dawn broke, a bat leaving my son's fire-place flew through the passage and circled over my bed. The circles grew in circumference. I had the impression that it was trying to tell me something and in an effort to understand I went to open the window. It immediately flew out.

As it was cold and at last I wanted to sleep, I closed the window again and put out the lamp. The room was filled with grey light. Another bat now flew through the passage and began to perform evolutions over my bed.

'Very well,' I exclaimed. 'Wait a moment.'

And I opened the window again.

This comedy was repeated four times. I thus learned that four bats inhabited my son's fire-place. At exactly four-thirty every morning, if my window was closed, I had to open it to let them out.

Their droppings covered the stone base of the fire-place and dirtied the teddy bears that used to live there.

H

Before leaving for London that summer I stupidly drove the four bats away from the fire-place.

This August something much more exciting happened.

My room, on the very first evening, was suddenly filled with the almost deafening sound of tiny squeaks as dozens of baby bats flew in through the open window and wheeled round my bed. It was about nine o'clock. I knew they were babies, not only because of their small size but because they were less clever at turning and banking than the four who had come to live with us in May. One or two gave the impression of only just having learned to fly. One flopped down on my bed, rose again, but a moment later became wedged behind the radiator. I tiptoed across the room in my night-dress: the baby's wings were folded back and it looked up at me piteously, baring its tiny teeth.

'Poor little velvet baby, wait!' I exclaimed.

I took it up and carried it to the window. It flew out immediately. I was not yet very sure of my reactions. One needs to overcome the first feeling of repulsion, but I was intrigued and ready to be friendly. It was not until I had learned a great deal more about them that the bats and I formed a passionate attachment.

I tried to close the window at various moments during the night, but as the passage and the two rooms were full of bats they would come and ask me in such a sweet way to release them that I had not the heart to refuse. Until dawn their radar squeaks formed a high-pitched background to the hooting of the owls. Then suddenly they disappeared and everything was quiet.

> Oh nuit, qu'il est divin ton silence.
> Quand les étoiles d'or scintillent sur ton front
> J'aime ton manteau merveilleux.

The babies came every evening. Actually they had no business to come in through the window. Their home was in the eaves between the half-timbering and the slate roof, but as they were so very young they mistook the aperture. I never quite discovered where they hung by day, for though the attic was full of their droppings I could not find any velvet wings, but then my house, being over four centuries old, was full of hiding-places.

Françoise Vincent, my notary's young daughter-in-law, came with her teen-age sister Anne, to drive us in her little car to the aerodrome of St. Gatien, for I was taking my son back to England for the last ten days of his summer term at school. Françoise, twenty-one, already had two little boys. Anne was to be married in October.

Françoise and Anne were contrasting examples of the modern French girl. Françoise rode fearlessly, hunted, loved to dance, played tennis at Deauville, and when the rooks descended on my cherry-trees came at my urgent request, jauntily down my orchard, her blonde hair beautifully curled, wearing a smart white blouse, a shot-gun slung across her shoulder, holding her two-and-a-half-year-old son Guillaume by the hand. She left her car in the lane. We talked a moment, and as she told me the latest news from Deauville, started to load her gun. I watched her long feminine hands with the bright red varnish on the nails, and the bracelet with the dangling gold coin. Guillaume, terrified the first time he heard a detonation, now trotted beside his mother without fear. I left them to their noisy occupation, and when Françoise thought she had burned enough powder she lit a cigarette, slung her gun over her shoulder again, and returned to my house without a curl of her pretty head having been blown out of place.

Her sister Anne did not ride, did not hunt, disliked guns and cigarettes but drove a car. They were born at Bagnoles-de-l'Orne, passionately loved their damp Normandy with its thatched roofs and apple-trees, and had been brought up on the books of Mme de Ségur, who wrote *Les Malheurs de Sophie* and *Les Petites Filles Modèles*. Though very different from little girls of Mme de Ségur's time, they remained deeply religious, believed whole-heartedly in marriage, and spoke with great respect to elderly ladies. Françoise told me she would never dream of engaging a nurse to bring up her sons, considering herself far too good a mother to hand over what was most precious in her life to a stranger. 'I hate nannies,' she said, and this was not from any reason of economy, for Françoise and her husband were rich.

Anne was to marry a young engineer who, after the most brilliant student career, was helping to rebuild the great city of Caen. She would not have much time to dance, for he worked from eight in the morning till ten at night, and her future mother-in-law had said to her:

'My son needs a wife who is both elegant and practical. You are good-looking but you must learn to cook, my dear.'

So between visits to the dressmaker, she was learning to prepare the most succulent dishes. They would have a small apartment in a new block of flats in resurgent Caen—builders and makers of to-morrow.

The air-liner rose gently from the forest aerodrome of St. Gatien, and as we wheeled over the trees, setting course for the estuary of the Seine, I could see Françoise and Anne beside their tiny car, waving good-bye. In seventy minutes we would be flying down into the haze of London.

CHAPTER XXIV

MY SON FINISHED his term at school and flew back to my mother in Normandy. I was obliged to stay in London a few days to appear in the B.B.C. feature In Town To-night.

In Paris when one appears in a programme of this sort the whole thing is done 'live,' on the spur of the moment. The French, of course, are such natural chatterboxes that neither interviewer nor interviewed is ever short of words. One waits for the red light and then breaks into a voluble high-pitched argument that lasts happily until one is told to stop. This adds excitement to the programme; on the other hand, if one's time is limited to two or three minutes, it seems more considerate to listeners to rehearse beforehand, as in England, what one is going to say.

Mr. Kenneth Grenville Myer came to see me at my flat in Piccadilly, and a few hours later sent me a script which I saw no reason to alter. I read it over aloud several times to see how it sounded, and at four I went to Broadcasting House where those who were to take part in the programme were introduced to one another.

One is made to feel so much at home that it would be hard not to achieve one's best. One starts by wanting to please the producer. There were a cyclist, a singing policeman, an airman who had baled out of a blazing aeroplane, a famous actor, and an American woman film-star. Half-way through the programme I was to say my little piece. The room resembled a theatre, and a few members of the public came to sit in the stalls. From time to time they advanced diffidently to ask for autographs, and we pretended not to be flattered. A boy about fourteen years old asked me for mine. He had large black eyes and came from Paris. His parents had sent him to learn English and he thought he must be doing well because he had understood every word. I took this as a compliment. He was very sweet, and reminded me of my son.

The next morning I flew to Villers where my son was waiting for me at the top of the orchard. He had grown still taller and was burnt by the wind and sea air. I suddenly realized that I should never again be able to lead him by the hand as Françoise led Guillaume.

'Do tell me,' I asked eagerly. 'How did I sound on the radio?'

'Oh, mother,' he answered, laughing. 'Don't please be angry, but we mixed the times up and never heard you.'

I was stupidly disappointed but I answered bravely:

'Never mind. You didn't miss anything.'

'You should see Fifine's ginger kitten,' he exclaimed as he opened the gate. 'We call him the Douanier Rousseau.'

The next morning we went to market. The season at Deauville had started and our village was crowded and gay. Mme Montague, Ernest Poulin's sister, told me that her daughter Paulette, who was exactly a year younger than my son, and her boy Michel, who was a year older, had found themselves holiday jobs to earn pocket-money. Paulette was at the laundry checking in the baskets, while Michel packed the clean linen and helped to deliver it. A woman who worked for me occasionally, plucking the fowls and cleaning the stables, told me that her little grandson was selling vegetables at the greengrocer's. The butcher's son, aged eleven, delivered his father's meat. Everybody was hard at work, making money during the season.

'Ah!' exclaimed my son angrily, 'what would I give to work like everybody else!'

We went to the baker's. He continued to grumble. At heart I sympathized with him, but I exclaimed, laughing:

'The mustard is climbing up my nose! If you don't stop grumbling I shall tweak your ears.'

'How could you?' he asked. 'You're only a woman. You would have to let go your bicycle, and then what would happen to your precious shopping?'

I sent him to buy the bread and called on Mme Sorel, the pastry-cook's wife. She was filling her window with the most delicate cakes made with farm butter and fresh cream. She and her husband owned two shops in the village and a pretty kiosk on the beach.

'Mme Sorel,' I exclaimed, 'my son wants to earn his living. Have you any use for a smart lad?'

'Oh, Mme Henrey,' she said, spreading out her hands, 'what could I do with him? Your son has never learnt to work!'

I winced but quickly answered:

'He can make a *Moka* and I'm a pretty good judge of one. I would terribly like to see him apprenticed during the holidays to a pastry-cook—an artist like your husband.'

She preened herself, and then said:

'August is no time for my husband to take on an apprentice. You have no idea of the rush, madame. We might do something during the Christmas holidays when things are quieter. On the other hand, if he isn't proud, if it didn't embarrass him, he might help Mme

Hahn at the kiosk on the beach. She works there from nine in the morning till ten or eleven at night. Your son could give her a hand at week-ends, fetching the *croissants*, the chocolate rolls, and the ice-cream, and perhaps learning to serve the customers. How would it be if he came on Sunday after lunch and stayed till eight?'

'I have an idea that this is going to do him a lot of good,' I said to Mme Sorel.

After lunch on Sunday my son, after washing himself very vigorously, asked me for his best pullover and blue shorts. He was clearly anxious to make an impression and even asked me to cut his hair.

At two-thirty as he wheeled his bicycle to the top of the orchard, we waved to him like women saying goodbye to the man of the family. I worked in the kitchen garden most of the afternoon. The sun was strong and the work hard, but I refused to give in, for the rich soil produced the most magnificent vegetables that I desperately needed. We had to produce them ourselves, for a gardener's wages would have cost me more than the value of the food. The kitchen garden was, in fact, so important that it became one of the chief subjects of discord between myself and my son. As I received dairy produce from the farm and as my mother supplied us with eggs and fowls, we could be self-supporting. Cherries, apples, and strawberries paid for our groceries. My son was now almost as strong as a man. We used often to watch him demonstrate his strength on childish games, but he refused absolutely to help in the garden. People say that children should not be made to do manual work during the holidays, that it stunts their growth and narrows their minds, but nothing vexed me so much as to see my young giant playing with a cricket ball while my mother, who was crippled with rheumatism, tried to dig up the potatoes.

At six I came in for tea. The house seemed strangely empty and the cats for once could sleep peacefully without doors being roughly opened and closed. My mother was preparing supper.

'Imagine,' she said proudly, 'how hungry he will be! One must never keep a man waiting for his meal!'

I thought of her preparing my father's dinner when I was a girl, and by a strange coincidence she was this evening making stuffed tomatoes, so beloved by men in Provence. Through the open kitchen door I could see the farmers coming to milk a herd of cows grouped round the house. The milkers came in single file carrying their stools, while the donkey from whose flanks hung the churns ambled in the rear.

At eight o'clock my son came riding his bicycle down the orchard, ringing the bell to attract our attention, and when a few moments later he came into the kitchen, he placed a cardboard box containing a very large cake on the table, exclaiming:

'Here's my pay! Is supper ready? I'm starving.'

My mother looked at me with a triumphant air, and answered:

'What did I tell you?'

And to her grandson:

'There are stuffed tomatoes, and I've just been down to draw some fresh cider.'

For a few moments he ate silently, and I realized how relieved I was to see him back. While I had been at work in the kitchen garden I could distinctly hear the ceaseless roar of Sunday traffic on the main road to Caen, and I had pictured him crossing it on his bicycle.

Soon he began to recount his adventures.

The little boy whose mind during the last eighteen months had been influenced by the English preparatory

*H

school system with its traditions, prejudices, and over-emphasis on games had come up against an entirely new code of behaviour, the code of working with enthusiasm for one's living.

'One is not allowed to sit down,' he said. 'That was the most surprising thing. One must stand up smartly with the tips of one's fingers lightly touching the counter, for if one were to sit down, Mme Hahn said, the customer would have the impression that one was tired or bored. And children, who are timid, might be put off. But though one must remain standing one must be careful not to bend over the counter, for that would be unpleasant for the pastries that are laid out on it. You see there are rules. Would you ever have guessed it?'

He was impressed. This Mme Hahn, whoever she might be, had clearly filled him with unexpected respect for trade.

'As Mme Sorel's pastries are very expensive,' he went on, 'only a few must be displayed on the counter at a time. The sight of too much food might rob people of their appetite, or then again they might think our cakes were not selling so fast as those next door.'

From time to time Mme Hahn sent him off with a wicker basket to fetch new supplies of *croissants* and chocolate buns from the shop in the village. The pastry-cooks in white, with tall white hats, stood round M. Sorel in the kitchens, and there was a delightful smell of freshly crushed almonds and burning apple-logs, for a pastry-cook's ovens are not heated by coal but by apple-logs. He had been introduced to the cooks at three o'clock when he reported for duty. They were just finishing lunch, and as he shook them by the hand they gave him a pat on the shoulder to welcome him into the corporation.

'Won't it be wonderful at Christmas when I'm really apprenticed?' he exclaimed. 'M. Sorel asked me to sit down with the others and have a Plombières ice made with fresh cream from the Poulin farm. I think we ought to sell them our cream, don't you think, mother?'

This ice had freshly ground hazel-nuts and candied fruit and was popular on hot afternoons at Mme Hahn's kiosk on the beach. Mme Hahn had unlocked the door to let him in. It was a rule that they must lock themselves into the kiosk because of the till.

Mme Hahn taught him the price of everything, and how to squeeze lemons for the lemonade.

'It's not like in England,' he said. 'When a customer asks for a lemonade we take a fresh lemon which costs forty francs and squeeze it into a glass. Then I fetch a bottle of Evian water from the giant refrigerator and open it in front of the customer, who pours it himself into the crushed lemon in the glass. We have to work very fast, for at times there are lots of people, fat men with white linen ski caps (that is the great fashion), children who first come to ask the price of what they want, and then return holding the money tightly in their hands, and young women in shorts with silver bracelets.'

'Now,' said his grandmother greedily, 'you must cut the cake.'

My son blushed with pride.

'It is a Polonaise,' he said expertly. 'Mme Sorel gave it to me when I said good-bye.'

I was never able to make my son work at his Latin during the holidays, but I was determined that he should learn to write accurately both in English and French. Every day I gave him long and difficult French dictations: when they were finished I made him translate them into English. Like most temperamental women I was short-tempered and could not forgive him for spelling mistakes. Each misplaced accent, each wrong termination, struck me as a personal affront, and often I was convinced that girls were cleverer than boys. His lack of enthusiasm riled me. I would have been so terribly grateful at his age for the opportunities I was giving him.

He could now take down a page of French with reasonable accuracy, but after all any shorthand typist in Paris could have done as much. But as soon as he was left to himself, to write an essay for example, his style was original and full of colour, and this gift seemed inherent in him.

With the problem of his future continually in my mind, I began to wonder how his standard compared to that of a French boy of similar age.

M. Salesse was the local schoolmaster and his wife was head of the girls' school. They were both intelligent, and because the teaching profession was relatively a good deal better paid than in England they occupied a favoured position. Their daughter Michèle, who had been learning English, first near London and later with a family in Scotland, was of the same age as my son.

I asked M. Salesse if he would give my son a thorough test. There was an excellent college at Trouville; it would be interesting to know if he would be capable of taking his place there. On his return from this test my son exclaimed:

'You know, mother, it would be a pleasure to work with a man like M. Salesse.'

The next day M. Salesse and his daughter came down my orchard. I asked Michèle in English if she had enjoyed her stay in Scotland. She told me about the wonderful scenery and the porridge, while her father looked at her in admiration, for though he understood English he could not speak it. I asked Michèle if she had seen my farm and requested my son to show her around while I talked to M. Salesse.

The schoolmaster confessed that he had found my son's composition surprising.

'Some of the credit is mine,' I declared, laughing. 'I began teaching him when he was five, and even now we do a dictation every day after which he translates the French into English.'

'That is not orthodox,' he declared firmly. 'It would not meet with the approval of the teaching profession. We schoolmasters concentrate on analysis. We keep our dictations short and make the children analyse each word. Unless a child can explain, for instance, why he terminates a verb in a certain way, how can one be sure that he hasn't got it right by accident?'

'I don't know any grammar,' I admitted guiltily. 'I do everything by instinct.'

'No, really?' he cried. 'But you would never pass an examination. You would be ploughed. What would happen to you if you had to go back to school?'

His manner softened and he went on:

'Well now, we are discussing your son, not you. I feel that he might have some trouble with his handwriting if he were to go to a French school. His handwriting is so particularly English. We in France are very careful about giving each letter an elegant slope. Our professors are adamant about this. In mathematics your son appears to be up to standard, but then they add and subtract in such a curious way in England that though he got all the sums I set him right, I was quite unable to discover how he did them!'

The children came back from the farm.

'So you found it difficult to accustom yourself to Scotch porridge?' I asked Michèle. 'It's delicious with cream, but then, of course, there may not have been any cream. Food even in Scotland is still rather difficult.'

'Oh, but the table manners are so much better!'

exclaimed Michèle, looking severely at her father. 'One never hears a sound when English people drink their soup, and they never dip crusts of bread into the sauce.'

M. Salesse accepted his daughter's reproaches with an indulgent smile. He merely said:

'My darling, it was precisely for you to learn good manners that we sent you across the Channel!'

She looked up at him with gratitude and asked gently:

'May I stay and do a dictation with Bobby? Afterwards I could translate the French into English.'

She was already a little woman. Over her white blouse with its long white sleeves and Peter Pan collar she wore a laced bodice. Her wide skirt was beautifully cut and she was a picture of seductiveness. My boy was tall, fair, blue-eyed but still awkward and childish.

'I will walk with M. Salesse as far as the gate,' I said. 'My mother will give you your dictation.'

I was making a bonfire when the girl and the boy came through the scarlet runners towards me. Michèle held a sheet of paper in her hand.

'Here's my translation, Mme Henrey. I'm afraid I used the dictionary quite a lot whereas Bobby never opened it. We compared notes afterwards. He takes more liberties than I do. Father makes me translate everything word by word, whereas Bobby just goes for the sense. He *thinks* in both languages.'

She looked so very earnest as the sun shone on the prettiest cardigan thrown lightly over her shoulders.

'What a smart cardigan, Michèle. I love the design!'

She considered my statement with perfect self-possession.

'Many people admire it,' she agreed. 'Mother made it.'

She removed it from her shoulders and handed it to me. The stitch was new and intriguing.

'It's supposed to look like tweed,' she said.

My son had bent his blond head over us, anxious to grasp the mathematical plan of the design. When it suited him he was quick to understand. And here was my mother who had followed the children, as interested as any of us. Expert seamstress she had never tried her hand at knitting, convinced for some reason that she could not overcome the initial difficulties. Besides, she thought knitting tedious, but when she was shown a finished garment she was the first to exclaim in admiration. Michèle now told us that she was knitting a waistcoat in pink. It was quite adorable but . . . Here she closed her eyes, showing long black lashes:

'I'm dreadfully afraid I shan't have enough wool to finish it.'

'You must buy some more,' I said.

'But I can't, madame. That's the tragedy. Mother bought it before the war, and of course everything was so much better then. We all know that.'

Her voice sounded quite pathetic. What a serious person is a little girl!

'Michèle!' I exclaimed to change the conversation. 'You have the tiniest feet. How very elegant!'

'Mother's are even smaller,' she answered, blushing. 'Just consider! She takes an English two-and-a-half shoe whereas I take a three. Granny, mother, and I are all small women—with small waists, small hands, and small feet.'

The great important word had escaped her lips. She was already a *woman*. She knitted, she sewed, she could wear her mother's shoes. Her mother would not dream of making a dress without first consulting her. Mother and daughter—two friends, two women!

'Tell me, Michèle,' I asked, 'when you are quite grown up, will you be a schoolmistress like your mother?'

'I suppose so,' she answered sadly, 'but my dream was to have been a ballet dancer.'

She turned to my son and added enthusiastically:

'How lucky you were to act in a film when you were eight. If only the same thing could have happened to me!'

She sighed.

'I do so love the theatre!'

She looked at the boy admiringly but he, trying to appear modest, kicked awkwardly at the gravel path with the tip of his enormous shoe.

CHAPTER XXV

BECAUSE THE land is so valuable our farms are tiny. Sixty acres is a good size—undulating apple orchards in which graze our cows, here and there a rich hayfield, a half-hidden stream, and distant views of the sea. Ducks and chickens wander from orchard to orchard. The peasants are stubbornly and delightfully backward, deeply religious, and prefer to milk by hand.

My son was seldom happy away from his farm, for he enjoyed the same liberty as the animals round him. It was when I tried to harness his energy that our characters clashed. The most spectacular of these occasions took place one Sunday morning in September. He had come down late to breakfast, refused to listen to morning service on the radio, played golf amongst the hens with my mother's walking-stick, and made such a nuisance of himself that snatching the walking-stick I belaboured him and sent him off to bed without any lunch.

Towards two o'clock I was digging round the strawberry beds when his young friend Michel Gilles arrived.

'Good afternoon, ma'am.'

Then with spontaneous politeness:

'Do please give me the spade, ma'am, and allow me to dig. You can pull out the weeds.'

Michel Gilles, fifteen-year-old son of a locksmith, was a giant whose parents owned a few acres on the road to

St. Vaast. He and my son had arranged to bicycle to Deauville, and after a few moments Michel asked me where he was.

'I have punished him,' I answered. 'Tell me, Michel, are you ever rude to your parents?'

'No, ma'am. My father would beat the life out of me. All the same, it's a pity about Bobby being punished, for it's my last chance to see him before you go back to England.'

Michel went to school too, a technical school at Dives where boys tried one trade after another till they found one that suited them. Michel had decided to be a turner.

'Is that really what you want to be, Michel?'

'No, ma'am, but you know how things are. The bit of land my mother inherited isn't large enough to keep us. I pretend I'm glad for my father's sake, but it's not what I should have liked to be. It's so monotonous. And the large factories are very noisy. Still, one has to be reasonable, doesn't one, ma'am?'

His blue eyes interrogated me. I smiled sympathetically, and he went on, without ceasing to dig.

'My brother and I have grants from the government, and the food is wonderful, much better than at home. Roast beef twice a week, and on the other days roast lamb or veal, besides red wine, plenty of butter, and as much bread as we can eat, and as I volunteer to clear up after meals I'm allowed to collect the bread the boys leave and bring it home to mother for the chickens. Then on Saturdays I help a man at Dives to load his truck after market, and for that I not only have a lift home but I get a cake of soap for mother and a packet of cigarettes for father.'

He rested against his spade a moment and cried:

'To own a truck and sell at market, that's what I should like to do in life, ma'am. I wonder sometimes if

Bobby realizes how lucky he is, having enough money to buy a truck if he wanted to. What could be more exciting than to buy in one place and sell in another? Dad won't see that. He says that trade fluctuates, but a good workman is always sure of a job. Dad's for safety.'

'How beautifully you dig, Michel. Your rows are so straight.'

His mother, Deaf Gravé's daughter, had trained him well. There was nothing she did not know how to do, and she was very strict with her boys, putting them to work on the smallholding the very moment they came home from school. Sunday afternoon was their only time off. She could not stand seeing them idle, but what struck one most about the boys was their gallantry. They were as gallant with her as if they had been born a century ago. Michel's politeness was amazing. He could not see me doing anything, whether lifting potatoes or carrying a sack of grain, without immediately rushing to help. It was instinctive. But then, as Michel said, if he had failed in this respect he would have had the life beaten out of him.

At this point my mother arrived with her grandson following two paces behind.

'I gave him permission to get up,' said my mother, trying to excuse her leniency. 'It wasn't so much for him as for Michel whom I saw crossing the orchard. I didn't think it fair to spoil his only free afternoon.'

'Very well,' I said to my son. 'You may go.'

'Come on then, Michel. Good-bye, granny. Good-bye, mother.'

His voice was still stormy and heavy with resentment.

'You had better give them some money for their tea,' I said to my mother. 'They will be hungry after their ride to Deauville.'

'I have done so already,' she answered.

The two boys came back at six, their eyes bright with
pleasure. Oh, the wonderful things they had done,
watching the trawlers unloading fish at the quayside at
Trouville, mingling with the travellers from Le Havre
by the ferry, buying a loaf and some chocolate which
they ate in a fisherman's bar frequented by Michel's
grandfather, Deaf Joseph, and washing down their
collation with frothy beer.

That night, when he was in his pyjamas about to go
to bed, my son came into my room and asked:

'Can we say prayers? I'm tired.'

We recited the Lord's Prayer.

'Is that all?' he queried after a moment's pause.
'Aren't we saying anything else to-night?'

We were in the habit of reciting a prayer of our
own that I had composed when he was a baby. I could
not bring myself to change it, enjoying the illusion
of thinking him small, but to-night I was vexed and
said:

'Go on by yourself if you wish, but it has been a bad
Sunday.'

His eyes were full of defiance. He went to bed, but
not being able to sleep asked if he could go and fetch
Rousseau, the kitten.

'Certainly,' I answered.

Towards midnight I went quietly to his room to see
how he was. The ginger kitten was curled up in his
folded arm, and he was fast asleep. As I knelt beside
them, Rousseau purred. On the other side of the bed,
peeping out from the sheets, was the teddy bear he had
rather grudgingly brought from London. I kissed my
little demon gently on the forehead. The skin was cool
and smooth. He must be dreaming of the road to
Trouville. I kissed him a second time, for he seemed a

baby yet, almost unchanged since that year when he acted in *The Fallen Idol*.

I went back to bed but could not read. The radio was unable to soothe my nerves. I must have been terribly on edge. I took up the New Testament, and turning to the Epistle of St. Paul to the Ephesians, read:

'. . . provoke not your children to wrath: but bring them up in the nurture and admonition of the Lord.'

Was he really as naughty as I sometimes believed?

CHAPTER XXVI

AUTUMN IS the season in which London looks its best. As the plane-trees shed their leaves in the parks and the afternoons grow shorter, the theatres try out new plays, the dress-making houses send one invitations to their collections, and everybody appears anxious to get back to work.

My duties as a mother would now cease until the Christmas holidays. I became again a woman who thought and acted for herself. I was aware of a quickening tempo. My mail became larger, and the green folders from the cutting agencies fatter and more frequent. In other ways my existence in the heart of London was lonely. Presumably I myself was responsible for this state of affairs. I was far too concerned with the fear of slipping back. I am always so little satisfied that I have no capacity to enjoy the process of going forward. I would be intrigued to discover to what extent successful women are made happy by their success. I mean, of course, career women. The success brought about by marriage and motherhood is quite different, and much more likely to be satisfying.

I urge myself on towards success, however, with the seriousness that distinguishes clever girls in examinations.

They do try so hard! I want very much to be the head girl. I have not come all the way from the heat of Montmartre to be satisfied with a second prize. I dream of success in terms of an Eve Curie, a Jeanne Lanvin, or a Marie Laurencin.

England is the country, I think, where in literature a woman has the best chance to succeed, perhaps because most people are wise enough to know that she will never be a serious menace to the best men writers. The giants in literature are invariably of the male sex. London editors are very wise about this. Most of them make a point of having women review women's books. We are thus usefully reminded that our spheres are entirely different.

But whereas most men prefer to read books by men, women please their own sex by showing themselves much cleverer in describing the reactions and thoughts of women. This most natural state of affairs did not immediately enter my mind. As a young woman I rather envied the male writer. It takes one a long time to accept one's limitations and to become proud of them.

If I sometimes feel a little jealous of the tremendous ovations of a Claire Bloom or a Margot Fonteyn filling the lighted theatre, the slow progress of an authoress gives her an equal though more sober satisfaction. Autumn saw a new book go out under my name. January was to see *The Little Madeleine* produced in New York. There is a feeling that the quality of a writer's work depends on the slowness with which each volume appears. This, of course, is nonsense. The giants of the nineteenth century tumbled books out of the presses. You need merely consider the output of George Sand. The idea that you must take a long time between each book is modern.

Do men writers keep up amongst themselves a

delightful exchange of thought? Possibly. One recalls
the fine compliments between François Mauriac and
Graham Greene that enlivened the *Figaro* when M.
Mauriac received with such justification the Nobel
Prize for literature. The work of both men is powerfully stamped with the vigour that makes a man's work
supreme. On the other hand, Susan Yorke, whose *The
Widow* gave new dignity to the modern novel, writes me
such penetrating and delightful letters that I doubt if a
man could equal them. One must not be surprised if one
is a woman to find oneself mainly helped by other women.
Vera Brittain, whose *Testament of Youth* I consider the
finest autobiography of the century, undoubtedly continues to influence many women writers. Critics like
Edith Shackleton of *The Lady* and Margaret Pope of
Woman's Journal have nursed me since the days I wrote
obscurely under a pseudonym. The women's papers are
apt to show a kindness to women writers that reflects the
wisdom of such women as Dorothy Sutherland, Winifred
Johnson, Julia Cairns, and Joanna Chase. A famous
editress once said to me: 'In London one does not meet
any jealousy between career women.'

C. E. Vulliamy, possibly the greatest of the male
critics, criticized the Madeleine books in prose as exciting
as a mountain torrent. The conflict comes when men
find it difficult to accept the reactions of feminine women.
The Times Literary Supplement tried to be scathing about
Madeleine 'tottering on her high heels.' On the other
hand I, like columnist Eve Perrick, am basically uninter-
ested in Hemingway's misfortunes of a man and a fish.
Thus runs the difference between the sexes.

What is wonderful is the great eagerness of young
women to write, but their letters often betray a feminine
resentment against an increasingly scientific, warlike,
inhuman world—a world in which men appear almost
to take pleasure in doing without women.

Sanmarie,
5 Ross Street,
Boksburg West,
Transvaal.

DEAR MRS. HENREY,

I dined with friends in town. I remarked that whenever I picked up a magazine I found an article dealing with inter-space travel and exploration, or stars millions of light-years hence, or the terrific progress in the world of flight, and I said: 'It bores and frightens me.'

I know if I fall ill to-day and am taken to hospital I am grateful for the wonderful medical aids to kill pain and speed recovery, or if I have a baby the chances are greatly in my favour that everything will be normal. I am glad to switch on the electric light when it grows dusk, turn on the radio to hear the news and listen to music, heat the oven when I start to mix a cake. I like air travel, but in life I achieve less certainly than the women of fifty years ago who ran her home, sewed, cooked, and brought up a large family in peace and content.

Leontine Sagan once told me that I was 100 per cent feminine, and when I retorted that being a woman this was only natural, she laughed and exclaimed: 'It doesn't always follow!'

I am not South African but Rhodesian. My home was outside Umtali, a town on the borders of Southern Rhodesia and Portuguese East Africa. I was taken there at the age of six weeks, and the name of our village is Penhalonga. My father was Welsh from St. Asaph. He was not good-looking but was tall and charming. I was proud of him and loved to be seen out with him.

We lived half-way up a mountain. The climate was subtropical, and after lessons in the village school I would play alone with invisible children in the shade of the

garden, acting, talking, and dancing all the long, hot
afternoons.

At ten I went to boarding-school in Umtali, and there
spent five years in a lovely setting—curling, curving,
graceful mountain ranges, lush green vegetation, misty
mornings and hot days. I loved my girls' school. I
love it still, and when I close my eyes I see it. When
I was there beauty crept into my heart and stained my
soul.

After leaving school I went to Beira, a Portuguese port
where I worked in a shipping office and lived on £10 a
month—£7 10s. for board, £1 10s. a month bus fares, and
£1 for myself. I was young, pretty, and very gay.
I married Sandy, from Aberdeen, a man who was my
complete opposite.

We left Beira and came down here where I had a baby,
but I did not like the Transvaal. I still do not like it.
I had always lived in small places and had been a little
spoilt. Suddenly I was alone in what seemed to me a
'foreign' place. People looked hard and sour. I had
never run a house before and was bewildered. Sandy
was always busy. I was always alone. I wanted desperately to make friends, but it was like leaning across
a wide gulf trying to clasp hands and never succeeding,
and I envied other young women.

I missed the colour of Beira, the warmth I had been
accustomed to, the constant interest of the ships in port.
Beira had a mixed population and, because all my life
I have admired feminine beauty, I loved to watch the
picturesque and lovely women, Portuguese, Flemish,
French, who were so beautifully dressed. The winters
in the Transvaal froze my brain. I was miserable in the
bitterly cold high-veld winds, and with all my heart I
longed for the velvet softness of the tropics.

My baby, though pretty to look at, cried constantly
and no doctor could tell me why. I looked after my

home and read. I taught myself to sew beautiful
lingerie with fine pin tucks, insertions, and lace, and in
this way I found a little peace.

When my son was six I joined a theatre group, and as
soon as I started to act I seemed to spring alive. I
played Bess, the sister, in *They Walk Alone*, and I was
very pleased because I believed I looked the perfect
farmer's wife. South Africa was then forming her first
national theatre. Leontine Sagan and André Hugenot
were travelling round the country holding auditions.
On the opening night of our play Leontine Sagan was
there. Two months later she sent for me to play Lady
Caroline in the National Theatre's first production, *Dear
Brutus*. I sent my son to boarding-school, and three
days later was in Cape Town for rehearsals. Thus began
a delightful experience.

We opened at the Little Theatre, which is attached to
the university. The theatre stands in a lovely garden
under the majesty of Table Mountain. The Governor-
General and all the Cabinet were at the first night. The
play was successful, and with true feminity I seized hold
of all the loveliness that the Cape has to offer. We then
toured thirty-eight towns, some large, some mere dorps,
ending in Johannesburg.

Three years ago we moved into the house from which
I write this letter. It is in the country two miles from
Boksburg, fifteen from Johannesburg, and we built it
ourselves. The Transvaal, except for the eastern part,
has little beauty but here there are trees and it is green
in summer. I do not go out much because I can seldom
have the car, but I still act when I can.

I want urgently to become like you, a woman writer.
All my life I have had the desire. Lately it has become
overwhelming, and if I am to be faithful I must do
something about it. I will always act when the opportunity presents itself, but when one writes one needs no

play, no producer, and no assembled audience. Besides, women want to create things that last.

I have a lot of free time, for we have two good servants. Jack, the houseboy, has been with me nine years, a small, crumpled little African. He speaks little English and I do not speak Afrikaans. Neither does he understand that Rhodesian which we call 'kitchen kaffir,' but as he is faithful, clean, stupid, and kind, we get along very well. Jonas, the garden boy, is very young. He comes from Nyasaland, is intelligent, and blind in one eye. He looks after the fowls, the turkeys, and the dogs.

I read enormously, for I am in the stage when the woman who is to write reads everything she can lay her hands on. There is a lovely library in Boksburg. Mrs. Dix is the chief librarian. One day when she and her staff were discussing new books, one of the girls said: 'We must get *The Little Madeleine* for our women readers. Mrs. Mitchell would like it.' That is how I first came to read the book.

Our house is built in the shape of a U, and in the courtyard I have a private garden of my own. Camellias, white and pink, grow in tubs, and because they stand under broad eaves they are sheltered from the frost and have blooms throughout the winter. Madonna lilies grow in clumps between paving-stones, so do irises, white, amethyst, and pink, and in the centre are hydrangeas and an orange-tree.

The rest of the garden has a broad lawn on one side (the heavy rains have just made it emerald green), and on the other side two shallow terraces, the higher one having a rose garden, the lower one having twin cypress-trees, mauve Pride of India, Bottle Brush, Snow Ball, and gold and purple irises.

I grow my own vegetables and several fruit trees are beginning to bear. I also have an orchid. Early this year, while lunching out of doors on a farm in north-east Transvaal, I noticed an orchid growing in the fork of a tree. My hostess, seeing my delight, offered me a section of the plant. I brought it carefully home, placed it in a pot filled with pure peat moss, and stood the pot on another in an aluminium tray filled with pebbles, sand, and two inches of water. The tray remained in the courtyard till April, when we went to Rhodesia on holiday. Before leaving it I carried it indoors and placed it under a north-facing window where it now stands. Two months ago it began to bloom, five greenish-lemon flowers, speckled with deep orange spots, on one stem. The leaves are long and pointed.

Shall I tell you what I look like?

I have very long red hair and my complexion has the milkiness that red-haired women have. Your mother must have been the same. My eyes are blue. I have, of course, to use a lot of make-up on my lashes and brows, for they are colourless. As a very little girl I would not play in the sun for fear of ruining my complexion, and even in the Transvaal I never go into hot sunlight without a wide hat, sunglasses, and a sunshade. I thus look my best in the evening, because I can lower my neckline and discard the glasses.

And now I have embroidered you a small handkerchief. Will you please accept it with my love and put it immediately in your hand-bag?

MARY MITCHELL.

My son now passed very creditably his common entrance examination and I made arrangements for him to go to Downside in January. The fact that he was bilingual and that I was anxious for him eventually to learn Spanish, convinced me that he would be happy at this famous school beside the monastery of St. Benedict.

CHAPTER XXVII

I DECIDED towards the end of February to spend ten days at Gstaad in Switzerland. I had been ill with conjunctivitis followed by the prevailing influenza.

Snow was falling irregularly when I arrived at London airport and it was my first morning out of bed. After the various formalities, we entered the Geneva–Milan aeroplane. The air hostess showed us to our places, enjoined us to fasten our safety-belts, and handed round the morning newspapers. She was very slim in her grey uniform and I began to wonder what sort of life was hers, half on the ground, half in the clouds. I recalled how often when I was a little girl my mistresses used to shout: 'Come down from the clouds, Madeleine, and be more attentive!'

The engines made a dreadful noise as we bumped awkwardly on inflated tyres along wide avenues of tarmac. We turned at right angles, then stopped. A few wisps of smoke came out of the pilots' compartment and the air hostess asked us to unfasten our safety-belts and follow her down a little ladder to the tarmac. Snow was still falling and we were swept by a cruel wind. The women passengers grouped together: the men stayed by themselves. In due course the pilot came to tell us that it was nothing, nothing at all, but it was better to have noticed it on the ground than in the air. The coach would come and take us back to the airport. He seemed very pleased and beamed with satisfaction. What were we, ignorant passengers, not to be equally delighted that whatever had happened had happened at such an opportune moment?

Ten minutes later we were back in the waiting-room, seated in osier arm-chairs. The company would treat us to coffee. The passengers cheered up. It is always pleasant to get something for nothing. A young woman in a beige coat, her hands in her coat pockets, alone appeared rather anxious, but very sweetly she came to ask if she might bring me coffee when she went to fetch hers.

She was Indian, born in Calcutta. Her dark eyes were soft and beautiful, but I was chiefly fascinated by the long plaits, shiny and black, which wreathed her forehead like a diadem. I congratulated her on the beauty of her hair. I imagined the lovely picture she would make in native dress, for her loveliness shone out in spite of her beige coat, and I asked her if she had been long away from the country of her birth.

Yes, she answered, quite a long time. Before the war she used to return home to visit her family. It was a long journey that needed much preparation. Now one could leave London in the morning and be at New Delhi the next day. One ceased to be surprised at this marvel. But in spite of this she did not desire to return home, for her country was ravaged by massacres and famine. She told me about girlhood friends who had been dragged out of railway carriages, raped, robbed, and murdered, but how could English people living in comfortable houses in Surrey understand these things when they read about them in the paper? India, in spite of air travel, was so far away, and English people were so very concerned with the butter ration, the £25 travel money, and the football pools. They were always so proud of what they did. She had learned not to talk about her troubles. Was it not, to a great extent, the fault of the Indians themselves, if they were being massacred?   There were, of course, Englishmen who until they lost their jobs had spent most of their lives in India.   They understood.   They sympathized.   They had hearts.   Their heads were not crammed with madcap political ideas.   Really, madam, you should have seen our country when it formed part of the empire—the colour, the wealth, the retinues of our maharajahs.   Our costumes are so lovely and our race so noble.

I looked at her dark hands: she wore a wedding-ring.

'Yes,' she answered.   'I embraced the Christian faith and I am a widow.   I have a little girl.'

'How old is your little girl?'

'Twenty-four,' she said quietly.   'She is learning to be a doctor.'

I must have shown my surprise.   She appeared so very young.   I shall never believe people again when they tell me that eastern women lose their beauty when they are still almost girls.   My companion had a smooth, unwrinkled skin, her eyes sparkled, and her hair was vigorous and black.

A loud-speaker broke into my thoughts.   Were we bound for Geneva or Milan?   The company regretted to inform us that our flight would be delayed for another two hours at least.   We were invited to take lunch at the company's expense.

My companion remained looking for a moment with pained eyes at the inanimate square box from which the suave voice had come.   Then turning to me:

'I shall miss my train from Milan to Florence,' she said. 'I am going out to fetch a friend who is desperately ill. This was to be my first journey by air, but they all told me it was so much quicker to fly, and here I am losing precious hours.   I might even arrive too late.'

The restaurant, with its vast windows overlooking the tarmac, was animated.   I also would miss my connection at Geneva. The snow had ceased and the sky was almost blue. There was even a suggestion of sunshine. I was vexed to think that the weather had nothing to do with our delay. Swissair must already be nearing Geneva. The men said that our radio had been faulty and one wondered why the fault could not have been discovered earlier.

The air hostess had reserved a table for the four women passengers. A neat little woman, very slim, finding herself beside me, exclaimed in an impeccable French which I nevertheless judged to be Swiss:

'And to think that if it had not been for all this business we should already be nearing Geneva! As it is the second part of my journey, which is relatively so short, will end by taking the longest time. Consider, madame, that only yesterday I was in Montreal, and that we reached London in thirteen hours. One can't help being amazed, don't you think? I have to talk about it. When something surprises me, I feel that everybody should join in my surprise.'

She had no trouble to enthuse me. To begin with I passionately love Canada, especially the province of Quebec, and was only too willing to talk about Montreal. The other two women at our table warmed to our excitement, though only one spoke French. My Indian friend understood not a word, but I selfishly, after a journey to India in my wicker arm-chair in the lounge, now flew across the Atlantic and up the St. Lawrence waterway. My companion, I noticed, was deaf, for very unobtrusively she had placed a tiny box, like a gold cigarette-case, on the table-cloth. She would talk, then listen carefully for my answer. I have always felt an immense sympathy for persons isolated by deafness. Moreover in my experience they are invariably intelligent, sensitive, and full of imagination. They live a second life within themselves and read enormously.

I

'I do so apologize,' she exclaimed, turning to the Indian woman, 'for not speaking English.' My Indian friend smiled, having sensed the meaning of the words by the deaf woman's gestures. 'Indeed I should speak English,' she went on, turning to me, 'having spent four and a half years in Canada, but it is because of my difficulty in hearing, and if it were not for my good friend here'—she tapped her fingers on the little box—'I would be quite cut off from my own people who speak French and German—the German we speak in Switzerland, you know.

'Yes,' she continued, as our conversation became more personal, the other two women talking by themselves, 'I am not married, and believe me, it is all my own fault. I loved my father and my father loved me, and when my brothers left home I took the place of my mother who had died. I would accompany my father on excursions up the mountain. We would take our bicycles and ride off with our hearts full of laughter. I never had the slightest trouble in hearing him. I suppose I was accustomed to his voice. Every winter we would skate and ski but that did not prevent us from working hard, for we owned a restaurant where we served a cheese dish that was famous all over the canton, and we had what you might call an honourable fortune.

'Five years ago my father died. He was seventy-eight. I felt very lonely and, as both my brothers had made their homes in Canada and were very anxious for me to join them—one is a dentist in Montreal, the other has an hotel at Three Rivers—and I adore them both, I sold my father's restaurant, filled five enormous packing-cases with my books, the photographs of my family and all my personal treasures, and off I went.

'How can I describe to you my first impressions of Canada?

'The forests have no beginning and no end. A walk

in a wood leads nowhere. This sensation oppressed me. I was crushed, made to feel very small. Then when I took a bicycle to go for a picnic as I used to do with my father in Switzerland, I found the roads impossibly dusty. Cars sped past at high speed, for what had their drivers to look at but miles upon miles of forest trees? What charmed me most were the trains. Every evening we heard the great bell of the approaching train, and all the township would troop to the station to see it arrive. That was adorable.

'In Montreal I was amazed by the beauty of the women and the waste paper strewn about the streets. Canadian women practise very seriously the art of looking their best. They are no more intelligent than we are: they merely see things in a different way. They are born, they grow up, and are beautiful. I would have felt ashamed, for instance, to appear before my sisters-in-law with no varnish on my nails. They have all the latest labour-saving devices in their homes. In French Canada the women call these devices by one general affectionate term. They speak of their "moulin"—their mill. One sees picturesquely a corn-mill, a water-mill, a windmill. They do not say "I must put my husband's shirt in the washing-machine!" but "I must put it in the mill." They polish the floor with a mill, clean the carpets with a mill, dry their hair with a mill, take the ice cubes out of a mill.

'They have so many that they do the housework in no time after which they attend to their beauty, but they never sew. I lost my thimble the first week I was there, and you would never believe how many shops I had to visit to find another. Thimbles have become extinct. The women continue to wear a dress till they decide to throw it away.

'My Canadian sisters-in-law are female idols. They reign over husbands who adore them, and they do things which my brothers would never have tolerated in Swiss women. My brothers were quite right to marry Canadian women. They became in this way more quickly assimilated into the Canadian manner of life. They have the loveliest children who will never have anything Swiss about them.

'The women of our countries are so terribly reasonable. French women, Swiss women, are brought up from girl-hood to do without things. We mend our clothes and make them last. We sew, we knit, we run up a dress, we unpick a pullover. We cook a meal. We hate things that come out of tins. We are not nearly extravagant enough. A Canadian man is driven to success by the insatiable requirements of his Canadian wife.

'In spite of my brothers' kindness, I never felt at home. I am too Swiss. I was staying with one of them who had a lovely country house to which I had taken my five packing-cases full of treasures when on a winter's night, when we were all asleep, fire broke out. We escaped in time, but my little kingdom, represented by the five packing-cases, was wiped out.

'I had dreamed a lot about Canadian winters. I planned long expeditions by ski, but the country where I found myself was too flat, too wooded. However, there were unforgettable moments, my first sight of the tracks of wolves, for instance, on early morning snow.

'Then this:

'Late at night our house, imprisoned in the vastness of winter's snow, was fast asleep. I who am deaf heard what seemed a metallic sound at the back door. I went quietly to the window and looked out. There was a full moon. A female bear had lifted the cover of the garbage can and was licking the cover of a tin of Golden Syrup. Three baby bears were playing at her feet.

'The next evening I filled the garbage can with golden syrup and maple sugar: to my immense joy the mother bear returned, bringing her children who growled sweetly while she fed them. The family came back every evening. I was terrified that some hunter would come along with a gun, for I loved my bears and would have felt responsible. Then the thaw came and they disappeared.'

The air hostess arrived and suddenly we were all in a hurry, even leaving the coffee undrunk on the table. That is the whole essence of air travel: one takes a taxi to the air station, one runs, one waits, one sets off, one comes back, one waits again, and then suddenly one cannot go fast enough. So for the second time we took our places in the Elizabethan. The engines roared. We taxied down the avenue and finally took off. Now here we were high above the clouds in brilliant hot sunshine.

Evening came on and now at last we saw the lights of Geneva. My Indian friend, who was continuing her journey to Milan, came out for a moment on the tarmac. 'Thus,' she said, 'I shall have walked a little in Switzerland!' I wished her a successful journey, and as she was a Christian I added:

'God bless you.' Her beautiful dark eyes thanked me, and she stood watching me until I had entered the customs shed.

My Swiss friend went to change some money. I heard her saying: 'I have just come from Canada. Yesterday I was in Montreal.' She needed to hear the sound of her voice in the country of her birth. Meanwhile a page from the cable office was calling out: 'Mademoiselle Rose S—— Mademoiselle Rose S——' and, receiving no reply, he continued: 'Fraulein Rose S—— Fraulein Rose S—— Miss Rose S——' His eyes then fell on my companion's luggage and he stooped down to read the labels. Thus I learned, the cable having been safely delivered, that my friend's name was Rose.

When we were in the coach, Rose said to me:

'Madame, it was indeed fortunate that the little page saw my luggage with my name written so clearly on the labels. Otherwise he might never have found me. I hear with my eyes rather than with my ears, and just then I was talking to the man at the Exchange counter.'

She had folded over her lap a beautiful beaver coat and, after explaining to me by what route we were to enter Geneva, she said:

'Though I am returning to my own country, I have not a single relation left here. Happily I have many friends. I shall travel with you as far as Lausanne. You will change there for Montreux, and from Montreux you will take a mountain train for Gstaad.'

She had taken charge of me entirely, and I was glad of her friendship. The Swissair office is just inside the railway station at Geneva and, while I was inquiring about our rail tickets, I noticed that Rose was searching for something in her hand-bag.

'I must have dropped my purse in the coach,' she said. 'I will ask them to telephone the garage. I expect the driver will find it.'

Ten minutes later a man arrived with her purse. I marvelled at this piece of honesty.

'Oh, but I was never in the least frightened,' she said softly. 'The Swiss are not thieves. Nobody has yet taught them to steal.' She added:

'All the same, I am glad the man found it so easily because I had changed one hundred Canadian dollars at the airport.'

At Lausanne, where I had an hour and twenty minutes to wait, Rose decided that I must dine with her. We ate a succulent steak and drank exquisite Valais wine in the second-class buffet. When I wished to pay the bill, Rose said:

'No, no. Let it not be said that on returning to my country I failed in the laws of hospitality. It has been lovely to meet such a patient friend.'

She put me in the train to Montreux, choosing a compartment where she thought I would be well, and asking a gentleman in a corner seat to help me with my luggage and, whatever happened, not to let me go further than Montreux where I must change again into the mountain train. I had once more the impression of being a little girl. Rose had to tell the gentleman in the corner seat about her flight from Montreal and how delighted she was to be back in Switzerland.

'You are very fortunate,' I said to her, 'to have such faith in your country.'

'Yes, indeed,' she answered. 'You see, we have only been here a few hours and yet everything seems so secure. When we open a newspaper and read that another French government has fallen, we of Geneva or Lausanne, who have such affection for the French, who admire their intelligence and their excellent taste, cannot feel but a little angry. They have so much, and govern themselves so badly.'

This criticism which I hear so often in England and which I dismiss with a shrug, hurt me coming from this woman who made it not with contempt but with deep affection. We bade each other good-bye and she went down the platform to the subway, turning back several times to wave. Then my train slipped out of the station.

My companion was smoking in his corner seat.

'And so,' he said, 'you are going to Gstaad? I sometimes go there to ski over the week-end, but our week-ends are rather rare. We work pretty hard in Switzerland.'

I smiled in agreement.

'As a matter of fact,' he went on, 'I represent an

important London firm, but each time I go to England I am shocked to find that they do less and less work. Those people still think they own a vast empire. There is only one country left that can make its empire pay, and that is Belgium. There's a country for you, small, highly industrialized, and obtaining from the Congo the raw materials it needs most. It can even sell its surplus to other nations. If only Switzerland could have a tiny piece of Africa as wealthy as the Belgian Congo. You would see how we would make it hum! Switzerland is prosperous enough as it is but consider that we must buy almost everything from abroad. Well, I suppose, the best we can say is that never having stolen anybody else's land, our consciences are at least clear. We stand before history with our hands clean.'

'I am not very good at politics,' I answered.

My companion smiled and began to talk about the vineyards which unfortunately I could not see because it was night. He said that this part of Switzerland, between Lausanne and Montreux, had been much favoured by English tourists in the days when there were no currency restrictions, and he added:

'The English no longer have enough money to spend their holidays here. Even suppose they could manage a cheap hotel or a *pension*, what would they have left to spend in the shops. Nothing here is cheap. The Germans are rich, and as they work extremely hard they spend a lot and want to play as hard as they work. Many Italians also have made big fortunes with the Americans.'

Here was Montreux. My companion helped me with my bags and showed me a little mountain train on an adjoining platform. How lovely the country air smelt and what a splendid thing is the electric train! These stations without smoke, without dust or litter, so clean and pretty, smelling so good, are indeed a joy! But how cold it was as soon as one left the splendidly heated compartments.

A porter led me to a long first-class car with low twin seats back to back on either side of a central corridor. I chose a place beside a little girl who was reading a book and as I sat down she looked up at me and smiled. The train moved off immediately, for it had probably been waiting for the connection from Lausanne.

I very soon became aware that the compartment beyond mine was full of Italian teen-agers with their hair cut in the poodle way in front and the duck's tail behind. Their laughter filled the coach. They would climb on the seats to haul down their bags from which they would bring out a coloured scarf, a wool beret, a pair of ski-ing gloves, or some other amusing thing which they would all try on in turn amidst cries of enthusiasm and joy. Their slender wrists were cluttered up with gold bracelets from which dangled and jostled gold coins and hearts speckled with semi-precious stones. Their voices trilled like a mountain stream, clear, enchanting, musical. I could see their heads and shoulders when they stood on their seats. Occasionally one of them would dart out in the centre corridor. They were clearly of aristocratic birth, wealthy, and brimming over with youth and vitality.

In my own compartment, facing the little girl next to whom I was sitting, an extremely elegant woman was reading a novel from which she only lifted her eyes to look, from time to time, at the little girl who was obviously her daughter. Her nose was pronounced, her hair beginning to turn white, but as she wore it very long and gathered up at the back with a multitude of hairpins, the whole chignon meticulous, one looked at it with pleasure.

Between myself and the little girl was a Mickey Mouse in Italian. I looked down at it, intrigued by the title, but

*I

I did not, of course, permit myself to touch it. Suddenly the little girl, who, because all children are curious, had been watching me, took up the book, and offering it to me asked me rather falteringly in French:

'Vous le voulez, madame?'

Then, quite terrified by her forwardness, she turned back feverishly to her own book. A moment later she looked up nervously at her mother for approbation of her act. Her mother, in answer, smiled indulgently as if to say: 'You did very well. You are perfectly brought up, and you must not be afraid to speak a language that is not your own.'

Emboldened by this mute scene between mother and daughter, I turned to the little girl and asked in a low voice how old she was.

'Eleven,' she answered.

The teen-agers in the adjoining compartment continued to laugh and to talk. One of them had a heavy cold, and each time she sneezed all the others broke out into merriment. The little girl beside me, tired by her long journey, the lateness of the hour, and the heat of the compartment, laid her book on her lap and closed her eyes. Her mother said gently:

'Come to me!'

The child in the Tartan slacks and thick white socks placed her head against her mother's arm and stretched out her legs on the vacant seat. Soon she was fast asleep. Her mother did not cease reading her novel, but her arm slowly encircled the child's bust, and each time the train jolted the arm encompassed her a little more. Mother and daughter wore the same coloured pullover and cardigan.

After a while a teen-ager jumped up on her seat in the adjoining compartment, and dark eyes under a poodle coiffure peered over the partition. No longer seeing the little girl in her corner, the eyes searched round till they met the sleeping figure of the child nestling against her mother. Then the whole expression changed. From extreme gaiety, one read consecutively surprise, tenderness, enchantment. Quickly she signalled to the others to climb up and take a look. Half a dozen poodle-dressed heads now peered over the top of the partition. Eyes of young women who would soon be mothers, filled with veneration. All the laughter and the youthful cries were hushed. One heard only the swish of the wheels against the metal rails as the electric train climbed the mountain pass. The picture was truly exquisite—this Italian adoration of a sleeping child. Large tears fell down the cheeks of one of these wealthy, sophisticated girls. How delightful to find oneself in a country where women are tender beings, not afraid to reveal their sensitivity.

At the far end of our compartment an aged woman, dressed in black, her hands folded on her knees, was also watching the sleeping child. She was, I suddenly realized, the nurse. The teen-agers, one by one, slipped down and resumed their seats, but now they spoke only in whispers.

Suddenly the whole picture changed once more. The train was running into Gstaad. The nurse woke the child and helped her to put on a bright red coat with a white fox collar. All her sleepiness had gone. Her eyes shone with excitement and she ran into the corridor where she was surrounded by the teen-agers who were chattering louder than ever, preparing to leave the train. The mother closed her novel and slowly put on an amber-coloured felt beret decorated with an old-fashioned jewel, not very valuable perhaps, but clearly a family piece. The nurse in her sombre black clothes was standing up patiently holding a big fur coat into which she presently wrapped her mistress. She lifted down the luggage without effort, her peasant stock having placed wiry strength into her arms. She also gave me my bags, and

lifting up my coat placed it over my shoulders without a
word but smiling in the sweetest way.

Now all the teen-agers were in front of the open window calling out:

'Facchino!   Facchino!'

The porters came running up.   The whole station was
illuminated as if for a public rejoicing.   Thick snow
crunched under our feet: flakes fell indolently, dividing
us by a muslin veil from what lay ten yards ahead.
Sledges, with bells joyously ringing, came swinging into
the station yard.   Each had a closed hood and leather
sides so that when I was closed into mine I experienced a
moment of delicious fear.   I imagined myself a pretty
village girl being carried off to satisfy the whim of the
wicked owner of the castle.   Stories of this kind greatly
excited me when I read Russian tales as a little girl.   I
tried to find an aperture at the side of the sledge to look
out on the snow and the pine-trees, but I could find none
and it was terrifyingly dark.   I could feel us skidding
gracefully from side to side as the horses plunged forward,
bells tinkling.   I thought of Germaine de Staël fleeing
from Coppet to escape the fury of Napoleon.   I had
always admired and envied this great woman writer.
This feeling of mystery and fright was delicious, quite
delicious.   Faintly came the sound of a clock striking.
It was midnight.

CHAPTER XXVIII

THE OWNERS of the Hôtel du Parc at Gstaad have a very pretty chalet of their own in which they accommodate certain guests during the height of the winter season. I was given a tiny room here, not much larger than a convent cell, but so warm and clean that I took to it at once. On my first morning, looking for a bell to ring for breakfast and finding none, but hearing a great noise in the hall, I opened the door and found myself facing a small band of servants eager for the privilege of serving my neighbour, Field Marshal Viscount Montgomery of Alamein, whom they all referred to by the affectionate title of *nôtre maréchal*.

Often I saw the field marshal sitting on his balcony looking across the snow or reading a book, and I was surprised that a man so famous should remain far from the crowd and, to all appearances, lonely.

On Sunday Gstaad is full of husbands who have come from Lausanne, Milan, Paris . . . all the cities where men work so hard during the rest of the week. Young wives, their cheeks flushed with happiness, speak softly to their children. They have looked forward eagerly to this day. There was a time when, according to the novels, rich women in mountain resorts took lovers. Now after six days of feminine companionship they make themselves attractive to welcome their husbands.

I lunched very quietly at the Hôtel du Parc. Each

table had father, mother, and the children, flowers growing in pots, and a bottle of wine.   The table-cloths and
napkins were as formerly in England, sweet-smelling
linen not only hand made and hemmed, but washed by
hand, dried in the sun, and ironed with due respect for its
beauty.   At my chalet I saw cupboards full of this magnificent linen, and it struck me that we should be thankful
to certain countries for keeping up habits of good living
that tend to slip elsewhere after each new stress of social
agitation or war.   I had the same agreeable impression
when each shopkeeper, after the smallest purchase,
accompanied me to the door of his shop, opened it, and
said good-bye to me on the pavement.   Two generations
ago that might have happened in Bond Street.   One can
be both democratic and polite.

Two Airedales, belonging to the owners of the hotel,
lay on the carpet of the hall.   They were delightful
animals and I used to meet them everywhere.   They
liked to follow guests who had children so that their
intelligent heads could be in line with the children's
shoulders.

I thought I would walk for an hour before the cold set
in.   A steep road climbs to the ice rink, a steep winding
road up and down which come sleighs pulled by one or
two horses with foxes' tails tied to the harness behind
their ears.   The brushes seemed to dance a weird ballet
in the cold air.   Down came the toboggans and the skiers
so swiftly that I sometimes lost my nerve and threw
myself against the soft snow of the banked sides.

A professional skater wearing tights and a short red
velvet skirt was making figures of eight on the rink.   I
sat down and soon a great number of young women came
to change their shoes, or leave some garment on the
bench.   They spoke at least four languages with ease,
and wore their hair like the young Italian girls in the
train.   The duck's back coiffure and navy blue ski-ing

trousers are here the mark of the international young woman as, not so long ago, the 'bob' or the 'Eton crop' and the short, waistless dress were the pride of the girl of twenty.

The bevy of skaters took to the rink and a young woman, all by herself, came to sit beside me. We smiled at one another, and I asked her where she came from. From Fribourg, she answered, and she had a little boy of three. Her husband had bought a chalet at Gstaad so that she could come with the child whenever she wished, summer or winter.

'I have put in so many labour-saving devices,' she said, 'that I don't even need a charwoman, and there is no dust, to be sure. We use Diesel oil for the central heating which eliminates smoke and soot. I learnt my lesson from my apartment at Fribourg which is also extremely modern—central heating, washing-machines, electrical ovens, and so on. Domestic labour in Switzerland, as everywhere else, has become uneconomic. If I had wanted a maid in our Fribourg apartment, my husband could not have afforded to buy me a chalet at Gstaad. So we get up an hour earlier in the morning, and go to bed an hour later at night, and do all the work ourselves. I can run my chalet for a week for what it would cost us to spend a night in an hotel.'

She blushed charmingly, anxious to explain that though she was careful with the money, her family did not lack anything. No, on the contrary, she and her husband were young and her good management allowed them to go about and see other countries. Last year they had let their chalet and gone to Spain, a wonderful country, but they had been obliged to keep all their bags locked, and on one occasion, when she was kneeling in church, a man even managed to rob her. Her husband had caught a man picking his pocket in a tram at Barcelona. These two incidents spoiled their journey.

We got up and walked down the winding road. My companion chose the dangerous, slippery side, and when I pointed this out to her she answered:

'But it's only natural. I'm more accustomed to walking on snow and ice, and I can protect you better like this.'

I had brought a good deal of work from London and we parted outside my own chalet. During the next few days I tried to get better in the clear air. I would visit the shops to buy knitting-wool; each afternoon I would write for three hours, and then sew, but on one occasion I felt over-excited and tired and asked the *maître d'hôtel* if he could serve me dinner in my room. He said:

'Ah, madame, I have my field marshal to look after. This evening a few friends have come to see him.'

'In that case,' I answered, 'pray do not bother. I can manage without dinner.'

'But madame, it is not because I have my field marshal that you need go to bed hungry. Have no fear, madame, you will have a very fine dinner—a *côtelette Pojarsky*, a salad, and an ice . . . but I will serve you after I have served the gentlemen. Will that be all right?'

He came in a few moments with the mail. Ah! Here is a letter from my son who is at Downside. His letters have become quite remarkable and he is both intrigued and deeply impressed by the Benedictine monks.

DEAR MOTHER,

I am very glad that your eye is so much better. The monks are continually asking me for news about you. Last week I had told one of them about your conjunctivitis. They became quite alarmed. So you see that many people have your health at heart.

We hardly did any work on Monday, it being the Purification of the Virgin Mary. At 9 a.m. we set off in the direction of the church, but instead of passing through the monastery arches we went into the monastery itself which normally we are not allowed to do. I was tremendously impressed by the monks' pretty cells. You should have seen how impeccably clean they were, how comfortable, how filled with learned books! I have seldom seen so many books, and the walls were covered with paintings, old maps with Latin inscriptions, and newspapers printed before the battle of Waterloo. How I would have loved to wander at will through the monastery! We then went into the church up spiral stairs and many mysterious turnings.

After a short time a choir-boy unrolled a carpet about ten yards long in front of the altar. All the monks were dressed in white. We then went forward, twenty by twenty, to kneel on the carpet. When the distribution of candles was over (it took about twenty minutes) we lit them, and while we prayed with our candles in our hands, the monks walked round the aisles singing. The church was thus illuminated by 500 candles, but as mass lasted an hour and a half I became a little tired.

I laughed tremendously at seeing Sir Alexander Korda's film *Henry the Eighth* again. I do love the way the fat king throws the chicken bones over his shoulders. I think when I saw it at Shepperton (while I was making *The Fallen Idol*) I hardly realized what a splendid film it was.

I kiss you one thousand times,

BOBBY.

I feel suddenly very lonely and long to have my son with me. Was the field marshal lonely when I saw him reading on his balcony?

Here comes the *maître d'hôtel* with my dinner tray! There is suddenly a great noise in the hall. The field marshal is going off to a gala accompanied by many gentlemen with deep voices and heavy steps.

'Do not forget, madame,' said the *maître d'hôtel*, to look out of your window to-night. Thousands of lighted candles in little red jars line the field marshal's triumphal route from the chalet to the hotel. The snow at the foot of the mountain glows pink. It is very beautiful, madame.'

CHAPTER XXIX

I RUN UP the moving stairs of the old Tuppenny tube and blink in the sunshine of Newgate. The bells of St. Paul's Cathedral come crashing, leaping, pealing, over the fern-covered wasteland of town turned by the bombs and fire of twelve years ago into country. I hesitate for a moment, arranging landmarks in their right places, then turn on my heels and trip quickly off in the direction of the General Post Office.

In my hand-bag is a letter for my friend Jenny Bell of New York, and I think that if I post it here she will receive it faster. Three days? Two days? Even less than that? What a miracle of speed! Will she realize that I hurried down Newgate? Oh, this strange juxtaposition of yesterday and to-morrow.

The bells of St. Paul's fill the waves of the morning air. They are important, resounding, and possessive. All this territory is theirs, and I wonder if this pealing has something to do with the young queen's coronation which is getting nearer every day. The West End is already garlanded, but Newgate, and the countrified path leading to St. Paul's churchyard, keep nature's decoration of wild flowers and bushlike trees that might turn this part of London back to what it looked like in the days of the Ancient Britons if little acorns are allowed to grow unmolested into great trees!

I break into the cathedral stillness of the General Post

Office and am somewhat abashed by all this white and green marble and the absence, for the moment at any rate, of the democratic queue which in other post offices seems to wait eternally for insurance stamps and to register fifty parcels at a time. All the young men here wait to serve me, and I can choose the one I like best.

He smiles. I am his.

He places an express tab on the envelope, takes my money and, running off with Jenny Bell's letter, calls back over his shoulder:

'You see, it's already on its way.'

In the centre of the pillared hall is a table on which the *habitués* come to weigh their own letters. There are two scales, one of old-fashioned design with little black weights carefully graduated—father, mother, right down to little sister Anne; at the other end of the table the sort of scales my grocer uses to weigh three rashers of bacon. These delightful toys, that personally I would never dare to touch, add to one's sense of importance at being in the General Post Office. Here is the interpreter's desk. He is not here just now. Perhaps he is having a cup of tea? On the other hand, when he is here he can *habla espanol* and *spricht deutsch*.

At all events, my air-mail letter has gone, and how good it is to be in the sunshine again!

Bright red vans, a bright red pillar-box, and a bronze statue of a gentleman in a frock-coat with a pencil poised above a note-book. An old-fashioned newspaper reporter? No! This is Rowland Hill who, in 1840, founded the uniform penny post.

I am charmed by my little adventure. Here is a plaque to say that the building from which I have just emerged was begun just a year before I was born. The foundation-stone was laid by Edward VII, King of Great Britain. . . . King of Great Britain! What a splendid-sounding title!

Up and down, over and yonder go the bells of St. Paul's, filling my mind with thoughts of the coming coronation. This General Post Office, the plaque goes on chattily, was built on the site of Christ's Hospital founded in 1552 by King Edward VI.

Like a schoolgirl I recapitulate.

King Edward VI.

King Edward VII.

Then comes King Edward VIII.

Who was King Edward VIII? Why, of course, he is . . . Oh, what a strange, surprising business! From what distant land will he be watching the young queen's coronation?

There is an oasis on the other side of the road. A lovely garden with fig-trees whose milky juice, touched by the sun, fills the air with the perfume of the country-side. This is the garden of St. Botolph-without-Aldersgate, and I am suddenly reminded of an amazing thing: that my father-in-law was a curate here before the General Post Office was built.

I must hurry across the road and make a tardy acquaintance with the garden of St. Botolph under whose spreading elm-trees is a notice signed by the vicar, saying that this garden is known as *Postmen's Park*. Yes, indeed, several postmen are sitting round the sundial, smoking their pipes and blinking at the lilac and the blue irises. My goodness! How the birds in London can chirrup and sing! How sweet it is to hear the sound of water falling from a fountain into the dark waters of a pond skirted by long grass and bulrushes!

There is an arbour with tablets commemorating brave, everyday deeds done sixty and seventy years ago. I am intrigued and look up and down the wall on which they were displayed.

Walter Peart, the driver, and Harry Dean, the fireman,

of the Windsor express 'whilst being scalded and burnt, sacrificed their lives in saving the train.' This deed, recorded in curious English, took place on a summer's day in 1898. Samuel Rabbeth of the Royal Free Hospital tried to save a child suffering from diphtheria at the cost of his own life in 1884, while two years later a little boy of twelve supported his drowning playfellow and sank with him clasped in his arms. And would you be surprised to learn that Alfred Smith, a police constable, was killed in an air-raid while saving the lives of women and girls—in June 1917!

Here is the gardener who lives in a rustic garden house.

'All those tablets? They were to do with a memorial to G. F. Watts, the painter, but the money ran out and no more brave deeds were recorded.'

Curiouser and curiouser, said Alice!

He was the painter who did the magnificent portrait of my husband's grandmother, Lady Lindsay, that I had removed from the Tate and hung above my writing-table in my Piccadilly apartment.

'What is your name, Mr. gardener?'

'Charles Bennett, ma'am. I've been around here since 1906.'

'That was the year I was born—in Montmartre, under the shadow of the Sacré Cœur.'

'This black-trunked tree full of sprouting leaves is a black poplar. About eighty years old, I reckon. Not old, is it? In that pond there lives a $4\frac{1}{2}$-lb. carp that a retired police inspector gave me. There's also some goldfish but the carp don't eat the goldfish. Nice fish, ma'am, friendly and all, but we've got no name for him.'

'I think perhaps I would like to see the church.'

But, of course, like many Protestant churches when one wishes to visit them, the church was closed.

Said the gardener: 'The verger don't come that early.'

I must return to Piccadilly. The bells of St. Paul's are silent. I had not noticed. The air was full of sound one moment. Only the birds chirruped the next. There is hardly any traffic down Newgate.

From King Edward Street St. Paul's is visible in all its beauty. I do not know if it is beautiful, but one loves it. Those of us who saw it ringed with flames love it as a mother loves a child she has nearly lost. On my right is the burnt-out ruin of Christchurch Greyfriars. These gutted City churches are beautiful. I am not sure they are not the most beautiful things I have ever seen. Like what is left of a medieval monastery, they make one greedy for the past. On the site of these charred walls, for instance, stood the Grey Friars 1225–1538.

Now Jenny Bell is young. Jenny Bell is new. She stands up for herself in the whirling, vital, ultra-modern city of New York.

Her friendship came to me suddenly in an air-mail letter, but it was different from other air-mail letters of the kind mentioned in this book, in that it was devastating and purposeful. Jenny Bell never had any doubt about me becoming her friend. Her letters are exciting with the excitement of being a young woman, ambitious, in love, and just about as alive as it is possible for a human to be. Jenny makes one feel that a young woman's lot is the loveliest in God's garden, and that the world is a terribly nice place to live in, especially when one has to fight for a bit of standing room.

In three letters she progressed rapidly from 'Dear Mrs Robert Henrey' to 'Dear Madeleine,' from 'Sincerely' to 'Lots of special love'—and after that—in an air-mail parcel—came the petticoat!

Now that she has given me permission to do so, I shall give these three letters as I received them so that you

can share some of my enjoyment, and decide for yourself
if the art of letter writing is dead.

> 184 East 75th Street,
> New York City, N.Y.

DEAR MRS. ROBERT HENREY,

Having just finished your *Little Madeleine*, I am writing
to ask you for another one quickly. What happened to
your cousin Rolande? What happened to you? Whom
did you marry and where is your mother?

I too was a poor little girl with an ambitious and
beloved mother. I went to work at sixteen, which is
unusual for the United States in the forties, and my
mother and I both worked so that I could go for a short
time to a fashionable college—an investment which has
paid dazzling dividends.

At eighteen I became a model for the American fashion
magazines and now, at twenty-six, I am a well-known
New York designer. My life has been rich in the
gratifying experience of hard work and now I am proud
but tired, and wonder what can come next. That is why
I am so interested in knowing what came next to the
little Madeleine?'

> Sincerely,
>
> JENNY BELL.

DEAR MRS. HENREY,

What a wonderful letter you sent me! I am waiting
impatiently for *Madeleine Grown Up*. Your books will
mean more to me now that you are my friend.

Your letter was waiting for me when I returned
Sunday night from two weeks in Florida. Had I known
it was here, I am sure I would have come home sooner,
for never have I had a happier thing happen to me.
I want so badly to meet you. Your picture in *The New
York Times* was lovely.

I live here in New York with two other young women, one of them, Ella King Russell, brilliant and very beautiful—tall, with black hair and pale skin, very animated, a member of the U.S. Legation to the United Nations; the other Ceciley Youmans, the late Vincent Youmans's daughter. Our house is lent to us by friends who have many other houses, and only occasionally use one room of this one. It is far too big for three girls in New York, but it is a wonderful place for parties. Wouldn't it be fun to have one for you?

On many week-ends I go to Philadelphia to see my mother who is a semi-invalid. Our home there is across the street from the hairdresser and around the corner from the grocery and street car. My mother longs for a small low house in the country.

I am quite happy now, but I am in love and I am not sure how it will turn out. However, I have been in love with people before, and it has not worked out, and so I ought to know how to take it, but I never wanted anyone before as desperately as this. Isn't it difficult, no matter how hard I work, it won't do, because of all the things you can get by working, love is not one.

Every day at lunch time, or at 6 p.m. I go to a ballet class run by a white Russian who speaks no English. I go for two reasons, because it makes me feel so wonderful, and because it is good for my French—not because I have dancing aspirations. To amuse myself I make up animal jingles, for example, *The Porcupine*.

> A hedgehog's a hodge-podge
>   Of prickles and bristles.
> His fur is all whiskers,
>   His whiskers are thistles.
> Take care not to scare him with
>   Whispers and whistles.
> He might use his thistles and bristles
>   For missiles.

I am sending a page advertisement from a New

York newspaper showing my new dresses and separates in cottons with crease-resistant textures. And then because I want you to have something of mine, I am sending you one of my petticoats. I think it might fit you, or at least be easily altered.

I took to designing petticoats just after leaving Sweet Briar, the women's college, in Virginia. Actually, the first thing I did in New York after leaving there, was to work as a model. The fashion was for clean faces rather than handsome ones. The 'scrubbed look' they called it, and my face was scrubbed until the bones shone through. I found it easy to get jobs with the best photographers and magazines. But my mother was appalled that her girl was supporting herself by her figure instead of her head. Mother was convinced that Park Avenue was paved with primroses and that every time I had a fitting, a large and lascivious audience looked on. So together we designed petticoats, all white and virginal, trimmed in lace and blue ribbons. They were the first petticoats New York had seen in thirty years and they were a tremendous hit. All the other models, all the fashion editors, all the girls I lived with, wanted to buy them. And when I went back to Sweet Briar, the American College Girl wanted to wear them.

I would like to know your dress size because some of the gay little inexpensive things we make might amuse you to wear in the country. Also tell me your stocking size. I can send you nylons when you need them. I'll stick them in an envelope with an air-mail stamp, and you'll have them in no time.

I hope I don't sound to you like a success story. I am not a success at all yet. In fact, at the moment, I feel immensely defeated. Often I think there is no success on Seventh Avenue—our garment centre—only knocks and bumps, and skinned knees and broken finger-nails from that endless climb. I have not told you anything at all about the years behind the blouse counter in a store, and the struggling and the pushing and toughening before you build any sort of reputation, and the constant things that happen to remind you that you're really not there. If you tell the truth, nothing is ever easy,

With love,

JENNY BELL.

DEAR MADELEINE,

When I was in Paris my friend who I was visiting said that in Europe you don't call people by their first names unless you know them very, very well, and have been asked. Do you think it's all right to say 'dear Madeleine'? I wish the petticoat would arrive. They told me at the post office it might take four weeks. Next time I shall wear whatever it is for a short time first, so that you don't have to pay too much duty. When I read that you liked to make your own lingerie I was a little embarrassed. You and your mother do beautiful work, and my mother and I just rush things through to be copied.

It's warm and lovely in New York, very beautiful, and lots of exciting things ought to be happening, but I'm going to tell you that the most exciting possible things are these letters from you. I won't say it again, but I think it's important for you to know. And after a thousand letters, it will still go.

I would love being part of *Madeleine's Journal* but I have forgotten everything I said in the last letter. My father is a Pennsylvania Dutchman. He comes from a German farm family that settled years ago in a beautiful rolling section of Pennsylvania among the 'plain people' —Mennonites, Schwenkfelders, and Amish religious sects who will not wear trimmings on their clothes, ride in automobiles, or use electric light to this day. They speak a low German dialect, are very thrifty and clean, but my father's family was not strict. They sent all their children away to school and had electric light, and even a bath-room.

You ask about my friend Ceciley Youmans. Her father was the famous American song writer who wrote *Drums in My Heart*, *Hallelujah*, *Tea for Two*, and many others I am sure you have hummed and danced to.

24 hours' interruption.

Yesterday was a complete loss!

I did nothing I should have done, and all because it was such a beautiful day! And I wanted to play tennis!

You ask me if I can read French fashion magazines easily—why, yes. The language of fashion, like ballet, is universal. When I was in Paris I met Madame Lazarus of ELLE, and she had my picture taken for the famous magazine. She wanted to buy the clothes off my back for her daughter, but since the clothes on my back were the only clothes I had with me, I couldn't sell them. I had come to Europe with one overnight bag to satisfy the American magazine that had done a picture story of me going away with this one suit-case. Fortunately Marguerite Labouret, whom I was visiting, and I are the same size, and she opened her wardrobe for me. Also I had a friend who was then designing for Balmain who lent me party dresses from there which was a great thrill. Don't forget to send me your measurements. We have some checked gingham things with ruffles that I think would be fun for the farm in Normandy. Do you like sleeveless things? Some women don't, but I do because it leaves more area to get tan on.

Sweet Briar is a women's college in Virginia that dates from 1906, the date of your birth. It has a bigger and prettier campus than most—2,800 acres with a lake. It was once a Southern ladies' seminary and the original plantation site was such a riot of wild roses that it became known as Sweet Briar. When I was sixteen some girls at my school were asked to be aides at a ball. I had never been to a ball before, and it was a wonderful night for me although we were not guests but, as it turned out, waitresses who took orders for the drinks. Still, I had a white party dress (with a lot of petticoats underneath), and an excited happy face which caused a handsome army lieutenant to ask me to take off my apron and dance with him. Completely Cinderella! He was very nice to me all the evening, and I was enchanted. During the conversation he asked me where I was going to college, and I said I didn't know. 'Well,' he said, 'I went to the University of Virginia, and I think you look like a Sweet Briar girl.'

So that is how I went to Sweet Briar. Sweet Briar and the University of Virginia are neighbours, you see. Of course, by the time I went to college, that influential lieutenant had been killed in Italy.

I am going to Philadelphia this afternoon, and shall take the Madeleine books with me. I shall lend one to my mother who loves you.

There is a school across the street from us. My desk is opposite a window facing the classrooms. It's diverting to see the hands shooting up and down when the nuns ask questions, and the pencils being sharpened, and the trouble they have getting the blinds adjusted in the morning. Now they all seem to be saying their prayers.

This 75th street where we three girls all live in this big house, is a nice street with trees and pretty town houses which have not all become apartments. In the back we overlook pretty courtyards and gardens.

It's getting late. Into my grey suit and out into the pale day for me!

Lots of special love,
JENNY BELL.

I am now in the train to Philadelphia reading *Madeleine Grown Up*. On page 21 you speak of singing *No, No, Nanette*. That and all the music for the show was by Ceciley's father.

Ten days later the petticoat came.

The postman had knocked early one morning when I was still in bed. He was a little man with a sad expression and he stood at the open door holding the flat brown-paper parcel in both hands, as he said almost with a sense of guilt:

'There's one pound twelve shillings and a penny to pay.'

'Have you change?'

'No, lady.'

'Can I give you a cheque?'

'Not unless I take the parcel away.'

'Well, I'll tell you what. Take a short cut down the back stairs and ask them at the newspaper shop in Shepherd Market to pay you.'

He looked at me dubiously.

'You really think they would?'

'I think so, and to make sure I'll telephone.'

He stretched out a hand to take back the parcel he had momentarily put down.

'Oh no!' I exclaimed. 'You simply must leave the parcel. Then you won't need to come back.'

He thought a moment, and then said:

'Well, at any rate you can't run away, lady. Not yet.'

So this was Jenny Bell's petticoat!

The postman departed and Ella, the pretty girl at the newsagent's shop, paid him the money. She also is sent things like nylons from friends in America. She understands.

No wonder that all the girls at Sweet Briar are crazy about Jenny Bell's petticoat!

Adorably starched and white, its folds of organdie tumble about my hands. Buttoned by a wide band to the waist, it billows out in descending tiers of threaded pale blue ribbon and *entre-deux* to the wide hem of scalloped lace. And on the skirt, here, there, and everywhere, are lace butterflies poised delicately, realistically on delicate antennae. There are also the prettiest bunches of sweet-briar roses and forget-me-nots, their pink and blue daubing the great expanse of white.

A turn on the heels, a swish—the lace butterflies flap their wings, the roses turn over lazily, showing minute foliage and tiny buds. How lovely to feel the starchy whiteness brush against one's knees and the top of the legs!

Oh, Jenny Bell, how right you were to go to college!

At least, they taught you something really useful. I would prefer to have created this than take a 'double first.'

I remove the petticoat and examine the waistband.

A little pocket cut in the form of a heart with a coloured design of sweet-briar roses contains within— a sachet of scented powder. The powder falls on my carpet and suddenly the whole room smells of sweet-briar.

So the petticoat is scented! The sweet-briars of Virginia bring me all their delight!

What fun girls have in America!

There are some words written across the heart, in and out of the roses. I feel a tingling of pride as I read:

DESIGNED BY JENNY BELL

CHAPTER XXX

THIS SUMMER will go down as coronation summer. Our children will read about it in history books. But we have lived through it. To prove that it is not merely a fairy-tale we shall be able to remember the cherries and the strawberries in their normal loveliness, the corn ripening amongst poppies and cornflowers in the fields, the hay cut once again by farmers. The August holidays suddenly arrive. We shall soon be in the process of looking back on something that is gone. Delightful winter will be upon us with the lights of Piccadilly Circus reflected on smooth wet pavements, theatrical first nights, red buses jammed between taxis and cars, exciting new books to read, Christmas just ahead.

The coronation of Elizabeth II with its inevitable throw-back to the reign of the great Queen Bess, the obvious analogy with the girl Victoria whose reign was to prove so long and so rich in achievement, has dominated us, dazzled us, almost overpowered us. The transformation from austerity, class-warfare, rationing, and the one doubtful egg a week, to this splendour, this plenty, this return to all that was picturesque, noble, tremendous, in our island history; from foreigners shunning a London where the food was bad, life not very gay, and people depressed and rather rude, to these relays of air liners filling up at Orly, depositing at London airport, even at midnight and 2 a.m., men of all nations, and the prettiest, smartest women from Europe and North, Central, and South America, all excited, all looking forward to their arrival in the great capital upon which the arc-lights of the civilized world were blindingly focused—these violent contrasts left us gasping.

Millions of words have been written on the splendours of the Abbey service and the pageantry of the streets, but the great, the magnificent thing is the resurgence of the British spirit. The bus conductor whistles a tune, the shopkeeper smiles, good humour breaks in revealing ripples over the town, and the young woman trips along the pavement with a new air.

My village in Piccadilly will not mind if I say that other parts of the West End may have hung up more bunting, but we had a maypole to recall the one in 1716. Old prints show the first maypole amongst the shops and booths of May Fair, a very tall pole with what appears to be an acrobat climbing up one of the streamers. There are two houses with inn signs, a Swan and a Mitre, and somebody is leaning out of a first-floor window displaying a piece of material on which are painted two naked women. There are soldiers with red coats and black hats. Half a dozen people are dancing at the foot of the maypole, and there is a platform on which an actor and a child are performing.

The arrangements for our new maypole were made by Mr. Hal Gutteridge who was recently mayor of the city of Westminster, and who lives in a house in Curzon Street at which King Edward VII was a frequent visitor when Prince Soltykoff owned it. The house was the last of a row of aristocratic dwellings (of which one was the then newly built mansion of the lovely Duchess of Marlborough, now Consuelo Vanderbilt Balsan): after them came the little shops of Shepherd Market. To

K

protect King Edward from the gaze of these shopkeepers when he went to visit his friend, a wooden screen was put up which you can still see.

Against one side of the screen a flower seller warms herself on cold days with an oil lamp, but the shops behind were destroyed in the Battle of London, and pretty weeds and trees, now almost fully grown, flourish in deep cavities.

My friend Mrs. Waller, the builder, having paid a deposit to the council 'for possible damage to the pavement,' dispatched men to dig a hole three feet deep, insert a nine-inch-wide drain-pipe, put in pegs and concrete, and plant the maypole. To prevent little boys from tugging down the streamers, these gay things were nailed out of reach, so that our maypole looked like a smart lady holding up her crinolines in order not to dirty the hem.

The nailing up of the streamers gave rise to a rumour that the authorities frowned on street dancing, but Mr. Hal Gutteridge denied this, saying that he hoped to make our maypole an annual affair on the queen's birthday, and that he would be delighted for us to dance our feet off. The shopkeepers who contributed to the maypole, which cost £50, came out to see the present mayor perform the opening ceremony, and even Edward, my butcher, appeared for a moment with his carving knife.

Had it been in the nature of our people to dance, their hearts would certainly have prompted them to do so. The drab, suspicious years were being rubbed away. I remembered moments when we were all so bad-tempered that I wished again for the thunder of the guns, for had I not seen my village proudly and joyously standing up, it is said, to more bombs and incendiaries to the square yard than rained down on any other part of London? A good place for a woman with a baby to live in with such a brave community to make a fuss of her! Could it be that these same people were unable to surmount the troubles of peace?

Now this coronation summer had miraculously brought back their smiles. A pretty young woman in slacks and an apache's red scarf, and two men assuming swift disguises with false beards, false moustaches, and more hats than the Prime Minister owned, appeared one sunny morning in our market-place between the vegetable stall and a baby sleeping in her pram outside a millinery shop. The music was very gay, and out came Sylvia from the newspaper shop, and Edward complete with white apron and carving knife.

The strolling players were unconsciously re-enacting the scene portrayed in the famous print of 1716 and were singing, acting, and dancing on the same spot. The little market-place has really not changed in centuries. The vegetable stall has an almost theatrical background, with Shearn's famous newspaper shop and the covered passage leading to the bakery and to Curzon Street in the centre; and a café with open-air tables, and other charming shops and passage ways in the 'wings.' The tiny square fills up every morning with the picturesque knife grinder, the ventriloquist, the vendor of porcelain, and the conjurer—not to mention the huge van bringing carcasses for the various butchers whose shops have been a feature of the May Fair for three hundred years.

The important thing is that laughter fills the air. As soon as one set of musicians goes, another comes, sometimes a solitary one, playing his reed like Pan. Our market has rediscovered its soul. We are resurgent. The white-coated employee at Hayward's says to me:

'Madame, our new-laid eggs are excellent. Would you like two dozen?'

He smiles, he is polite, he is eager. Oh, what a lovely

thing it has become again to be a woman with a shopping-basket!

The young queen's picture smiles down upon us from every little house and shop. Suddenly, clatter . . . clip . . . clop . . . down narrow Shepherd Street into the market square comes a shining, well-groomed horse, a magnificent brougham and a coachman so erect that if he did not hold his whip in his hand I would be tempted to think he had swallowed it.

The brougham draws up behind a van filled with frozen carcasses of lamb for Edward, and a lady steps out. By the time I reach the carriage, this lovely reminder of a more elegant age, half a dozen shopkeepers are round it questioning the coachman with the eagerness of children. Is it difficult to drive such a spirited horse through the crowded streets? Who is the lady who has just gone on an errand? Is she a lady-in-waiting?

The coachman without altering the dignified erectness of his body, leans a little to one side, and answers diplomatically:

'She is a person of quality in Her Majesty's entourage.'

We are hushed. We do not hiss or boo. We are not envious. We merely admire. What lovely things are tolerance and mutual estimation, and what a hideous nightmare we have left behind! A young assistant in the oil store says:

'I reckon it's even smarter than a Rolls.'

'And rides as smooth as anything, I bet!' says somebody else. 'Amazing springs, I should think.'

At this moment the lady returns, and putting a gloved hand on the door, says sweetly to the last speaker:

'You are quite right. One is very comfortable inside. The springs are wonderful.'

Then turning to the coachman, she gives her next destination.

'Very well, m'lady!' he says.

He shakes his reins, the door closes, the brougham goes off clatter, clip . . . clop . . . down narrow, winding Whitehorse Street and into Piccadilly.

Some of the facets of these amazing days and weeks are symbolized for me in a wide balcony overlooking the gardens of Berkeley Square.

The house has tall french windows and bright green shutters against a façade of warm red brick. A gilded coat of arms, the Royal Warrant, is attached to the balcony railing along which also are banked white marguerites, red geraniums, and blue pansies in great profusion.

The gardens are magnificent and their importance overshadows the traffic in the square. Tulips splash the lawns with colour, and paper garlands of 'old' rose, the distinctive decorations of Berkeley Square, wind in and out of the leafy branches of the plane-trees. There is an arbour in which strange and lovely birds are flying, their cage so tall that they appear to be free, birds they say from distant lands to compensate for the British nightingales which must not be placed behind prison bars.

A dog barks and there are women's voices. I return through the french windows into the millinery *salon* where Millie, one of the Rita sisters, finds me the prettiest hats when I want to make a special impression at lunch. The three sisters, by a coincidence, are all here together, and as I have known them through the difficult days of war and peace, I feel a satisfying mixture of pleasure and affection in their presence.

Millie is dark, slim, sweetly pretty, and is wearing a close-fitting wine-coloured velvet suit, with three ladybirds on the lapel. Her voice has the warm, coaxing ring of the Londoner born. One feels that she is in tune with the throb of the town through all its layers from the lowest to the highest. This is her *salon*. Her hats are the prettiest in town.

Her sister Katie owns the Scotch terrier who is begging for an enormous bone that Edward, my butcher, must have provided. Katie's *salon* is on the floor above. She makes beautiful dresses for many of the people for whom Millie makes hats. The dressmaker and the milliner always strike me as one and indivisible. Katie's voice is deeper than Millie's and her friendliness is just as warm but of a different sort. I plague her just now to show me the peeresses' robes and dresses, and to tell me the stories of amazing discoveries of coronation robes in medieval castles. I marvel at her patience, and like a little girl I want to cry: 'More! More!'

Ruby de Oliva, the third sister, has just flown in from New York where at her shop at the corner of Sixty-fourth Street and Madison Avenue she sells suits, skirts, jackets, and top coats made in America out of British woollens and tweeds coloured to her own design. They are dressmaker's suits, soft and feminine, and they cost little more than in London or Paris. She does not like browns and beiges with which I thoroughly agree but, being herself a gifted landscape painter in oils, invents her own tints. When she fills her windows with yellow and blue jackets and skirts she ties ribbons of the same colour on her two poodles which she took over from England by air, and as her poodles love to sit in her shop windows to watch the crowds in Madison Avenue they often attract a crowd.

In late summer when New York becomes too hot Ruby takes her poodles and her prettiest tweeds to North East Harbour, 500 miles away in Maine, where she has a house—four bedrooms, a living-room, and a garden. Multi-millionaires keep their sea-going yachts in North East Harbour, and so Ruby is able to keep in touch with her distinguished clientele.

As Ruby, smiling under her adorable curly hair, talks to us about the wives of American millionaires and what one should do to keep a husband happy, her eyes suddenly fall on Millie's day-book in which the appointments are listed, and she gives a little cry of admiration.

'What! All these this afternoon, Millie?'

'All who?' asks Millie, coming back from the work-room where her girls are sewing to the lilt of the radio.

'All these,' reiterates Ruby. 'The Duchess of Devon-shire, the Marchioness of Hamilton, the Countess of Dunraven, the Countess of Meath, the Countess of Westmorland, the Countess of Dalhousie . . .'

'Oh, I know,' says Millie. 'The last four probably want to know about their coronets. I have discovered rather a good way for keeping the coronets firmly on their young heads.'

'How *is* it done?' I asked.

'Like this,' says Millie, taking up a coronet and placing it carefully on my head. 'In the old days all women had buns and masses of hair into which it was quite easy to stick large pins. A coronet was therefore anchored firmly into position and stayed there. Your own hair is a case in point. You wear it so long that if you were a peeress you could certainly attach your coronet in the old-fashioned way. But most modern women have not nearly enough hair. Imagine, for instance, trying to spike long pins into a young girl's poodle crop which is now so much the fashion! So this is what I advise them to do.'

Millie picked up a pair of combs, each two inches wide and an inch deep, and said:

'We fix these combs with elastic ribbon on either side of the coronet, and then turn them sharply inwards. The coronet is thus safely anchored and cannot topple over the tiara which,' she added, laughing, 'would be most undignified! Do you understand now?'

'Wonderful, Millie!'

'It is they who are wonderful,' says Millie with that look in her lovely eyes that bewitches me. 'A young countess went off yesterday carrying her magnificent diamond tiara in one box, her coronet in another, her hat in yet another, and her hand-bag I know not how. Of course, with London so crowded she could not find a cab, so she hurried down the steps of the Underground as she is accustomed to do on her way to work.

'They are all so delightfully busy. I love to see these young girls coming even for a short time into their own. One feared so much they would never have their spell of youthful glory, a glittering taste of their noble inheritance. Take, for instance, a day last week in the life of one of my young customers, a twenty-two-year-old maid of honour to the queen who will help to bear Her Majesty's train. She came to me. She picked up a hat. She rushed to the hairdresser. From the hairdresser she ran to Norman Hartnell for a fitting, from her fitting she rushed to a rehearsal at Westminster Abbey. She took her lunch standing up in a snack bar. She then hurried to Buckingham Palace for some other rehearsal. From the palace she went to another fitting —and finally, happy with triumphant youth, she went home to dress for the magnificent ball at which Her Majesty was present.'

'Millie, I suppose that most of your customers have old and valuable coronets which have been in families for many generations, and that it is then merely a question of arranging them and fitting the combs, but do you ever make an entirely new one? Or would that not come within the competence of a milliner?'

'Yes,' she answered, going over to her private table and bringing back a coronet. 'Here is one I have just made for the wife of a baron. As you see, it is of red velvet and imitation ermine, and it will not cost more than nine guineas. One might feel, I suppose, that it would be more fun to wear some heavy, historic piece, but this one would sit much more lightly on your head. I think it is in some ways more feminine.'

Katie is being dragged round by her dog, Jock, who is so well fed that he is no longer interested in his magnificent bone. He is probably asking Katie to take him for a walk in Berkeley Square, but first I long to know something.

'Katie, will you not tell me about the cedar-wood box that Lady Saye and Sele brought to you?'

Lord and Lady Saye and Sele live in one of Britain's oldest inhabited castles, Broughton Castle, near Banbury. Lord Saye and Sele's family have had their castle now for 502 years. How stupendous is this island's history! A great event like the coronation brings one face to face with stirring facts. Then one is suddenly overcome with fear, for is it not the opinion of great men that, because of senseless taxation, we shall lose the inheritance of past ages? Our nobles will be ruined, our castles will fall into decay, and our sovereign will be increasingly isolated? Is it possible that laws are such that a noble family may keep a castle 502 years and then perhaps . . . No, we must hope that in this case at least Broughton Castle will not for a long time be separated from its barons. From Broughton Castle came the cedar-wood chest that Lady Saye and Sele took to Katie in Berkeley Square. There was no question of a find. Lady Saye and Sele knew exactly what was in the chest. They were the beautifully packed robes worn by her mother-in-law at the coronation of King George V in 1911, consisting of a white lace dress, the kirtle—a red velvet coat with short sleeves trimmed with two rows of ermine—and the mantle—a red velvet cape that has the long train.

Though it was only just over forty years old, and

Lady Saye and Sele had opened the chest on several occasions, much of the lace fell to pieces when the dress was taken out. The kirtle and mantle were in perfect condition. This coronation was proving that the red velvet used in days gone by was so magnificent that centuries could not hurt it. One doubts if such velvet could be made to-day, and Katie, for one, claims that it is a lost art.

Lady Saye and Sele had a new silk slip made and old lace put all over the front of it.

Her mother-in-law who was tall had a waist measuring only eighteen inches! This set us wondering whether our mothers and grandmothers had slimmer waists than we have, the average now, according to Katie, being about twenty-four inches. This happens to be my measurement to-day, but when my mother was young my father could span her waist with his two hands. Yes, certainly, women had more feminine bodies forty years ago, slimmer waists, larger busts and hips. Perhaps we are still paying for the waistless, corsetless, bobbed-hair craze of the twenties!

The dress that was being talked about most at this period was one eventually worn in the Abbey by the beautiful Duchess of Devonshire who was looking for something in the metal chests at Chatsworth, where a great many ceremonial clothes are carefully kept, when her attention was drawn to a red velvet off-the-shoulder dress dating from at least 1800.

As in the case of the cedar-wood chest at Broughton Castle, there was no question of a find. Those in charge know very well what is at Chatsworth, but though the duke supposes that this dress was made for a coronation it might presumably have been worn at one of George III's courts.

The fact that it was of red velvet gave it this amazing span of life. The beauty and freshness of the dress caused many people to think that it had never been worn.

The absence of shoulders singled it out from the usual dresses worn under the kirtle and mantle, and indeed the Duchess of Devonshire asked Millie to make her six yards of white organza to cover her shoulders.

One heard many rumours about this dress. Some people thought it might have been made for Lady Elizabeth Foster, the dark and alluring daughter of the Earl of Bristol with whom the fifth Duke of Devonshire, husband of the fabulous Georgiana, fell in love, and whom he married in 1809 after Georgiana's death. This was not the case. More romantically still the dress was almost certainly made for the beautiful Georgiana, Duchess of Devonshire, herself.

The present young duchess is so very beautiful, and made so lovely a picture wearing this dress on coronation day, that the imagination weaves endless dreams around the thought that she was adding lustre to a court dress worn more than a century and a half earlier by a Duchess of Devonshire whose beauty is legendary. And if this is indeed the case, in what particular year must we imagine Georgiana herself wearing the dress? At the time she was painted by Thomas Gainsborough wearing that magnificent wide-brimmed hat with the satin ribbon and feathers? Or when George Romney painted her with the almost identical hat? Or in 1788 when Sir Joshua Reynolds made the immortal picture of her playing with her baby girl?

It would indeed be lovely if the present Duchess of Devonshire were to be painted in the dress for future generations.

By now, I expect, the dress has gone back to Chatsworth to sleep in its box for the space of another reign. We must hope, meanwhile, that some happy discovery in the archives will conclusively tell us what we want to know. Was it Georgiana's? Was it not? Some members of the duke's family point out that the dress is the same shape as the one worn by the Duchess of Buccleuch at Queen Victoria's coronation, but this resemblance may be entirely fortuitous. Certainly first impressions are that it is 1800 or earlier. What fun to think that such delightful mysteries can still exist!

History has now written itself. The coronation is over. The inhabitants of Shepherd Market, if they had no privileged seats to watch the procession, stayed indoors with television until the queen's coach arrived at the top of Piccadilly. They then dashed down Whitehorse Street or Down Street carrying kitchen chairs, saw what they could, got soaked in a sudden shower, and came tearing back to see the rest on the screen.

Now Ruby has flown back to New York with her busy mind full of pageantry and new ideas for making suits and top coats out of British tweeds. Here comes the Derby. Soon, too, will pass also the pageantry of Ascot.

Millie moves deftly, silently, amongst straws and organdie while the warm breeze rustles through the dark green boughs in Berkeley Square.

'Show me the hats for Ascot, Millie!'

She smiles and her eyes are full of pastel shades.

Will it rain? Will it be fine? We do not know, but we must make provision for either eventuality. A twenty-year-old maid of honour, invited by the young queen to the Windsor Castle house party, has just been trying on six hats, three large ones and three small ones, that now surround me in adorable, tempting confusion. Which shall I take up first—the large ones? A white straw? A wide-brimmed black crinoline (the French call it *cran*, which is horse-hair) in five delicate layers with a velvet crown? A pale pink straw (known as 'exotic' because it was first made by the Chinese under water) trimmed and bound with black velvet?

'This hat,' Millie whispers, as if it were a dark secret,

'she will wear with a pink shantung dress with black *etceteras*.'

'I love them, Millie, but what I like best of all is this little bonnet of pink exotic straw with the white organza fluffy bow behind.'

'She is having it in black with a red organza bow,' says Millie.

We laugh. Why do we laugh? Because life is such tremendous fun, and she suddenly says:

'You remember that red concertina straw from Jacques Fath that I lent you to wear at that important lunch? Well, I sold it yesterday.'

'Oh, Millie!'

The decorations come tumbling down. They break up like meccano sets. The grass in the parks starts to wither. Oh, for the tang of the sea and the smell of clover and hay!

Mrs. Terry is back in my apartment, pushing her carpet-sweeper back and forth.

'Madam,' she shouts to drown the noise of the machine, 'there's an American woman in the house. She says everything is wonderful. She goes on thanking and thanking me for everything I do for her. She thinks London's grand.'

Mrs. Terry switches off the machine, and adds reflectively:

'Mum's had a lovely time too. But mum's lucky. Went to have a look at Buckingham Palace, and out comes the queen! Bless my soul, we'll never hear the end of it.'